Preaching the Poetry of the Gospels

Preaching the Poetry of the Gospels

A Lyric Companion to the Lectionary

Elizabeth Michael Boyle, O.P.

LITURGICAL PRESS

Collegeville, Minnesota

www.litpress.org

Design by David Manahan, O.S.B. Cover illustration: 10th cent. ivory of Gregory the Great. Kunsthistorisches Museum of Vienna.

1	2	3	4	5	6	7	8

Library of Congress Cataloging-in-Publication Data

Boyle, Elizabeth Michael, 1927–
    Preaching the poetry of the Gospels : a lyric companion to the lectionary / Elizabeth Michael Boyle.
        p. cm.
    Includes bibliographical references and index.
    ISBN 0-8146-2891-5 (alk. paper)
    1. Bible. N.T. Gospels—Criticism, interpretation, etc. 2. Catholic Church. Lectionary for Mass (U.S.) 3. Christian poetry. I. Title.

BS2555.52.B69   2003
226'.06—dc21

                                                          2003041638

TO

MY MOTHER

WHO INTRODUCED ME TO

THE POETRY OF THE LITURGICAL YEAR

AND TO

SUZY

THROUGH WHOM GOD GIVES HER BACK TO ME

CONTENTS

ACKNOWLEDGMENTS

To all those, living and dead, who have deepened my understanding of the Gospels and challenged my response to them, I am deeply indebted, for they are a very real part of this book.

In particular, I wish to thank those who have most recently contributed to these pages:

—the president of Caldwell College and the Leadership Council of the Dominican Sisters of Caldwell, who entrusted me with time, space, and resources for contemplative study

—the homilists in my Dominican community, who have inspired me with the passion and poetry of great preaching

—the faculty poets of Caldwell College, whose balance of criticism with encouragement forced my own poems to birth

—all those poets who generously granted permission to publish their work

—Linda Maloney of the Liturgical Press for taking a risk with a new author

—John Schneider for his courteous and meticulous copyediting

—Sister Mary Joseph, O.P., and Kathleen Buse for proofreading

and above all

—Carol J. Dempsey, O.P., my director, producer, agent provocateur, sister, and friend, whose affectionately relentless attention to every detail of this project my words can neither describe nor repay.

INTRODUCTION

Long before any human tongue stammered a coherent sentence, God spoke. Using the visual nouns and dynamic verbs of the natural world, God wrote the first "sacred scriptures." Centuries before there were churches, there was prayer; before liturgies, a liturgical year. For eons human consciousness listened, pondered, and responded with desire as the seasons repeated their wordless theophanies, cyclically revealing the nature of a Creator in all its tenderness and terror, whimsy and fury, design and chaos. Even among primitive peoples, some more than others were attentive to these revelations and gifted in using symbols to communicate their intuitions about the One who could not be named. We called these visionaries poets. Then, as language evolved, the human family looked to them to translate the parables of earth and sky into rhythmic transmission for succeeding generations. Poets were our first theologians.

It is not surprising, therefore, that, when the Word became flesh, those who transmitted his story and his message to us chose literary forms as close as possible to God's "first language," the idiom of pattern, imagery, and symbol we call poetry. Following the psalmists and the prophets who heard God's voice in storm and calm and personified infinite love in titles like "Shepherd of Israel" and "Desire of the Everlasting Hills," the evangelists gave Jesus to us in a literary style that wove hundreds of strands from Hebrew poetry into what some have called a new genre.

Judging this style from its effects, we can infer that Jesus consistently used poetic devices to draw his listeners into a process of understanding that transcended prosaic exposition. The authors depict Jesus as having a preference for an interactive preaching strategy that led his audience from puzzlement to trust to commitment—and sometimes to rage. And, judging from its effects as pictured in the narratives,

Jesus' way with language worked. Although many people whom Jesus addressed were linguistically poor, the language they heard—rich in imagery, allusion, personification, irony, and paradox—was, more often than not, accessible to them. Rooted in concrete reality, this language also followed a literary tradition familiar to the first Christians. They were accustomed to hearing the language of the Hebrew Scriptures, where, as Raymond Brown points out, "human beings communicate in prose, but God communicates in poetry."[1] The authors render Jesus' life and message in a literary style combining simple, elemental vocabulary with all the sophisticated literary devices familiar to a rabbi. Those occasions when Jesus was *misunderstood* were precisely when his listeners took him *literally*.[2]

Yet, unlike so many who preach today, Jesus conspicuously avoided the phrase "In other words." The Gospels show Jesus appealing to his audience at three different levels. First, he enticed a response to language that was sometimes startling, rarely academic, and never boring. At this level he trusted his listeners to understand his poetic style gradually as they interacted with him orally. Secondly, he led them to read his significant *actions* as dramatic poetry. Finally, the evangelists make clear that, at the most intimate level, Jesus desired his message to be communicated fully only in that "primary zone" where one feels what one thinks and thinks about what one feels.[3] At this level of communication the model is Mary, treasuring in her heart the things she cannot understand (Luke 2:51). Indeed, the cumulative impact of Jesus' style for over two centuries attests that Jesus, the Word Incarnate, is best understood at that deep level to which the first cosmic epiphanies were addressed, that is, the meta-linguistic level from which poetry emerges and to which it returns. The Korean poet Ku Sang describes this intersection of verbal and non-verbal revelation:

> As the cataract of ignorance falls
> from off the eyesight of my soul,
> I realize that all this huge Creation
> round about me is the Word.[4]

Every version of Jesus' life that the post-resurrection Christians have left us makes apparent that they desired to embody not only Jesus' message but also the impact of a personality communicated through a mode of address that left their hearts burning within them (Luke

24:32). It is significant that even when the text reports that Jesus explained something, the evangelist preserves the poetic parable or narrative but omits entirely the teacher's prose explanation. Contemporary theologians have recognized the importance of literary sensitivity in Christian spirituality. Karl Rahner goes so far as to wonder: "Is there a preparation he [the catechumen] should undergo that turns out to be a receptive capacity for the poetic word?"[5] Moreover, Rahner insists that this sensitivity to language involves a more-than-academic imperative: "The power to hear means that one has heard the poetic word and abandoned oneself to it in humble readiness until the ears of the spirit are opened for it and it penetrates to one's heart."[6]

The whole range of literary choices through which the evangelists attempted to perpetuate their experience of Jesus' style is what I choose to call "the poetry of the Gospels." About this biblical mode of speaking the poets among us have much to teach those who seek intimacy with Jesus through the Word. Speaking to thousands at the 1998 Dodge Festival in Waterloo, New Jersey, the poet Robert Pinsky said: "The *medium* of the poem is one poet's body." To bring readers of the Gospel into contact with the living Body of Christ is the hope of every homilist; to persuade readers to offer their own bodies as the medium for the poetry of the Word is the humble ambition of this book.

But before elaborating on the spiritual objectives of this work, let me clarify my use of the term "poetry" in relation to all four Gospels. Twentieth-century form criticism has contributed much to our understanding of how *genre* functions in relation to meaning. Scripture scholars have pointed to certain poetic "events" and sub-genres within the narratives, for example the canticles in Luke. But, on the whole, critics designate the Fourth Gospel alone as "poetry," and rightly so. In fact, for me personally, so strong was John's literary impact that for most of my adult lifetime, I neglected the Synoptic authors to read exclusively the poetry of John.

Without questioning the preeminence of the author of the Fourth Gospel as poet and the scholarly value of generic distinctions, however, I hope to demonstrate that for pastoral purposes a poetic approach to *all* the evangelists can be especially enriching. For, as literary critics have further pointed out, the *literary* experience of the Gospel is the one in which the reader/hearer really enters into contact with something more than a historical or quasi-historical reality. Moreover, the Gospels, like all works of literature, engage the reader at multiple levels. Poetry can be defined as a way of *seeing* as well as a way of *saying*. Poets not only speak but also see and listen in a combination of language and silence that engages the dynamics of the whole person. When novelists and essayists achieve this holistic effect, we hail their writing as "poetic prose."

Poetry, according to Robert Frost's oft-quoted definition, is "what is lost in translation." The purpose of this book is to reclaim the poetry lost by three types of well-intentioned preachers who can obstruct the efficacy of the Word: the *paraphraser,* the *scholar,* and the *entertainer.* Paraphrase effectively denigrates the artistic design of a poetic text and dismantles its most potent metaphors. Although most people appreciate information that elucidates unfamiliar contexts, lengthy, complex, scholarly exegesis can obscure or evade the I-thou contact that completes the homily in the listener's personal prayer. The autobiographical detours of some raconteurs lose not only the poetry but often the Gospel itself. Although a robust audience response can be deceiving, anecdotal evidence attests that the entertainer is the type of preacher *least* appreciated by the community of believers, one of whom instructs his spouse, "Wake me up if he ever mentions Jesus." (Wit is, of course, a welcome seasoning for a sober homily, but when laughter is the only reaction provoked or expected, a congregation can feel exempted from taking the preacher seriously.) It is my hope that bringing the enthusiasm and insights of poets to bear on homiletics will persuade some who recognize themselves in this paragraph, either as "perpetrators" or as "victims," to hone their instruments both for preaching and for prayer through a serious engagement with poetry.

This book has also a secondary, educational objective. Preachers perform a great educational service when they use the homily to enlighten those in the congregation who have yet to accept that the Gospel was never intended to be received as an eyewitness account. But even in the twenty-first century, efforts to correct literalism will continue to meet strenuous resistance. Why do the most erudite citations from original languages and historical contexts often fail to revise a pedestrian understanding of a cherished Gospel? Perhaps one reason is that commentators do not go far enough. Unless preachers replace poetry with poetry, they simply substitute one literalism for another. A poetic approach should help Christians to avoid both extremes of literalism: exaggerating the facticity of the Gospels on the one hand and reducing the Gospels to mere facts on the other.

This book does not presume to instruct biblical scholars, except, perhaps, those whose erudition and/or pursuit of deconstruction for its own sake sometimes dilutes the sacramental action of Jesus' simple words. Many people would, perhaps, applaud the Dominican Timothy Radcliffe's courage when he asserts that "when theological discourse is profoundly boring, it just might be bad theology."[7] While this book can be a useful tool for scholars and preachers, its primary audience is the quotidian Christian for whom reflection on the Scriptures, alone or in groups, provides the "daily bread" for personal growth. For the average Christian who reflects on the Gospel and/or listens to a Sunday homily, the quest is not for the Jesus who *was*, but for the Jesus who *is*.

In this quest, the quest of a lifetime, the poets can be enlightened guides and companions. Reading poetry and developing a poet's relationship with language often give the reader fresh insight, but more importantly, such a relationship with language, since it facilitates the encounter with the living Word, can be a remote preparation for prayer. Regardless of what a specific pericope contributes to our knowledge of the Jesus of history, each text can be the locus for a genuine encounter with the Jesus of faith. Among educated Christians, many are poets and teachers of poetry who have never formally studied biblical theology. But when they read the literary approach of Johannine scholars, like Sandra Schneiders, for example, they feel a strong sense of affirmation for the theology they have gleaned from a lifetime engagement with the Word as literature.[8] For many, her most luminous insights are so informed by a deep understanding of poetry that they elicit the response: "Yes, this is how poetic language works, and this is how the language of Scripture has always worked for me."

Hence our exploration of the poetry of the Gospels begins by asking: What do poets *know* and *do* that we can use to unleash the power of language in the Christian community today? That question will be answered incrementally throughout the pages that follow. Here I would like to point out briefly four things that poets know about the nature of language:

- Poetry tells the truth.
- Poetry listens to the truth.
- Poetry uses symbols to express what is beyond words.
- Poetry, like prophecy, acts in the present and often makes things happen.

First of all, poets know that truth and poetry are not discrete categories; they recognize poetry as a way of seeking and saying truths that go beyond facts. Perhaps the best way to illustrate this point is to compare the way we react to a newspaper article with the way we react to a poem. How often we respond to the day's headlines with exclamations like "Incredible!" "I don't believe it!" By contrast, our most common reaction to a good poem is "That's so true." Moreover, poets know from experience that truth is not the opposite of imagination. As the poet-convert Denise Levertov has said, "Imagination, the chief of human faculties . . . which energizes intellect, emotion, and instinct, is the perceptive organ through which it is possible, though not inevitable, to experience God."[9]

Second, poets know that the purpose of their language is neither to transmit information nor to simplify complexity, but rather to provoke an experience, to elicit an affective response, to create the intellectual and emotional environment for an encounter with the Word-as-Presence. Whether or not they have studied a philosophy of language, poets have experienced what Heidegger means when he says "it is language that speaks and we who must listen to it."[10]

Third, poets know, intellectually and viscerally, the nature and power of symbols. They understand that showing is "truer" than saying, that symbolic meaning is not necessarily the opposite of literal meaning, and that symbols always mean more, not less, than facts. For them, facts are "truer" when they become symbols of deeper realities. Those who surrender themselves to Scripture as poetry do not compromise their experience of Scripture as truth. They experience symbols first hand, not as a form of fiction, but, as Sandra Schneiders maintains, as "a form of revelation" that involves a "subject-to-subject relationship with the transcendent."[11] The poet-evangelist of the Fourth Gospel models effective homiletics in scenes where Jesus interacts with Nicodemus (John 3:14-21), with the man born blind (John 9:1-41), and with the Samaritan woman (John 4:5-42). In no case does Jesus *explicate* the symbol and then discard it; he *immerses* the listener in the symbol and trusts the Spirit to continue the transaction in the listener's soul. When we are reading or preaching for transformation, symbols speak to us from all sides, and the daily newscast can be a symbolic call, a Gospel message translated into the vernacular.

Finally, poets understand that the act of writing the poem does not merely record something that has happened; the act of writing makes something happen. Biblical scholars know that the Hebrew term for "word" also means "event." So too, the act of preparing a homily is itself an event, a transforming encounter with Christ, and the act of preaching the homily is another transforming encounter with the Body of Christ. "In preaching the seeker and the sought come together, the lost and the found. God finds us in the midst of our very own words attempting to bespeak him."[12] Like many other human events, poetry is frequently prophetic. Throughout the following pages, numerous parallels between poetry, preaching, and prophecy will emerge. Poets themselves are the first to recognize these parallels. David Brendan Hopes points to the prophetic function of the poet:

> If you didn't hear the wind speak, you were not listening.
> If the stars did not warn you, you were
> safe at home with the doors locked tight.
> If you sought your soul and didn't find
> a small bird beating straight home forever
> where there is no road, you were seeking something else.[13]

Poetry, preaching, and prophecy are also similar in the way that each is affected by time and place. A single event in personal or communal history can infuse a poem, a Gospel, and/or a prophecy with new significance. Those who read and preach the Gospel regularly are often struck by how the Lectionary readings comment on the day's headlines. On September 11, 2001, most poets were stunned into silence. But at the same time, they reached into their memories of poetry from other times and places for words with which to penetrate the mystery of what was happening and in hopes of finding a key to survival.[14] In the weeks that followed, as the multi-faceted scope of apocalyptic nihilism unfolded, the prayer of the poet Rainer Maria Rilke, written at the dawn of the twentieth century, struck me with stinging force:

> Your first word was light,
> and time began.
> Then for a long time you were silent.
> Your second word was man, and fear began
> which grips us still.
> Are you about to speak again?

I don't want your third word.
Sometimes I pray: Please don't talk.
Let all your doing be by gesture only.
Go on writing in faces and stone
what your silence means.

. . .

Be our shepherd, but never call us—
We can't bear to know what's ahead.[15]

By the time these pages are printed, America's notoriously short attention span will have shifted to other headlines. That fleeting attention span demands that preachers capture the response to the headlines by appropriating the poet's power of *compression*. In his beautiful meditation on the life and work of Denise Levertov, the Franciscan poet Murray Bodo defines a poem technically as "a thing constructed of words that are the shortest distance between the maker and what is made."[16] Would that we could say of the Sunday homily that it creates the shortest distance between Jesus and us. How do poets *do* that?

That question will be answered incrementally as this book proceeds, but for now I'd like to answer by offering three alliterating verbs that might help to remember what poets *do* to carve their words into swift arrows piercing directly into the heart of the matter:

Describe, Design, Delete

Describe: Poems, like human relationships, begin in a specific place. Do we not designate one such cherished place as where we were "in love"? And do we not experience an immediate warm glow or stab of pain just by picturing that place again? Poets know how to suggest a whole emotional landscape simply by drawing a vivid picture. But the Gospels are, in fact, utterly bereft of physical description. This absence of specificity gives the narratives their timeless appeal, but we are such an intensely visual culture that we need to see to believe. Ignatius of Loyola, among others, stressed the value of what he called "composition of place." If you want to understand a Gospel, Ignatius instructs, go where Jesus was, see what he was looking at when he spoke these words, etc. Well, I too believe in the composition of place, but I prefer to say, "Go where Jesus is now." In a few vivid phrases, describe the landscape where this takes place today: the battlefield, urban ghetto, suburban desert, college campus, oval office, chancery office, or other venue where the furniture is different but the issues are the same, where Jesus needs to say the words or perform the miracle of this Gospel again. Sometimes the very act of mentally describing where Jesus was will lead you to a parallel contemporary universe. If for a certain Gospel place seems irrelevant, describe a face—either that of Jesus or the one talking to him—and visualize its facial expressions.

Design: A poem's visible design distinguishes it from prose. Stanzas divide the page into tidy blocks with refreshing white space around them. And right from the beginning, you can see where the poem will end. Because the members of a congregation cannot see a preacher's design, they can become restless with apprehension that the speaker has embarked on a journey without a map. The shepherd needs to reassure the flock that he knows where he's going and that he knows the way home. Telling a congregation that your homily has a design will dramatically improve attention. Something as simple and blunt as these openings will do:

> "Today's Gospel has a special message for two kinds of people."

> "All that Jesus said can be summarized in three questions that only you can answer."

> "Four symbols in this familiar scene express the nature of God's mercy."

A statement like that tells your people that you are really prepared, that you won't digress, and that you know when to stop. A design is a promise. And people will pay attention, if for no other reason than to see if you can keep it.

Delete: Design demands discipline. The preacher who hopes to be effective must learn to excise brutally every sentence, phrase, word that deviates from the design. The person who meditates, too, must resist the temptation to explore every avenue of thought. (File the discarded ideas away for another homily, another meditation.) Like Jesus, the poet never says everything. Preachers, like poets, compel more attention when they trust something to the Spirit who acts in the silence the words create. By way of demonstration, the Gospel reflections in this book range in length from six hundred to one thousand words, that is, from three to eight minutes. They are designed to give the preacher who is inspired by them ample room to adapt them to a looser, oral style—but always resisting digression.

Regarding style, Poet Laureate Billy Collins's complaint about students might describe some professorial preachers who "tie the poem to the chair with a rope and torture a confession out of it."[17] By contrast, those who experience the power of both poems and Gospels without fully understanding them learn not to resist a process that "begins in clarity and ends in mystery."[18] Understandably, some ardent preachers, seeing people begin to nod, reach for bombast to recapture attention. Poetry offers a more effective option. "Beauty summons us without bullying. It has its own authority, which is more profound than argument."[19] The preacher who appropriates the perspectives and techniques of the poet will spend longer and richer time in preparation to produce shorter, more powerful homilies. From the poets we will learn that language that elicits an affective response is compressed, allusive rather than exhaustive, incantatory rather than expository, and designed to engage the memory and imagination in such a way that the poem is completed within each listener.

How to Use and Abuse This Book

First of all, a few caveats are in order about what this book is *not*.

a) the subtitle, *A Lyric Companion to the Lectionary,* indicates that the Gospel reflections follow the *order* of the liturgical texts used in most Christian Churches, but the source for all quotations is not the Lectionary itself but the New Revised Standard Version of the Bible—Catholic Edition. Moreover, this "companion to the Lectionary" encompasses the Sundays of the liturgical year only as far as Ordinary Time. Finally, it does not treat the A, B, and C Cycles discretely. Some reflections traverse the three cycles, treating all three versions of a single event; others select the text most hospitable to poetic interpretation. Both for preaching and for meditation, you will find it helpful to read several versions and/or translations of the Gospel and choose the one you find most rhythmic or most meaningful in the context of your homily or your life.

b) The approach outlined here does not pretend to be better than other solid approaches. Since preaching on the same texts to the same audience year after year is difficult and preaching to yourself can numb the power of language, I offer one of many alternatives for your repertoire.

c) My reflections on the Gospels do not contribute to current theological debate; I try to focus on those aspects of current theological consensus that seem most conducive to inspire a spiritual response.

d) Homilists will not find here a "quick fix." These pages cannot substitute for one's own engagement either with the Gospels, with poetry, and, above all, with the People of God in their constantly intensifying struggle on the frontiers of human suffering. Rather, these pages are intended to be used either as a *preparation* for prayer and/or a *preparation* for preaching. The first step in that preparation is always a thoughtful reading of the Sunday's Gospel, a prayerful reflection on the text and on its wider contemporary context.

As a Preparation for Preaching

❖ Every preacher must speak in his or her own voice to a specific audience at a specific time, just as each Gospel speaks to the soul and to the community in a specific existential moment.[20] Before you can find the right words to speak, you must learn to listen to everything around you as Word. Nothing in this book can substitute for the habit of reading your own soul, your relationships—both intimate and professional—and your moment in time as revelation. The reflections and poems in this book will simply drop like pebbles into the pool of your own subconscious and ripple with associations.

As "the medium of the poem is one poet's body," so the medium of the homily is one preacher's body. The more you strengthen your physical bonds with nature, with others, and with language, the more your bond with God is made concrete. While preparing this manuscript, I found that a process of cross-pollination occurred between the words of the Gospels and the words of the poems, and the more physical contact I had with each text, the more it opened up and spoke to me. In my reading I soon discovered that my experience was not unique. Among those who promote poetry as prayer, for example, I found references to Simone Weil's experience with George Herbert's "Love Bade Me Welcome," which she memorized, recited, and wrote out in her own hand. Weil wrote that during one of her many recitations of the poem, "Christ himself came down and took possession of me."[21] Writing or typing the poem will draw your attention to the poet's use of line-breaks for emphasis and double meaning. From this exercise the preacher will learn to use the line-break's vocal equivalent, the pause, as a more subtle and effective means to capture the attention of an audience than amplified volume.

For all these reasons, therefore, I recommend that you begin your physical contact with the Gospel by reading the text aloud. Then, write or type it out and carry it around with you all day. Compose brief, rhythmic prayers that respond to each Gospel, or use a compelling line as a mantra. Follow the same steps with one of the poems. Gradually you will find this delightful remote preparation for preaching enhancing your command of a compelling vocabulary, of timing, and of voice. As preaching professor Honora Werner, O.P., explains to her seminary students: "Since no one can speak of God except in metaphor, the preacher must read and imitate the poets who constantly enrich our language with fresh metaphors. The preacher should aim for a language which is concrete, evocative, colorful—anything but bland."[22] After this remote preparation, use the following questions as tools to find and probe the two things in particular that distinguish poetry from prose: symbolism and design.

- Above all, ask not *what do the words mean?* but *what do the words do?*

- Then ask not *what do the words say?* but *what do the words leave unsaid?*

- Do the words demand an act of imagination or an act of faith or both?

- To what texts in Hebrew Scriptures do Jesus and the evangelists allude, and how might understanding their allusions cast new light on the text?

- Do the words take you somewhere? How do they take you there?

- Do the words make you feel that *there* is like or unlike *here*?

- Where do the words take you from here? Inward? Outward? Both?

- Do images or actions within the text "rhyme" with each other (or with the first reading)?

- What response does this "rhyming" or parallelism invite?

- What central image do the words create? What associations does that image evoke?

- How do images relate to each other? To the speaker? To you?

- What polarities does Jesus (or the evangelist) set up within the story?

- Do these polarities produce paradox, irony, contradiction?

- What expectations does Jesus reverse, frustrate, replace?

- What popular values do these reversals subvert?

- Where is the most rhythmic phrase? What happens when you repeat it?

- What happens when you accent a different word?

- What change in your home, your place of work, your relationships would occur if you took that phrase with you as a mantra?

❖ Don't let the length of this list discourage you. One or two of these questions will suffice for each Gospel. As soon as the question "What do the words do?" becomes automatic, you are thinking like a poet and will no longer need to return to these questions.

❖ If you decide to include some lines quoted from the poetry, be sure to use them to draw attention not to yourself but to the person of Jesus and/or our relationships in him.[23]

❖ When a poem appeals to you, write or type it out. This will connect you to the words bodily in another way. You will discover that forming physical bonds with the poetry gives you a different kind of energy. Take that energy with you into the pulpit.

❖ Finally, as you read the poems, you will notice that even though many begin in the poet's own voice, most end by casting a wider net. Study the poems to learn how many different ways poets create a net that ensnares and implicates the reader. If you never preach in a way that makes someone mad or uncomfortable, do not consider that an achievement.

❖ Never consider a homily "finished" until you have asked:
What emotion will my Description evoke?
What Design imposes a Discipline on my words?

Who will feel that I am speaking directly to him/her?

Who will be consoled, disturbed, challenged?

If you are faithful to this process, you will eventually be free of process. You will have reclaimed for yourself and others the "original language" of the Gospels.

As Preparation for Prayer

❖ All that has been said above about establishing a physical relationship with scriptural and poetic texts applies also to preparation for prayer. However, those who are born loving language will sometimes find their passion for words intruding into the silence where the Spirit speaks. I believe that these readers will find it helpful to use the words of Scripture and/or the words of the poet to drive out their own inner noise.

❖ Individuals or groups that use the Lectionary as a starting point for prayer will also benefit from replacing the question "What do the words mean?" with the question "What do the words do?" For the meditation phase of personal prayer, you might find the questions above useful. But do not allow intellectual engagement to distract you. For personal prayer, only one question is necessary "What do the words in the Gospel text do—or try to do—to my relationship with God and with others?"

❖ Above all, remember that this book is merely a means to an end. When a simple reading of the Gospel text takes you immediately into the presence of the Divine or into silence, reading an analysis and/or a poem is a step backward. In such an event, postpone reading the commentary and poetry until the end of your prayer time. Then the poetry might provide a few lines to memorize and carry with you into the rest of the day like a mantra.

God's first language was wordless poetry. Reading and responding to the Gospels with a poet's eyes and ears can help us recover the beauty and power of God's first language.

NOTES

Introduction

[1] Raymond E. Brown, *A Retreat with John the Evangelist* (Cincinnati, Ohio: St. Anthony Messenger Press, 1998) 20. Throughout this book, words attributed to Jesus should be understood to mean words used by the four evangelists to communicate Jesus' message.

[2] "Misunderstanding" is itself a literary device that John's Gospel especially employs to lead an audience into an understanding of spiritual reality. John 2:19: "Destroy this temple . . ."; John 3:3: "without being born from above . . ."; John 4:14: "those who drink of the water that I will give them will never be thirsty."

[3] Edward Hirsch, "Poet's Choice," *The Washington Post Book World* (June 23, 2002) BW120.

[4] Sang Ku, "The True Appearance of the Word," in *Wasteland of Fire: Selected Poems of Sang Ku,* trans. Anthony of Taizé (London: Forest Books, 1989).

[5] Karl Rahner, "Poetry and the Christian," in *Theological Investigations,* trans. Kevin Smyth (Baltimore: Helicon, 1966) 4:357.

[6] Ibid., 363.

[7] Timothy Radcliffe, O.P., "Letter to the Order," *International Dominican Information* (IDI, May 2001) 135.

[8] Sandra M. Schneiders, *Written That You May Believe: Encountering Jesus in the Fourth Gospel* (New York: Crossroad, 1999).

[9] Denise Levertov, "A Poet's View," in *New and Selected Essays* (New York: New Directions, 1992) 246. Both poets and Scripture scholars understand that poetic truth is not less than historical truth, nor does it exclude it. For example, Joseph Fitzmyer, "Gospel-truth cannot mean historical or literal truth. Each literary form has its own truth." Citing Cardinal Bea, he continues: "Truth in a literary context is gauged by the form of genre employed. It is legitimate to speak of gospel-truth, i.e., that religious and salutary truth expressed by the evangelists which may indeed make use of history as well as many other kinds of truth." *A Christological Catechism: New Testament Answers* (Ramsey, N.J.: Paulist Press, 1982) 118n.

[10] Martin Heidegger, "Language," in *Poetry, Language, Thought* (New York: Harper & Row, 1971) 190–192; 215–216.

[11] Schneiders, *Written That You May Believe,* 67. In my judgment, Schneiders' chapter "Symbolism in the Fourth Gospel" (63–77) is the best exposition of scriptural symbolism in print.

[12] Donald Goergen, O.P., "Preaching as Searching for God," *Dominican Ashram* (March 2000) 17. "Then the word of God as preached is the coming of what is preached." See also Karl Rahner, "The Word and the Eucharist," in *Theological Investigations,* trans. Kevin Smyth (Baltimore: Helicon, 1966) 4:202.

[13] David Hopes, "Birdbones," in *The Glacier's Daughters* (Amherst: University of Massachusetts Press, 1981).

[14] Dinita Smith, "The Eerily Intimate Power of Poetry to Console," *New York Times* (October 1, 2001) E1–4.

[15] Rainer Maria Rilke, *Rilke's Book of Hours: Love Poems to God,* trans. Anita Barrows and Joanna Macy (New York: Riverhead Books, 1997).

[16] Murray Bodo, O.F.M., *Poetry as Prayer: Denise Levertov* (Boston: Pauline Books and Media, 2001) 1.

[17] Billy Collins, "Introduction to Poetry," in *Sailing Alone Around the Room* (New York: Random House, 2001).

[18] Billy Collins, personal interview with the author, Caldwell College, April 2, 2001.

[19] Radcliffe, "Letter to the Order," 128.

[20] ". . . for theological exegesis the basic 'hermeneutical principle' is human need. . . . Translation means finding the place where the biblical text can strike home. The role of hermeneutics is to remove all distortion so that the text can effectively speak to readers." Raymond E. Brown, "Hermeneutics," in *The Jerome Biblical Commentary* (Englewood Cliffs, N.J.: Prentice Hall, 1968) 71:54.

[21] Simone Weil, *Seventy Letters* (London: Oxford, 1965), cited in Peggy Rosenthal, *Praying the Gospels Through Poetry: Lent to Easter* (Cincinnati: St. Anthony Messenger Press, 2001) 60–61, and in Robert Waldron, *Poetry as Prayer: The Hound of Heaven* (Boston: Pauline Books and Media, 1999) 105. A photograph of the poem in Weil's handwriting appears in Simone Petrement, *Simone Weil: A Life,* trans. Raymond Rosenthal (New York: Pantheon, 1976) 194.

[22] Honora Werner, O.P., personal interview with the author, April 21, 2002.

[23] "Christ is present in his word since it is himself who speaks when the Holy Scriptures are read in the church." Second Vatican Council, "Constitution on the Sacred Liturgy," in *Vatican II: The Conciliar and Post Conciliar Documents,"* new rev. ed., ed. Austin Flannery, O.P. (Northport, N.Y.: Costello Publishing, 1998) no. 7.

Chapter 1

INCARNATION
Advent to Epiphany

The Sundays of Advent

Before we reflect on each Sunday Gospel individually, some general observations about this first liturgical season will be useful. First of all, the season as a whole is rich in poetic imagery in a way that the first Gospels of the liturgical year in themselves are not. In the Introduction we proposed that each of the Gospels embodies the perceptions and techniques of the poet, and that reading the New Testament as poetry rather than as history can not only illuminate some prosaic texts but also, more importantly, help to initiate a deeper personal encounter with the living Word. Advent's opening Gospels, however, present an immediate challenge to that central premise. For, in the readings for the first three Sundays at least, most of what the general reader recognizes generically as poetry appears, not in the Gospels, but in the verses from the prophets selected for the first readings. These verses of Isaiah and Jeremiah, having inspired the great classics of Advent and Christmas music, have become deeply embedded in both Jewish and Christian consciousness and elicit a very desirable emotional response. The poetic power of this prophetic literature should never be neglected.

I hope to demonstrate, however, that the prosaic exhortations of Matthew, Mark, and Luke can also have poetic impact when we read their words as poets would read them or when we translate the evangelists' imagery into the language of the unconscious. Moreover, although Scripture scholars have legitimately emphasized the parallels between the promise of the Hebrew prophets and their fulfillment in the person of Jesus, an appreciation for antithetic parallelism and ironic

1

juxtaposition can help a preacher to understand how these devices reso-
nate with what poets call affective meaning. Irony will have a particular appeal to a community of believers struggling to experience Advent
in a post-Christian culture.

Secondly, since Advent is the beginning of the liturgical year, it
would be appropriate on the first Sunday, and even on each Sunday of
the season, to meditate on the mystery of time itself. Every year, for
the average person, the month of December imposes extreme stress in
relation to time. Liturgies during this season should be a respite from
that stress. To give everyone a full sixty seconds of silence in which to
experience "the fullness of time" might be the most eloquent, memorable, and compassionate gift a preacher can give. To make this silence
your distinctive signature at the conclusion of a brief Gospel reflection
can be a very concrete "act of faith" in the power of the Spirit to reach
where you cannot go.

Geoffrey Hill responds to the urgency of the Advent invitation
with a prayer of moving honesty in which the speaker recognizes that
the "Christmas rush" is really a form of procrastination.

> What is there in my heart that you should sue
> so fiercely for its love? What kind of care
> brings you as though a stranger to my door
> through the long night and in the icy dew
>
> seeking the heart that will not harbor you,
> that keeps itself religiously secure?
> At this dark solstice filled with frost and fire
> your passion's ancient wounds must bleed anew.
>
> So many nights the angel of my house
> has fed such urgent comfort through a dream,
> whispered "Your lord is coming, he is close"
>
> that I have drowsed half-faithful for a time
> bathed in pure tones of promise and remorse.
> "Tomorrow I shall wake to welcome him."[1]
>
> —Geoffrey Hill

Skytides

I

The sky is at low tide this morning.
Pearl-grey ripples wash, hush, hesitate,
half-awaiting sandpipers.

Out in the mist, hills ride at anchor;
gulls wheel above buried hulls
and slack sails haul cargoes of subtle color.

Here and there
      a drunken steeple
           a detached mast
                lists
                    sobers suddenly
                        finds a steady deck

and sweeps through breakers that
move from rose to mauve and then
drown the whole fleet in amethyst.

II

The sky is at high tide tonight.
Anthracite boulders crash, crush, annihilate
a cumulus penninsula.
Among the ruins, scattered flares ignite and die.
      Dark on dark
          black
          coral
          spars
          emerge.
The meek armada drowned at dawn surfaces.
Below suspended seas, lambent windows:
incandescent coins with which each
native of Atlantis purchases a hearth for time.

No matter how relentlessly
        then
        now
      and soon to be
        converge
        upon
       each midnight
       the tense for sky
        for you
        for us
        is aorist.

—Elizabeth Michael Boyle, O.P.

The Greeks have five different words for "time," each of which in itself could be the text for an Advent homily: *chronos,* the exact time; *kairos,* the opportune time; *hēmera,* this very day, the time of God's action; *hōra,* the appointed hour; *hēlikia,* life span, all the time allotted to you. The Greeks also have a special tense, the aorist tense, for events that happened once. The poem reminds us how the uniqueness that makes each sunset precious applies to this Advent, this Christmas, this child, this relationship: not one of them will ever happen again.

FIRST SUNDAY OF ADVENT

Matthew 24:37-44   Mark 13:33-37   Luke 21:25-28, 34-36

The Gospel Speaks:

On this first Sunday of the gentlest season of the year, as we prepare for the coming of a God who chooses to appear as harmless as an infant, what do the words of the evangelist *do?* They reverse the sentimental Advent expectation and shock us to attention by giving Jesus what the poets would call a "persona" or mask. Matthew, Mark, and Luke, all three Gospels for this Sunday, transform Jesus into a Cotton Mather with a voice of fire and brimstone. This voice at first repels us until we look at what the words of Jesus *do.* First, he invokes the collective memory of his audience by alluding to the well-known symbol of salvation—Noah's ark (Matt 24:38-39; Gen 5–8). Jesus' use of allusion exemplifies a style respectfully attuned to his audience. Unlike poets of the Eliot / Pound school, who pepper their discourse with arcane allusions to showcase their erudition, the evangelists show Jesus using only the most familiar allusions as literary shorthand to unify the present with the past and to establish continuity with the emotional history of his Jewish brothers and sisters.

Having invoked the spiritual past of his listeners, Jesus next provokes their collective imagination to envision the future with a series of symbolic little scenes in which daily work is interrupted and security threatened (Matt 24:40-43). All these scenes have one thing in common, with each other and with the legendary flood: they all juxtapose redemption with disaster. Each juxtaposition contrasts what we expect and hope for—the coming of love incarnate—with its opposite: a storm, an abduction, a burglary, a cosmic disturbance, a trap. Before Jesus can save us, he must first disrupt our quotidian complacence.

In Geoffrey Hill's poem cited above (p. 2), he designates the "heart that will not harbor you" as one "that keeps itself religiously secure." Religion as a security blanket, the poet hints, actually shuts God out. Mercifully, Jesus alerts his people to what is at risk. "Watch out! The coming of the long-awaited one will be so quiet you could easily miss it." Like so much good poetry, the language of the Gospel acts by way of paradox. The stern voice of Jesus invites us to a totally new life by warning us of death. He announces the arrival of an eternal kingdom by pointing to a moment in time as unobtrusive as the heartbeat of an infant in the womb.

The Irish novelist Nuala O'Failan understands this Gospel's strategy. Living in the absolute solitude of a seaside cottage, she enjoys all year round the kind of peace and quiet for which most people merely yearn in Advent. "More than silence or a beautiful landscape, there's something I need if I want to really go inside myself," she says. Then she describes how she leaves her peaceful isolation and goes in search of silence in the noisiest place she can find, city streets and subways. "When you live in the middle of mayhem for so long," she explains, "you grow to need mayhem to construct peace within it."[1] Can we not use the noise surrounding this stressful season to make "peace out of mayhem"? Perhaps then the threat of the Son of Man will invert into a promise. When we stop searching for an unrealistic Advent, he will come into the heart of each of us when we least expect him.

The Poets Respond:

Thomas Merton, the Trappist monk and poet whose writings drew so many young men to the monastic life after World War II, is an example of the poet as prophet. The two poems below echo the contrasting tones of threat and promise in the first Gospels of the liturgical year. Moreover, in the first poem, written decades before contemporary theology began emphasizing "cosmic redemption," Merton calls all creation to prepare for the quiet miracle of a traditional Christmas. Again and again, by urging us to imitate the virtues of stones and beasts, the poet's metaphors and personifications level all the different "tiers" of the natural world. He exalts animals and "inanimate" creatures, on the one hand, and humbles humanity on the other. Decades before the strident prose of green politics, Merton's gentle poem anticipated a spirituality of non-threatening cosmic interdependence. Reading this poem aloud invites us to unite our souls with all creation in an act of quiet expectancy.

Advent

Charm with your stainlessness these winter nights,
Skies, and be perfect!
Fly vivider in the fiery dark, you quiet meteors,
And disappear.
You moon, be slow to go down,
This is your full!

The four white roads make off in silence
Towards the four parts of the universe.
Time falls like manna at the corners of the wintry earth.
We have become more humble than the rocks,
More wakeful than the patient hills.

Charm with your stainlessness these nights in Advent, holy spheres,
While minds, as meek as beasts,
Stay close at home in the sweet hay;
And intellects are quieter than the flocks that feed by starlight.

Oh pour your darkness and your brightness over all our solemn valleys,
You skies; and travel like the gentle virgin,
Toward the planet's stately setting
Oh white full moon as quiet as Bethlehem![2]

—*Thomas Merton*

During Advent in 1968, Thomas Merton died of electrocution. Many years before his sudden death, he seemed to predict the violence of it. But the final stanza responds to the warning, "at the hour you least expect, the Son of Man will come," with an exclamation of joy.

. . . make ready for the Face
that speaks like lightning,
Uttering the new name of your exaltation
Deep in the vitals of your soul.
Make ready for the Christ,
Whose smile, like lightning,
Sets free the song of everlasting glory
That now sleeps, in your paper flesh, like dynamite.[3]

—*Thomas Merton*

Since September 11, 2001, lines like these have become fraught with searing relevance and will be read, perhaps, more with pain and irony than with consolation. As Denise Levertov points out, at moments of historic disaster God's apparent silence is simply a different language.

Immersion

There is anger abroad in the world, a numb thunder,
because of God's silence. But how naïve,
to keep wanting words we could speak ourselves, . . . perfect freedom
assured other ways of speech. God is surely
patiently trying to immerse us in a different language,
events of grace, horrifying scrolls of history
and the unearned retrieval of blessings lost forever,
the poor grass returning after drought, timid, persistent.
God's abstention is only from human dialects. The holy voice
utters its woe and glory in myriad musics, in signs and portents.
Our own words are for us to speak, a way to ask and to answer.[4]

—Denise Levertov

December 8

FEAST OF THE IMMACULATE CONCEPTION

Luke 1:26-38

The Gospel Speaks:

As the mother of Jesus, Mary has inspired more poetry and art than any other woman in history, but to my knowledge, not one poem has been inspired by the event in the womb of her mother Anne, Mary's Immaculate Conception. Nor does a single verse of Scripture refer to the dogma the Catholic Church celebrates on December 8. Luke's account of how Mary consented to her election as mother of the Messiah, the one Gospel chosen for this feast in all three cycles, celebrates, not Anne's conception of Mary, but the conception of "the Word become flesh" in Mary's womb. The choice of this Gospel might very well be responsible for the fact that an embarrassing number of practicing Catholics believe that the term "Immaculate Conception" means that Jesus was conceived in the body of a virgin. Therefore, Catholic preachers should first take the opportunity to correct popular "misconceptions" and then invoke the poetry inspired by the mystery of the Incarnation.

As Luke opens the dramatic narrative, he grounds his story in a particular human time and place and a specific human family: "In the sixth month the angel Gabriel was sent by God to a town in Galilee called Nazareth, to a virgin engaged to a man whose name was Joseph, of the house of David. The virgin's name was Mary" (Luke 1:26-27). The very syntax of that sentence pays silent homage to Mary's position in history, for it is so structured that an angel, a husband, and a king go before her like an escort of acolytes, and Mary, the most important person, comes at the end of the procession. And because Luke offers not a single detail of physical description, artists throughout the centuries have given Mary the beauty that they imagine God would want

to give her. In fact, one poet imagines Gabriel so stunned by her love-
liness that he forgets why he came:

> . . . She is sitting near the window, doing nothing, unaware of his
> presence . . . her face as pure and luminous as a child's . . .
> Ah, wasn't there something he was supposed to say? He feels
> the whisper far back in his mind, like a mild breeze. Yes, Yes. He
> will remember the message, in a little while. In a few more minutes.
> But not just now.[1]

Throughout this Gospel, poetry obscures poetry, for the facts are
more stunning than their symbolic dramatization. Gabriel's message is
more spectacular than the glorious wings with which imagination has
encumbered him. Throughout the ages, all those who have experienced
a personal encounter with God have groped for words to express a
reality beyond hyperbole. The language of the mystic Simone Weil
embodies the evangelist's struggle to express the same kind of encounter: "I felt . . . a presence more personal, more certain, and more
real than that of a human being; it was inaccessible both to sense and
to imagination, and it resembled the love that irradiates a loving
being's most tender smile."[2]

By contrast, Mary's practical question brings us down to earth
and assures us that she knows exactly what's going on: "How can this
be, since I am a virgin?" (Luke 1:34). Poets have avoided the popular
controversies concerning the term "virgin" in this text, and preachers
would also do well to reserve biological / theological speculations for
private conversation with their more sophisticated congregants, since
these questions are irrelevant to the theme of today's liturgy: the mystery of the incarnation of the Word in Mary of Nazareth *and spiritually in the humanity of each of us.*

Luke's command of the devices of poetic understatement is im-
pressive here. By contrasting the grandeur to come and the stark reality
of its impact on Mary's life in a dialogue that alternates glory with
terror, he compresses into a few words the central paradoxes of what it
means to be a Christian. The poems gathered here and after the Fourth
Sunday offer a wide variety of responses to these paradoxes. Any one
of them, when read slowly and reverently with motivated pauses, could

be in itself a short, powerful homily on Annunciation and Incarnation as personal contemporary events.

The Poets Respond:

In one of his "Sonnets to the Unseen," Christopher Fitzgerald, playing with the double meaning of the word "conception," produces a "metaphysical conceit," that is, an elaborate metaphor for a complex of thought and emotion. Within the economy of the sonnet form, the conceit unites all the "conceptions" in this chapter of salvation history: in the eternal mind of God, in the womb of Anne, and in the womb of Mary.

> In Mary's body miracles took place
> Expressions, Yahweh, of Your holy plan.
> She danced in You before her life began,
> Conception sweetly clean, without a trace
> Of sin or imperfection, full of grace.
> As conceived, so conceived in Anne;
> So conceived the way the Son of Man
> Would enter time, would join the human race.
> In Mary's body, normal flesh and blood,
> A spirit lived unburdened, free to love.
> Normal soul and body, hand in glove,
> She was as You intended: simply good.
> Singularly normal in this wise,
> She bridged the gap from earth to paradise.[3]

> —*Christopher Fitzgerald*

In her first poem below, Luci Shaw renders Mary's struggle for a language to express what has happened to her—and to all creation. Her repeated "as if" seems to replicate God's need for a Word to make explicit a relationship that has existed "from all eternity."

In the next poem, Shaw contends that light and darkness are not opposites: darkness is the human mind's reaction to brightness too wonderful to comprehend.

Virgin

As if until that moment
nothing real
had happened since Creation

As if outside the world were empty
so that she and he were all
there was—he mover, she moved upon

As if her submission were the most
dynamic of all works; as if
no one had ever said Yes like that

As if one day the sun had no place
in all the universe to pour its gold
but her small room.

The Overshadow

". . . and the power of the Most High will overshadow you." Luke 1:35

When we think of God, and
angels, and the Angel,
we suppose ineffable light.

So there is surprise in the air
When we see him bring to Mary,
in her lit room, a gift of darkness.

What is happening under that
huge wing of shade? In that mystery
what in-breaking wildness fills her?

She is astonished and afraid; even in
that secret twilight she bends her head,
hiding her face behind the curtain
of her hair; she knows that
the rest of her life will mirror
this blaze, this sudden midnight.[4]

—*Luci Shaw*

As they re-imagine this scene, many visual artists have focused on a symbolic rendering of the incarnation of The Word in the will as well as in the womb of Mary, and artifacts are more frequently the poet's inspiration than the Gospel narrative. William Butler Yeats is captivated by an image popular in Byzantine mosaics, where impregnation by the Word is symbolized by ". . . a fallen flare / Through the hollow of an ear." Yeats comments: "She received the word through the ear, a star fell, and a star was born."[5] The artist seems to anticipate Vatican II's emphasis on the real presence of Jesus in the Word.[6] We cannot imitate Mary's unique exemption from sin, nor her unique biological relationship to Jesus, but as we listen to the Word of God proclaimed in each liturgy, we mimic receiving this "fallen flare through the hollow of an ear." In faith and with attention, we can participate realistically in the ongoing mystery of Incarnation.

From *The Mother of God*

> The three-fold terror of love; a fallen flare
> Through the hollow of an ear;
> Wings beating about the room;
> The terror of all terror that I bore
> The heavens in my womb
>
> What is this flesh I purchased with my pains,
> This fallen star my milk sustains
> This love that makes my heart's blood stop
> Or strikes a sudden chill into my bones
> And bids my hair stand up.[7]

—*William Butler Yeats*

Denise Levertov, a poet whose life history embraces the main events of the twentieth century, was converted from agnosticism to Catholicism through her involvement with Christian activists in the peace and justice movement and in the environmental advocacy based upon the spirituality of eco-theology. The following short poem will repay close reading and re-reading, for here the poet reverses for a moment the position taken by those who reject the notion of "lower life forms" to embrace no less humbly humanity's unique responsibility in the order of creation.

On the Mystery of the Incarnation

It's when we face for a moment
the worst our kind can do, and shudder to know
the taint in our own selves, that awe
cracks the mind's shell and enters the heart:
not to a flower, not to a dolphin,
to no innocent form
but to this creature vainly sure
it and no other is god-like, God
(out of compassion for our ugly
failure to evolve) entrusts,
as guest, as brother, the Word.[8]

—*Denise Levertov*

Thomas Merton, assuming the persona of Mary, gives voice to the contemplative soul's desire for absolute transparency in and for divine love.

From *The Blessed Virgin Mary Compared to a Window*

Because my will is simple as a window
And knows no pride of original earth,
It is my life to die, like glass by light:
Slain in the strong rays of the bridegroom sun.

Because my love is simple as a window
And knows no shame of original dust,
I longed all night, (when I was visible) for dawn my death:
When I would marry day, my Holy Spirit
And die by transubstantiation into light.
. . .
Therefore, do not be troubled at the judgments of the thunder,
. . . And do not fear the armies and black ramparts
Of the advancing and retreating rains:
. . .
Although it is the day's last hour
Look with no fear:
For the torn storm lets in, at the world's rim
Three streaming rays as straight as Jacob's ladder:

And you shall see the sun, my Son, my substance
Come to convince the world of the day's end, and of the night,
Smile to the lovers of the day in smiles of blood:
For, through my love, He'll be their brother,
My light—the Lamb of the Apocalypse.[9]

—Thomas Merton

Merton's startling phrase "die by transubstantiation into light" foreshadows the unique form of death in which hundreds of bodies disappeared in the historic explosion of New York's Twin Towers. In stark contrast with the mystic's voluntary self-immolation and the involuntary "burnt offering" of terror's victims, Jeanne Murray Walker chooses to reflect on a playful possibility: Was Mary God's first choice, and if not, what kind of woman said "No"? The tone of the poem moves lightly from serio-comic irony to honest admiration for the pedestrian heroism of ordinary Christian living. The poem can be the starting point for many different meditations, depending on the life-situations of individuals and groups.

Portrait of the Virgin Who Said No to Gabriel

She looked up from the baking that morning, hearing
his feathers settle and his voice scatter like gold coins
on the floor. Then, seeing his forehead, sweaty
from the long trip, she guessed. *Me?* She scoffed, *Oh sure!*

But after he walked away, she couldn't forget
the strange way his feet rang like horseshoes on the stones.
What she had been wanting before he interrupted
was not the Bach Magnificat, I can tell you, not stained
glass. Nothing risky. Just to keep her good name.

Small as she was, how could she keep in her heart
those centuries of praise? But I praise her,
anyway, for wanting a decent wedding
with napkins folded like hats and a good Italian wine.
I praise her name, Lenora. I praise the way

she would practice carefully making the L.
like a little porch, where she could imagine standing
to throw a red ball to some children she loved.
I praise the way, year by year, she let herself see
who that visitor was. Think of her collecting

belief slowly, the way a bird builds her nest
in an olive tree. Then finally how one year,
after the leaves fell, she was an old woman
looking at the truth, outlined against
the salmon sky, knowing it was true.

For not despising her own caution then, I praise her.
For never feeling envy. And for the way, once,
she walked through her fear to hand a cup of water
to a carpenter who was fainting by her door.

In every room of this gallery I think I see her picture.

—*Jeanne Murray Walker*

SECOND SUNDAY OF ADVENT

Isaiah 11:1-10; 40:1-9   Matthew 3:1-12   Mark 1:1-8   Luke 3:1-6

The Gospel Speaks:

Many commentators on the readings for the next two Sundays of Advent explain the significant parallels between Isaiah and John as prophets; others place the mission of the latter in its theological / historical context; still others emphasize the challenge to contemporary values represented in polarities between the Baptist and the leaders of his culture (Luke 3:1). When I now suggest that we consider Isaiah's imagery and the imagery of the Baptist and his landscape as Jungian archetypes of the unconscious, I do not pretend to offer a "better interpretation," but simply a poetic alternative that might elicit a deeper understanding of ourselves. In the poetry that the Christian liturgy has appropriated for Advent, Isaiah, the poet of the Old Testament, pulls out all the stops:

> Then the wolf shall live with the lamb,
>> the leopard shall lie down with the kid,
> the calf and the lion and the fatling together,
>> and a little child shall lead them.
> The cow and the bear shall graze,
>> their young shall lie down together;
>> and the lion shall eat straw like the ox.
> The nursing child shall play over the hole of the asp,
>> and the weaned child lay its hand on the adder's den. . . .
> for the earth will be full with knowledge of the LORD
>> as the waters cover the sea (Isa 11:6-9).

This lyrical description does not commit Isaiah to a utopian promise on which he cannot possibly deliver. His words propel us out of physical reality and into the realm of imagination. We know that none of us will ever live to witness the "peaceable kingdom" either in the natural world or in the social order; yet we listen to these beautiful lines over and over again each year with a profound sense, not only of yearning but also of possibility. Unconsciously, we recognize in Isaiah's menagerie the symbols that poets from William Blake to Carmen de Gatzold[1] have used as either fearful or playful objective correlatives for our own conflicting psychological states. Whether we can express it or not, we respond to Isaiah's poem with a wordless plea to God to reconcile and integrate the wild and the tame within each of us and within our disparate cultures.

The language of poetry, like the language of the unconscious, is the language of dreams. In a dream each place, each character, even each animal represents a part of the self. And as one critic has pointed out in relation to the poetry of Richard Wilbur, animals are: "'a live tongue' in which alone we can 'call our natures forth. . . .' These creatures are also a mirror in which we see ourselves as we are or want to be, in which we glimpse our own potentialities."[2] Today's Gospel of John the Baptist offers another dream mirror for the individual Christian, who asks: "Where is *my* desert? Does the dream call me to go *out* into the desert to pray and fast for personal purification, or does it call me to come *in* from my private desert and face my world responsibly?" As T. S. Eliot reminds us: "The desert is not remote. . . . / The desert is squeezed in the tube-train next to you, / The desert is in the heart of your brother."[3] Is the desert I see in the heart of my brother a "projection" of my own interior sterility? What can we see in the desert that we cannot see at home? Stars, for one thing. In the glare from our electronic landscape, do we miss the star that leads "true north" or the morning star that points to hope?

Closer to home, who in me is this wild man wearing animal skins (Matt 3:4; Mark 1:6)? What part of myself have I tamed because I fear to be judged unsophisticated? According to Carl Jung, the one who denies his animal nature is like the Pharisee who prayed, "I thank you, Lord, that I am not as this publican and sinner."[4] In a similar vein, poet Sara Hong compares those who are not honest with themselves to children playing hide and seek who think that when they cover their eyes, you can't find them. More than anything, Advent means "He is coming, ready or not. When we pout, he thunders in our pouting places."[5]

Continuing to read the Gospel as a dream, we ask, "What in me are these other forces represented by Caesar, Herod, Pilate (Luke 3:1-2)? Who or what has power over me, my family, my priorities? What alien power does the dream call me to renounce that I may control my own life and belong to the God who frees me?" Each of us will have different answers, but facing these questions will be the first liberating step on the Advent road to meet the one "more powerful than I [who] is coming" (Matt 3:11; Luke 3:16). Further, if we read this Gospel as a dream of the Church, we hear every day's headlines as a wake-up call to confront issues of justice and the abuse of power, even and especially within the Church itself. John did not go into the desert to escape, nor should we. Like John, we withdraw a little from routine to see ourselves and our world more clearly, and to strengthen ourselves for the service of God and others.

The Poets Respond:

Now, as in biblical times, prophets like Isaiah and the Baptist inspire mixed reactions. Now as always, the warnings and visions of prophets are dismissed as either too alarmist or too utopian. Poets take prophets seriously. Richard Wilbur rarely writes an overtly Christian poem. Yet he was recently honored by Saint Mary's Seminary in Baltimore, Maryland, for the prophetic stance of poetry that calls Christians to responsibility. In one of Wilbur's most popular poems, "Advice to a Prophet," he translates the Baptist's stern call to conversion into terms of two contemporary issues in relation to each other: the environmental and the nuclear crisis. In a 1968 interview the poet explains: "What I was trying to do in that poem was to provide—myself of course—with a way of feeling the enormity of nuclear war, should it come. The poem . . . comes at such a war through its likely effect on the creatures who surround us. . . . It made it possible for me to feel something beside a kind of abstract horror, a puzzlement, at the thought of nuclear war."[6] Unfortunately, after 9/11/01 no American can think of any kind of war as an abstraction. And realities worse than grimmest predictions have awarded prophets more respectful attention. Wilbur addresses modern prophets as he says: "When you come . . . to the streets of our city, / Mad-eyed from stating the obvious . . ." / you won't "scare us with talk of the death of the race . . .," because we can't "dream of this place without us." Contrasting the prophet's "global vision" with the myopic egotism that regards the whole created world as "these things in which we have seen ourselves and spoken," Wilbur concludes:

> Ask us, prophet, how we shall call
> Our natures forth when that live tongue is all
> Dispelled, that glass obscured or broken
> . . . in which beheld
> The singing locust of the soul unshelled,
> And all we mean or wish to mean. . . .
> . . . Come demanding
> Whether there shall be (anything) lofty or long standing
> When the bronze annals of the oak tree close.[7]
>
> —*Richard Wilbur*

In a totally different mood, Mark Doty hears Isaiah's vision evoked by Handel's music. Seated in the Methodist church at a pre-Christmas concert, he looks out the window and sees nativity images mirrored in nature. Clouds become "gleaming rags . . . torn and sunshot swaddling." Then, as he listens to the familiar chorus, human voices seem to "make the landscape / the text predicts the Lord / will heighten and tame." The whole "burnished oratorio" becomes a lyric reflection on the power of art to exalt our frail humanity, transformed by the Incarnation.

From *Messiah: Christmas Portions*

> . . .
> This music
> demonstrates what it claims:
> glory shall be revealed. If art's
> acceptable evidence,
>
> mustn't what lies
> behind the world be at least
> as beautiful as the human voice?
> The tenors lack confidence,
>
> and the soloists
> half of them anyway, don't
> have the strength to found
> the mighty kingdoms

these passages propose
—but the chorus, all together,
equals my burning clouds,
    and seems itself to burn,

    commingled powers
deeded to a larger, centering claim.
These aren't anyone we know;
    choiring dissolves

    familiarity in an up-
pouring rush which will not
rest, not for a moment
    be still.

    Aren't we enlarged
by the scale of what we're able
to desire? Everything,
    the choir insists

    might flame;
inside these wrappings
burns another, brighter life,
    quickened now,

    by song; hear how
it cascades in overlapping,
lapidary waves of praise? Still time.
    Still time to change.[8]

—Mark Doty

THIRD SUNDAY OF ADVENT

Isaiah 35:1-10; 61:1-2, 10-11
Matthew 11:2-11   John 1:6-8; 19-28   Luke 3:10-18

The Gospel Speaks:

Once again Isaiah, the visionary of the Old Testament, provides the lyric introduction to the more prosaic language of the Synoptics: crocuses burst forth from the desert sands; the blind, the lame, the speechless, and the liberated captives break into song. All nature, human and non-human, signals vibrant new life. The Gospels extend Isaiah's metaphors and translate his theme into a language of concrete action.

First, let us see how in Matthew, Jesus' interrogation by the Baptist's disciples initiates a lesson in the multifaceted "sign language" of New Testament poetry. Verbs point to and identify what is beyond verbalization. Asked if he is the awaited Messiah, Jesus declines to answer yes or no (Matt 11:2-5), for in fact Jesus has come to redefine that word. Instead, he points to the actions that are "signs" of his unique power over life and death, signs that allude to the miraculous actions in Isaiah. Then Jesus goes Isaiah one better: "the dead are raised, and the poor have good news brought to them" (Matt 11:5). Here the poetic device of *synonymous parallelism* between the Old and the New Testaments invests these words with added significance: the miracles of the physical order prefigure the greater miracles of the spiritual order. The Good News gives sight to the blind, voices the unspoken desires of the heart, energizes the weak to walk joyfully. Above all, the *position* of the climactic "sign" places hearing the word of Jesus on a par with being raised from the dead. Thus the raising of the dead itself becomes the "sign" proclaiming the spiritual regeneration that Jesus has come to make possible. And this new life is not reserved for a few miraculously exhumed from the grave, but for all who are open to the Word and live in its new fullness.

In Luke's interrogation of the Baptist, the emphasis is also on action as the sign language of discipleship. John highlights, not miraculous cures, but simple yet difficult interpersonal transactions, like sharing resources and collecting fair taxes (Luke 3:11). Read in conjunction with Isaiah, John's instruction parallels the miraculous actions of the Messiah with the pedestrian works of mercy. Those who perform these works become the blind who now see, the lame who now walk, the captives who are liberated into coresponsibility for the kingdom of God. In Luke's version the Baptist demonstrates his own gift for poetic imagery: "I baptize you with water . . . he will baptize you with the Holy Spirit and fire" (Luke 3:16). Then, using metaphorical imagery especially vivid for his agrarian audience, the Baptist returns their attention to the Messiah's action: "His winnowing fork is in his hand, to clear his threshing floor and to gather the wheat into his granary; but the chaff he will burn with unquenchable fire" (Luke 3:17). The words simultaneously caress and assault his listeners in phrases reminiscent of Isaiah's "signature style," tropes that conflate promise and threat, redemption and indictment in equal measure. The Baptist's blunt poetry erases false hope for a magic fulfillment of Isaiah and replaces it with a program of coresponsibility.

Strangely, it is in the Fourth Gospel, in the words of the most conventionally "poetic" of the evangelists, that John the precursor identifies himself plainly. Quoting the prophet Isaiah, he says:

> I am the voice of one crying out in the wilderness,
> Make straight the way of the Lord (John 1:23).

Is it John's straight talk, his passion, or his humility that endears him to Jesus and elicits this startling tribute: "Among those born of women no one is greater than John" (Luke 7:28). Was it his willingness to give himself totally and then get out of the way that attracted such crowds to the Baptist? Whatever John's virtues, Jesus assures us that the Baptist himself is merely a sign pointing to human potential as yet unrevealed: "yet the least in the kingdom of God is greater than he" (Luke 7:28). John's self-identifying voice crying in the wilderness is an apt metaphor for every committed Christian protesting the consumerism that annually invades our Advent wilderness. However, we can adapt his title as an Advent mantra both preparing us for Jesus' coming and reminding us of our role in bringing him to others, as we pray: "I am your voice, You are the word."

The Poets Respond:

One way the poet achieves new insight is to assume the persona or voice of a biblical figure and then imagine him or her in an unfamiliar situation. In the following poem, Pamela Smith, S.S.C.M., captures John's imagined transition from Jesus' boyhood companion to an adult who runs before, but always behind and below, his cousin. Most of us can think of a parallel situation in our own lives, for example a sudden shift or diminishment in expectations, professional position, or self-definition, where spiritual growth demands a humbling change in relation to others. Here the poet urges us to listen to such events as moments of grace, not so dramatic as the Voice from the cloud, but no less the voice of the Father.

The Cousin

John the Baptist:
It was when the water cascaded
through his hair and down his face
that the words crashed through, a shiver, a cloudbreak.
". . . My beloved Son. Listen to him."

When we were tykes playing in the sand,
and later, when we were ten or eleven,
we imagined palace houses, adventure,
tales of the East, ladders to heaven.

He said once that he would be a wise man,
and I pictured him on a camel, turbaned.
I thought I would serve in the temple, like Zechariah,
but I dreamed of digging out the ark or Eden.

That was before the wild skins and the tan
of searing weather and stark wilderness—
before I forefasted, before I foreran,
before the unrolling of the scroll of the plan
That is his Father's.

The voice which spoke this morn
was one I detected in the forlorn
night cry of the desert. I have heard it
before—before, it almost seems, I was born.[1]

—*Pamela Smith, S.S.C.M.*

The power of poetry derives from compressing into few words what prose says with many. One device of compression the evangelists mastered was association. Simply naming certain elemental images, rich in association, evokes a whole train of thought or feeling. One such word is "desert," a word with both positive and negative associations. Called the Garden of Allah, it was the traditional retreat of mystics and sages, the Desert Fathers. A landscape of severe beauty and of extremes of intense heat and cold, it became the testing ground of prophets and holy ones. In our own time, the desert has become the testing site for weapons of mass destruction, nuclear bombs, and germ warfare. The desert demands that we reorder priorities, focusing energy on simple survival. Perhaps most difficult of all, the desert forces us to face the one person we cannot escape and to rely totally on the One Person who knows us as we truly are. In its silence and loneliness, the desert evokes a sense of presence, human or divine. The voice crying from the desert is not always the voice of a prophet, but as Sister Maris Stella, C.S.C., reminds us, it is more frequently the voice of our own hearts:

This One Heart Shaken

It was only my own voice that I had heard,
But at first I did not know it for my own.
Although my lips had formed no single word,
And the voice seemed one that I had never known,
Still it was mine. I knew that it must be:
This secret voice that I had not surmised,
This cry flung from the unsuspected sea
Of loneliness by which I was surprised.
It was as though my other selves came thronging
To see this wonder washed up on the shore,
This one, heart-shaken with immortal longing,

That must possess its life forever more.
And over and over again one cry she made:
"I am afraid of silence. I am afraid."
To which, did I but listen, I should be
Afraid of nothing. Nothing could frighten me.[2]

—Sister Maris Stella, C.S.C.

In a work of expository prose, the setting is simply background scenery, but in a work of poetry or poetic prose, the setting often foreshadows, echoes, or underscores the theme. Hence, if we wish to hear the Gospel fully, we should get into the habit of listening to the setting. In his Intensive Journal Workshops, the Jungian psychologist Ira Progoff has demonstrated how rewarding it is to enter into dialogue with the places that have been significant in our lives. In such an imagined dialogue, the desert confronts a modern John the Baptist.

The Desert Speaks:

And what did you come out to see, John?
    Just how long you could survive on locusts?

Listen to me: there's more to it than that.
    Believe me, there's more to *you* than that.
    You can survive without
    the scraps that feed your ego:
    title
    corner office
    six figure income
    rooms jammed full of collectible stuff
    and collectible people:
    all the flimsy crutches from which
    you have constructed
    that reed shaken in the wind
    you like to call
    'identity.'

Dare to believe in who you are
just as you are
redeemable and worth redeeming.

Come out to the desert to *be:*
Exchange your crowded emptiness
for one authentic landscape
    free of mirages
    false prophets
    false profits
    and fraudulent 'necessities.'

Come out into the desert with Me.

Taste the wild honey.

        —Elizabeth Michael Boyle, O.P.

FOURTH SUNDAY OF ADVENT

Matthew 1:18-24   Luke 1:39-45   Luke 1:26-38

The Gospel Speaks:

Since Luke 1:26-38 was already covered for the Feast of the Immaculate Conception (p. 9), here we will reflect on the other two Gospels for this Sunday, which focus on the time between the Annunciation and the Nativity.

Strangely, Luke makes no mention of Joseph during Mary's pregnancy. We can be grateful to Matthew for at least attempting to speculate on an inevitable human question: How did Joseph take all this? (Matthew, of course, can only imagine how Joseph *would* take all this.) The evangelist assures us that he "took it" as any good man would: "Her husband Joseph, being a righteous man and unwilling to expose her to public disgrace, planned to dismiss her quietly" (Matt 1:19). Very often the power of poetic expression is in the silences. Though Matthew can assume that Mary has told her husband at least as much as she told Elizabeth, he does not name a single emotion in the heart of Joseph or a word between him and his spouse.

These silences represent a literary decision—and an inspired one. With amazing economy, Matthew tells us volumes about the relationship of trust between Mary and Joseph. Obviously, Joseph believes in Mary's innocence. But the simple phrase "unwilling to expose her" tells us even more about Joseph's love. It is stronger than his manly pride; his main concern is protecting her. Matthew frames the story in a familiar literary form: the archetypal "testing of the hero" narrative. Believing in Mary's virtue against all the evidence, Joseph passes the test. Only then does God have mercy on him and, through the poetic medium of a dream, reveals all that Joseph needs to know—and no more (Matt 1:20). In dream language the voice of the angel first confirms Joseph's personal decision and then places it in the larger context of salvation history: "She will bear a son, and you are to name him Jesus, for he will save his people from their sins" (Matt 1:21).

In Luke's account of the meeting between the two expectant mothers (the Visitation), both women speak poetically. Luke's talent for poetry is evident in a number of his literary decisions. For example, there is no reason to believe that Elizabeth, a mature woman, was so ignorant of the stages of pregnancy that she interpreted the Baptist's first kick in her womb as literally a miraculous feat of pre-natal cognition. Luke allows her a playful hyperbole to make vivid her own joy at Mary's news and her faith in what the Holy Spirit is revealing to her.

To Mary herself, Luke assigns the lyric medley of Old Testament verses that we know as the *Magnificat*. This canticle performs several valuable functions. First, by quoting from more than a dozen places in the Hebrew psalms and prophecies, it unites Mary and her unborn child to the whole history and hopes of her people. Mary's song also demonstrates how fragments of verse, stored away in the unconscious, rise to the surface at times of emotional intensity and give voice to feelings for which we have no words of our own.

But the *Magnificat* is more than a collage of quotations; its design reveals the hand of an accomplished poet. Luke seizes upon the setting for this encounter, the highs and lows of the Judean landscape, as metaphor for his theme. Then he sets up a series of contrasts that mimic this imagery. Echoing contrasts between pride and humility, hunger and plenty, power and dependence embody the revolution in values that Mary's son will soon bring about. Finally, the rhythm facilitates memorization. Almost every verse of the *Magnificat* invites repetition until incantation induces the appropriate emotion—or the more appropriate silence.

Both these pre-nativity narratives can be appreciated as brief symbolic poems translating the awesome mystery of redemption into intimate domestic relationships. For the average Christian this message will be enough: in our intimate relationships, God will become real to us, and through our struggle with pedestrian challenges, God's "kingdom" will be established within us and around us. Although the Lectionary stops short of Mary's *Magnificat*, however, we should include it in our meditation, for only in this song do we hear Luke's larger theme, echoed in each of the canticles in his infancy narratives—the theme of liberation.[1] The Mother of God sings her hymn of praise in joyous gratitude for the mystery taking place in her womb: "My soul magnifies the Lord, and my spirit rejoices in God my Savior" (Luke 1:46). But when she follows this exclamation with a series of chiastic contrasts that reverse the definition of greatness, she aligns the coming Redeemer on the side of the poor in emotionally charged language.

The words that break the virgin's accustomed silence deliver a promise of empowerment, especially for women. "He has brought down the powerful . . . and lifted up the lowly" (Luke 1:52).

The Poets Respond:

Thomas Merton's poetic response to the scene of Mary's visit to Elizabeth focuses on John in Elizabeth's womb and compares his vocation to that of the contemplative in his cloister. Imagery like "stone mountain" and "treeless places, and stone valley" embody the sense of the purely contemplative life as "barren." Although faith assures cloistered monks and nuns that their life is not in God's eyes sterile, it often feels that way. Advent is perhaps an appropriate time for Christians to remind themselves of the value of these lives hidden in the "eyeless dark" of heroic faith, lives whose "relevance" is sometimes underappreciated even by pragmatic Christians.[2]

But cloistered monks and nuns are not the only ones whose invisible service to others is embodied in Merton's lovely metaphors. By extension, the unborn John can stand for those among us whose quiet, listening presence is a sacrament or for the disabled and the elderly, whose helplessness, less attractive than that of an infant, delivers a "tongue-tied sermon" of resignation to God's will.

From *The Quickening of St. John the Baptist*

Luke 1, 39-45

. . .

You have drowned Gabriel's word in thoughts like seas
And turned toward the stone mountain
To the treeless places.
Virgin of God, why are your clothes like sails?

. . .

Her salutation
Sings in the stone valley like a Charterhouse bell:
And the unborn Saint John
Wakes in his mother's body,
Bounds with the echoes of discovery.

Sing in your cell, small anchorite!
How did you see her in the eyeless dark?
What secret syllable
Woke your young faith to the mad truth
That an unborn baby could be washed in the spirit of God?
Oh burning joy!
What seas of life were planted by that voice!
With what new sense
Did your heart receive her Sacrament,
And know her cloistered Christ?

You need no eloquence . . .
Exulting in your hermitage,
Your ecstasy is your apostolate,

. . .

Your joy is the vocation
Of Mother Church's hidden children—

. . .

Planted in the night of contemplation,
Sealed in the dark and waiting to be born.

Night is our diocese and silence is our ministry
Poverty our charity and helplessness our tongue-tied sermon.

. . .

We are exiles in the far end of solitude, living as listeners
With hearts attending to the skies we cannot understand:

. . .

Then, like the wise, wild baby,
The unborn John who could not see a thing
We wake and know the Virgin Presence
Receive her Christ into our night
With stabs of an intelligence as white as lightning.[3]

—Thomas Merton

Ruthann Williams, O.P., in her meditation on the visit of Mary and Elizabeth, focuses on the joys of motherhood, which always include thoughts of the unborn child's future. Like Luke, Williams uses the imagery of the Judean hills as metaphor. Her metaphors anticipate the sacramental life of the Church, through which we participate in this encounter. While Merton adopts the unborn Baptist as the embodiment of his own vocation to hiddenness, this poet clothes the two mothers in her own expressive nature as she boldly translates the mood of the *Magnificat* into a dance.

visitation

womb calls to womb
as sacrament begins
nascent eucharist
cries out to herald

i have come

loved cousins
leap
in blessed recognition
no thought now of salome
or calvary

this is the beginning
and the end
of testaments

woman's soul proclaims
the sacredness of life
the glory of beatitudes
while sky and hills rejoice
and spring winds blow
redolent with scent
of jesse's blossoming
laden with infinitude
of love

mother sings to mother
of her joy
and sandaled feet
leave dancing prints
in dust made holy
by his presence

while spirit
flying high above
sends laughter
to accompany the dance.

—ruthann williams, o.p.

Surely no Gospel passage elicits more human sympathy than Joseph's agony at the discovery that the woman he loved and to whom he was betrothed was pregnant. In the following poem Pamela Smith goes beyond speculating on Joseph's emotions during his trial period to imagine an interior monologue that occurs after he has been enlightened. Here she focuses on the emotional sacrifice Joseph's privileged place in God's plan demanded of him throughout a lifetime. In reflecting on this poem, we too should go beyond the obvious. Although Joseph is uniquely himself, he also fulfilled two other lifetime roles: the spouse to whom the partner is always (thankfully) a mystery and the parent to whom the child is inevitably (for better and worse) a stranger.

The Carpenter of Nazareth

Joseph:

The woman,
The woman I could never hold to
But have clasped forever, it seems, soul to soul;
The son who could never belong to me,
The boychild with his cryptic answers, his enigmas,
his perceptions, his everything astonishing,
The son who could never belong to anyone but One,
The man who no longer, at twelve, feels altogether at home. . . .

Over my sawhorse I muse,
Over my carpenter's tools . . .
The house of David,
This house in Nazareth,
"My Father's house,"
"My Father's business". . . .
Which is building.

(Though none would ever dream of angels and ancient texts
or imagine what any of them have to do with this.)
Building.

Someday they will surely say,
"Isn't this the carpenter's son?"
Merely . . .
"Isn't . . .?"
This boy who is expert in wood grains and weights,
Who fondles what he turns and hammers,
This boy who is an artist and tradesman
already, himself.
"Isn't this the carpenter's son?"

Unnoticed, I will insinuate that there is something undisclosed.
More secret than the secrets of my father and his and his
and the whole family line,
confided when a man grasps his firstborn around the neck
and blesses him . . .
Secrets of a craft and generations of faith . . .
. . .
The firstborn . . .
To consecrate and foster but never to father at all.

My wife, the maid
Who is a masterpiece of love and grace . . .
Both of us, the three of us, a bit against the grain.

And waiting, aging.
You might say that my life,
Like the form that wakes from the worker's wood,
Has been a keeping still and trusting
Another hand to cut and lathe, sand and shape.

O Maker, O Master,
O Adonai of David,
O one who duped and used
And fashioned and smoothed the prophets,
O Mystery who has made of my dead wood
A green, an infinitely flowering tree.
I praise, I hold to, Thee.[4]

—Pamela Smith, S.S.C.M.

CHRISTMASTIME

With the Christmas Vigil begins the second liturgical season, Christmastime. Christmas liturgies are characterized by an extraordinary emphasis on natural time: Vigil, Midnight, Dawn, Day. In the readings for the Midnight and Dawn Masses, the Synoptic writers seem intent on establishing the specific moment in human history when the eternal Son of God entered time. John, on the other hand, whose prologue the Lectionary assigns to the Mass for Christmas Day, reminds us that the Word-made-flesh during the reign of Tiberius Caesar had existed from all eternity. Christmas celebrates, therefore, the paradoxical union of timelessness and time in the life of Jesus and calls us not merely to commemorate his historical birth but also to actuate his spiritual rebirth in our hearts and homes. The imagery of the Nativity narrative helps to access these abstractions imaginatively by providing visual metaphors as a starting point for prayer.

The Gospel texts from Christmas Eve through Epiphany, referred to as "the infancy narratives," include some of the New Testament figures and scenes most familiar to Christian art—and Christian devotion: angels, shepherds, Magi; the flight into Egypt; the slaughter of the innocents; the prophecy of Simeon; and the finding in the temple. Twentieth-century scientific criticism has relentlessly assailed the historicity of these unverifiable vignettes from the childhood of Jesus. As a result, not a few contemporary preachers have become more intent on demolishing sentimental attachment to these stories than on exploiting their unique power to communicate Jesus' values. Raymond Brown, however, does not hesitate to assert: ". . . the infancy narratives are worthy vehicles of the Gospel *message*; indeed, each is the *essential Gospel story in miniature*."[1] To paraphrase Brown in the language of this volume, we can say that each of the infancy narratives is a symbolic poem compressing into vivid, evocative language what Christian teaching has always recognized as the essence of the Good News: that through the earthly life of Jesus, our earth and our earthly lives are made holy.

As poetry, these Gospels often express their themes through *patterning*. Literary critics like to illuminate theological intent by carefully tracing patterns within each evangelist's work and between Old and New Testament episodes. Preachers who have been personally enriched by these studies should enhance their homilies by demonstrating how pattern supports meaning internal to the text and also in practical situations relevant to the congregation. In my reflections on the infancy narratives, I will limit myself to what any intelligent lay reader can do with a Gospel text by studying observable patterns in the New Testament and in parallels to well-known Hebrew Scriptures.

CHRISTMAS EVE

Matthew 1:1-25

The Gospel Speaks:

The Gospel chosen for the eve of the Nativity divides into two parts that seem to contradict each other. In the first seventeen verses Matthew gives Jesus a respectable human pedigree, tracing his genealogy through Joseph, the husband of Mary. With the majesty of a trumpet blast, the record opens by announcing the most famous ancestors: "An account of the genealogy of Jesus the Messiah, the son of David, the son of Abraham" (Matt 1:1). In the next eight verses, however, Matthew demonstrates that Joseph is not the father, that, in fact, Jesus had no human father at all. At the time the Son of God entered history, a paternal genealogy was important, of course, to legitimize Jesus and his mother in the Hebrew culture God chose to be the locus for his Son's life on earth. But for contemporary Christians, for whom such perfunctory legitimacy is irrelevant, this annual recitation of unfamiliar names is at best puzzling and at worst boring. Since Gospels, like poems, never waste words, there must be some kerygmatic significance in these names, gesturing, however subtly, toward the true identity and mission of the Messiah.

Abraham, the father who was willing to sacrifice his only-begotten son, is a logical name to invoke at the outset of a list that will conclude with the Son who is eventually presented as the divine Father's ultimate sacrifice. But King David, from whose royal lineage the prophets have promised that the Messiah will descend, was a man guilty of adultery and contract murder (2 Sam 11). And apparently, the family of the Good Shepherd also had more than its share of other "black sheep." Those familiar with the Hebrew Scriptures will notice that the lineage Matthew claims for Jesus includes a number of relatives most families would prefer to disown. The cast of characters in the seventy-two generations includes liars like Jacob and the illegitimate offspring of "loose women" like Tamar and Bathsheba (2 Sam 2).

Therefore, the first thing the words of this Gospel *do* is ground the eternally begotten Son of God in a human family, in Jewish history, and, more importantly, in the reality of human sinfulness. In the manner of poetry, each of the figures named functions as a synecdoche, a part representing a whole class of human frailty. By introducing Jesus through an unattractive pedigree of saints and sinners, the texts tacitly suggest that family history opens our entrance into "salvation history."

Is it too bold to suggest that our participation in the world's salvation might very well hinge on our willingness to forgive the least forgivable members of our own families? Intellectually, all practicing Christians recognize that no one is beyond the reach of God's mercy. But that truth is hard to accept emotionally when it means forgiving those closest to us who have hurt and betrayed us. On Christmas Eve we are reminded that, for some of us, Christmas will begin the day we forgive an abusive or negligent parent or an ungrateful, self-destructive child. To take this challenge a step further, the genealogy suggests that God uses unlikely people as conscious or unconscious instruments in his plan for human salvation. Among these unlikely instruments, for better or worse, are members of the Church whose attitudes and actions are often stumbling blocks to the faith of the flock they are trying to lead to God. Perhaps for many of us, Christmas will begin the day we find it in our hearts to forgive that motley crossbreed of wisdom and ignorance, weakness and strength, pomposity and humility, sophistication and bad taste that many Roman Catholics refer to affectionately as "Holy Mother Church."

In the second section of this Gospel, Matthew's dramatization of the angel's annunciation to Joseph is the same text assigned to the Fourth Sunday of Advent, on which we have already commented (see p. 28). Here I will add only a few additional observations on Matthew's gift for poetic compression. Leaving to generations of poets the imaginative task of speculating on when and how Joseph learned that Mary was pregnant, the author focuses exclusively on how Joseph responded after he *did* learn. The two modifiers Matthew uses to sum up Joseph's character encapsulate his dilemma: Joseph is both "righteous" and "unwilling to expose her" (Matt 1:19). In poetry, juxtaposition produces a verbal shorthand in which each word highlights and comments on the other. Simply by juxtaposing "righteous" and "unwilling," Matthew delivers a powerful homily: the truly virtuous person never acts to reward his own virtue. As a "righteous" man, Joseph is legally entitled to end the betrothal contract with a woman who is bearing a child not his own. But Matthew's simple statement makes clear that Joseph is interested in neither vengeance nor publicity. He goes to bed pondering how to spare Mary disgrace. Then in a dream an angel comes to his rescue (Matt 1:20).

A modern psychologist would interpret Joseph's dream as the acting-out of his anxiety. The angel's words immediately address Joseph's fear and provide a way for love to act on desire: "Do not be afraid" (Matt 1:20). The angel answers Joseph's unspoken question by declaring that what is conceived in Mary is generated by the same Creator Spirit that shattered the darkness in Genesis. Then, using the words of the prophet Isaiah, the angel identifies Mary's unborn son as Emmanuel—"God with us" (Matt 1:23). Finally, he calls Joseph to his role in this mysterious drama, to take Mary as his wife and name her son his own. Matthew does not describe Joseph's emotions after waking or speculate on why he believed the dream. He sums up the whole of Joseph's reaction, and at the same time, the whole of Joseph's vocation in the simple statement: "He did as the angel of the Lord commanded him" (Matt 1:24). Matthew's silence invites us to explore the powerful emotions that must have accompanied that obedience in poetry and in prayer.

The Poets Respond:

Several twentieth-century poets have attempted to replace Joseph's reticence with invented thoughts and feelings. In some cases the poets give Joseph a personality emblematic more of the faith struggles of modern skeptics than of a devout biblical Hebrew. W. H. Auden, in his famous oratorio "For the Time Being" and Rainer Maria Rilke, in "Joseph's Suspicion," both envision Joseph arguing strenuously with the angel.[1] Auden's poem, with its demand for blind faith in a scientific impossibility, actually discards the revelatory dream. Joseph asks for "important and elegant proof" that Mary's word is true, proof the angel refuses to give. Rilke, on the other hand, imagines Joseph refusing to believe that Mary is pregnant, shaking his fist at the angel as he defends her honor. In his classic book-length poem *A Woman Wrapped in Silence,* John Lynch resists the temptation to speak for Joseph. Lynch makes poetry of what we do not know, yet he seems to capture what Joseph and Mary might really have been like with each other.

From *A Woman Wrapped in Silence*

What source we have of knowledge of her days
Is sparing, and has left us many days
Still veiled, and if there is enough to find
What Joseph found, and a few dear treasured words,
We must have more to lead us where our love
Would seek to go. And there is one sweet place
That distant watching eyes could fondly wish
To see and ponder on. Did Joseph come,
And with his sobs seek pardon for his fears?
And did he see how, suddenly, his love
Was greater than he knew and could be carried
Now along new pathways with his prayers?
God's kingdom now was four, and claimed again
Another life to be with Zachary,
To listen with Elizabeth, and then
With her to serve. O, glad, he was for strength,
And glad for honor, and for name, and glad
His hand was skilled enough to fashion walls
And build the smallness of a crib that now
Would cradle more than all the world could hold.
Dreams of all his fathers fell on him
In one bright dream, and all bright hopes were clear.
We may not know for sure, and yet, and yet,
May we not see how quietly he came
And spoke no word. And Mary saw him come,
Finding a new thing shining in his eyes.
And when quick tears of gladness and relief
Were done, she saw him kneel, lift up his hands,
Two hands that held invisibly, his life.
She may have reached her own pale fingers out
And found them . . . callused, generous, and *strong.*[2]

—*John W. Lynch, S.J.*

Within the past decade the Christian Churches have been experiencing a new phenomenon: couples bringing to baptism infants conceived in fertility clinics. These couples are aware that the institutional Roman Catholic Church disapproves of in vitro fertilization. Yet, their faith convinces them that medical technology alone cannot produce an immortal soul, that no child can be conceived without the cooperation of the Creator. To their traditional God they have prayed throughout a long ordeal. Now that their prayers have been answered, they desire to admit their child into the sacramental life of the Church. One morning in Advent, a few days after meeting one such parent, I was reflecting on this new mystery as I hummed my favorite Advent psalm:

> Heavens, pour down your waters from above:
>
> Let the Just One descend.
>
> Open up, oh earth, and let the savior bud forth.
>
>> The earth's fullness belongs to the Lord
>>
>> For all that is substance and breath.
>>
>> All things from pebble to star
>>
>> Are born from His love.
>
> Open your highways and gateways:
>
> Ancient paths and new roads, open!
>
> For the Lord of Glory is coming.
>
>> Who is this Lord of Glory?
>>
>> . . . The maker of all worlds
>>
>> He who lifts all creation
>>
>> Into the dance of life.

Through many Advents I had sung these words celebrating the unity of all creation in the love of the Creator. Recently, in the context of modern science, the familiar lyrics suddenly assumed fresh meaning. Then all these inspirations came together in the following poem:

Ages of Faith

"Joseph, do not be afraid . . . the child
conceived in her is from the Holy Spirit."

Some lines of scripture
capture the colors of sky:
or is it the other way round?

This December dawn's warm grey
streaked with ice, flaked with embers:
the can-it-be-true-at-last
fiercely-fought-for hue
of a fragile pregnancy test.
How strangely it touches me with
the cold / warm silences of Joseph
before and after the brief
white flame of the angel cooled
then burned to steady blue.

Some miracles of science
capture the colors of faith:
or is it the other way round?

In vitro, in utero:
"You knit me together in my mother's womb."
Deus incognito?
Deus abscondito?
Outside my window
the Advent sky
marries darkness to daybreak
heaven to earth
listens for an infant's cry
and asks no questions.

—*Elizabeth Michael Boyle, O.P.*

CHRISTMAS MIDNIGHT

Isaiah 9:1-16   Luke 2:1-14

The Gospel Speaks:

If any readings require no homily, the texts for the Christmas Midnight Mass should certainly qualify. And yet, at no time is a preacher more likely to command an attentive audience. At this moment people are counting on the liturgy to deliver for a few minutes the profound peace that a consumerist culture has almost, but not quite, banished from the event we struggle to remember as a silent night. On this night, therefore, the homily should be brief enough to motivate a long silence. Depending on the shared experience of each faith community on a specific Christmas, any one of the following reflections could provoke a thoughtful silence. *The best meditation or homily will focus on one suggestion and leave the others for another year.*

❖ The texts for Christmas Midnight affirm one of the central premises of this book, namely, that the Gospels reveal their full meaning through their *poetic design*. Imitating St. Ignatius's well-known "composition of place," the preacher might guide the congregation to listen and mentally follow the Gospel with their *eyes*. In particular, she should encourage them to imagine the Nativity scene, with its visual symmetries and polarities.

Tradition attests that Luke the evangelist was also a painter. This could account for the extraordinary sense of artistic composition in his version of the Nativity scene. In its upward and downward lines Luke's careful composition captures what Raymond Brown calls a "sense of geographical theology": the union of heaven and earth, the human and the divine, in the person of Jesus Christ.[1] Re-creating the scene within us, we unconsciously experience a tension between desire and reality in some area of our personal lives that mirrors the artistic tension between high and low, angel and animal, in the familiar Bethlehem scene. Many will also feel an emotional tension between childhood memories and adult realities. In the silence after the reading, we hand over our hearts to the transforming action of an artist who made a temple out of a barn and can make a home in the midst of our contradictions. Then we can relax in the embrace of a God who became incarnate to dissolve all distances and dualities. This is the peace of Christmas.

❖ Isaiah's prophecy "A people who walked in darkness have seen a great light" (Isa 9:2b) seems to prefigure the heavenly glow that announces Jesus' birth to the shepherds and the star that will guide the Magi. Read aloud, these words fall on a darkness that is a little different each year. We who walk most of the time, not in the darkness of evil but in a fog of spiritual oblivion, beg the light to penetrate the unique personal darkness in each of our hearts: the darkness of doubt, grief, loss of faith in one's self, one's world, or one's church, in a marriage, in parenthood, or in one's constantly postponed "interior life." In the silence simply repeat the words "A people who walked in darkness" as a prayer acknowledging your share in the human condition. This humble willingness to walk in darkness will call the light to your shores.

❖ ". . . all the garments rolled in blood shall be burned as fuel for the fire . . . and there shall be endless peace" (Isa 9:5-7). Isaiah's description of the messianic reign, a promise on which Christendom has never delivered, strikes the skeptics among us with bitter irony. Reflecting regretfully on the painful contrast between these words and almost any day's headlines forces us to focus on *that peace which the world cannot give, or earn, or buy.* In the silence reflect on a practical plan to bring peace into the only places within your control.

❖ Scholars and skeptics are disturbed by geographical discrepancies between Luke's and Matthew's versions of the Nativity. One evangelist locates the birth in Bethlehem and the other in Nazareth. Rejoice that the God-man has effectively frustrated the commercial impulse to make a theme park out of Christianity's birthplace. All that we're sure of is that the monumental Church of the Nativity bears no resemblance to the cave of Bethlehem. By subverting our desire for earthly permanence, our compulsion to lock God up in a place separate from our lived-in ambience, the geography of Christmas compels us to admit that it does not matter exactly where Jesus was born two thousand years ago. In the silence, open up the place where he chooses to be born today.

Those of us who have been attentive to the readings throughout Advent notice that the words "joy" and "rejoice" have chimed like sleigh bells throughout Luke's first chapter. We hear joy ring in Gabriel's announcement to Zechariah (1:14), his greeting to Mary (1:28), the Baptist's greeting to the unborn Jesus (1:44), and the "exultation" of Mary's canticle (1:47). At midnight all these little bells are joined by a clashing of cymbals as the Christmas angel's proclamation brings the theme to a glorious conclusion: "I am bringing you good news of great joy for all the people: to you is born this day in the city of David a Savior, who is the Messiah, the Lord" (Luke 2:10-11). Then the voices of a whole angelic choir transform the incident into a liturgical event. Joy, real joy, is not an isolated episode. Joy is a habit rooted in a lifetime of willingness to interrupt any agenda to pay attention to the presence of God within and around us. In the silence, receive this sacrament with a moment of complete attention.

❖ Significantly, the angels depart the scene, leaving the shepherds to become the first Christian faith community. The angel's message demands that the shepherds "trust but verify." Together they go to investigate the "sign" and assure themselves that they have not had a collective dream, and thus assured, to bear witness (Luke 2:15-20). But they do not bear witness to the actual birth of Jesus. Luke's account has spared us the prolonged, clinically detailed, noisy childbirth scenes that are a staple of soap opera. The reticence surrounding Mary's delivery underscores the ordinariness of Jesus' humanity and offers only one extraordinary detail—that she placed him in a manger (Luke 2:7). Is this the sign that this child is indeed creator of the universe: that he has and needs less than any of his creatures? In the silence, acknowledge that the surest access to Christmas peace is to have and need less of everything else.

❖ Out of the single detail "she . . . laid him in a manger" (Luke 2:7), Christian tradition has extrapolated many beautiful artifacts. Each Christmas Eve women spend hours in their homes and churches decorating the crèche until every detail is "perfect." Every syllable and every image is repeated like a magic incantation hoping to revive an ideal Christmas, a lost childhood. As the familiar narrative is read, one gets the impression that Mary and Joseph are following a script. Those of us with a gift for ritual try each year to repeat every detail of a personal or family ceremony, convinced that if we manage to follow our ideal script, the grace of Christmas will surely happen. What the Gospel cannot say, of course, is what script Mary herself had in mind. Yet one thing we can know for certain is that every detail of Christmas Eve contradicts a mother's ideal scenario for the delivery of her firstborn. In the silence, revise your Christmas plans to leave room for the unexpected. That way, you just might be blessed with a "real Christmas."

The Poets Respond:

America's penchant for excess electrifies our Christmas landscape with a dazzle of lights that almost obliterate the stars. Poets, fortunately, understand that darkness is the companion, not the enemy, of light. In fact, the poet-prophet Isaiah puts these words into the mouth of God: "I form light and create darkness" (Isa 45:6-7). With the possible exception of John of the Cross, perhaps, no other poet has embraced "holy" darkness more than Rainer Maria Rilke, who prays:

> You, darkness, of whom I am born—
>
> I love you more than the flame
> that limits the world
> to the circle it illumines
> and excludes all the rest.
>
> But the darkness embraces everything:
> shapes and shadows, creatures and me,
> people, nations—just as they are.
> It lets me imagine
> a great presence stirring beside me.
>
> I believe in the night.[2]

Two poems, one inspired by astrophysics and the other by ancient tradition, take us to a hillside that, for a few moments, becomes the center of the universe. Each poet restores darkness to its privileged place in creation, in spirituality, and at the heart of Christmas hope. Marion Goldstein's metaphysical lyric, besides being a meditation on dark matter, also demonstrates the process of association as darkness speaks to the soul.

In the Absence

"It is our habit of thought that confuses things with their names."
—*Simone Weil*

Just take the dark matter
of the cosmos
those enormous fields surrounding stars
they are absent
light
existing outside of time
not of this universe
where everything falls apart
and reclaims itself with a new name.

Pure mystery
it sends us back
our own questions
deflecting them like a mirror.

The archives of Auschwitz
tell the story
of a man
in the darkest of time
who lived in his head
and there his wife and children picnicked
on the Elb
the hamper filled with cheese and fruit
the bread warmed by the sun

and the lilacs even dying
transformed the hillside
with the glory of their blossoming.

So let us baptize the dark matter
Call it imagination
Call it love
Call it the tenth dimension
But call it
Let it ride the waves of gravity and pile itself
On every hillside you climb.

—*Marion I. Goldstein*

shepherd's field: Bethlehem

there is remembrance in this dark field
the tranquility of starlight
moon-silvered grass and somewhere
a quiet bell announces
dream-stirring animal
while angels leave their mark upon the sky.

the coolness of a cave
round and hard
as a woman ready
for birthing
drawing darkness in upon herself
drawing down deep darkness
deep into herself
deeply down
to heavy womb
she moans

a sudden thrust
a pain
a shout
and light breaks out
the echo of an infant cry

a light
shining in the darkness
that cannot overcome it
glory to God in the highest

was this the place?
no matter for *was* is past
and *Is* must be reality
this place is now
and I draw darkness
deep into myself
and pray for light

while in
the little town of Bethlehem
armed soldiers march

with guns
against the crowd
and stones like lamentations
hurl down the streets

no silent night
but rachel
weeping for her children
and a voice cries out in ramah
my god, my god
why have you forsaken us
and oh, where
is peace
for your people on earth?

—*ruthann williams, o.p.*

When St. Francis of Assisi arranged the first outdoor crèche, he was attempting to re-create the harsh realities of the original Nativity scene, complete with live animals surrounding the manger. In the ensuing centuries, Christians have incorporated the crèche into their elegant Christmas décor by reducing the austerities of the situation into something merely ornamental. Christopher Fitzgerald rejects any attempt to sanitize Jesus' embrace of "the human condition":

IT'S NOT FOR US TO KNOW if Mary's pain
Was dark or light, or how the labor went,
Or whether Joseph's energies were spent
Evicting some reluctant beast to gain
A corner of a manger's rich terrain
For purposes obstetric. Was he sent
To beggar, when the need was evident,
The help of women skilled in their domain?
It's left to our imagining to square
The rigors of the manger with the creche,
To hear the muffled cry, to mark the stretch
And push a birthing God might bring to bear.
The image of the creche is sweet and light,
But Lord, was there no blood and sweat that night?[3]

—*Christopher Fitzgerald*

Those familiar with the English sonnet form will recognize the poet's strategy here. Typically, an English sonnet consists of fourteen lines divided into two parts: three quatrains that raise a question, followed by a couplet that resolves it with a sage comment on the situation. Fitzgerald's first three quatrains raise the kinds of questions with which a skeptic entertains himself. Then he teases us with practical details that the Gospel leaves out. But the final couplet dismisses those issues as irrelevant and compels us to re-read the opening sentence: "It's not for us to know" about the details of that physical birth, because that's no longer where and how the Son of God is born on earth. We read our way back up the lines of the sonnet and acknowledge that the "sweat and blood," the "stretch and push" demanded are our own; that we might need midwives for our spiritual birth; that the "beast" to be "evicted" is within each human breast; that God is still "a-birthing" in our hearts and in our homes tonight and always.

CHRISTMAS DAWN

Luke 2:15-20

The Gospel Speaks:

Poetry is an art of compression. In less than twenty lines Luke delivers a proclamation narrative that also models for us the two principal modes of bringing Jesus to birth within each individual and each community: to internalize the Word in personal intimacy and to externalize the Gospel in concrete action. In the Mass for Christmas Dawn, Luke personifies this twin vocation in the shepherds and in Mary, the *animus* and the *anima* of an integrated Christian personality.

The text begins with the shepherds, who represent the first to whom the birth of the Savior is announced (Luke 2:8-12). Apparently, according to their behavior, the shepherds are not theologians. They do not analyze the angel's words or submit alternate interpretations to a vote of the Jesus Seminar. Luke does not picture them saying: "Let's see *if* what the angel said is true." Rather, without hesitation or reservation, they set out for Bethlehem and find the Savior right where the angel said they would (Luke 2:15). Then they joyfully spread the word to others (Luke 2:20).

These are men of imagination, men of faith, and men of action. The evidence that God has in fact visited his people is in the shepherds' incorruptible simplicity and transforming joy. Their example suggests that we need neither learned exegesis nor powers of persuasion to fulfill our Christian mission. In the familiar words of Marshall McLuhan, the medium is the message. All we need is authenticity.

Meantime, the silence of Mary, the mother of the newborn Savior, radiates from the center of this Gospel scene and communicates her authenticity to the shepherds. As she listens to the shepherds' account of the angel's proclamation about her child, we can imagine her understanding for the first time why she had to endure the inconveniences of delivering her baby in a stable shared with animals. Mary and the shepherds need each other. At the time of her own Annunciation, Mary needed to believe that the child in her womb would be extraordinary;

now she needs to believe that he has come to transform the ordinary. It is the shepherds' words she ponders in her heart (Luke 2:19). And her commanding silence gives them something to ponder too. Mary's quiet majesty lends credibility to the angel's claims for her child. The fullness of Mary's faith animates the shepherds as they go forth praising and glorifying God for their part in this amazing story (Luke 2:20).

Mary and the shepherds represent the contemplative and active dimensions of every personality, every family, every community, whether it be an office staff, a construction team, a school faculty. They also embody the places where Jesus desires to be born anew each Christmas. In the most intimate relationships of each human heart, the God of love is born again and again. But Jesus also desires to be found in a place where we least expect to find him: in the workplace. In a sweet reversal of the threat at the outset of Advent (Matt 24:40-41), the angel surprises the shepherds where they are "simply doing their job."

The shepherds' example warns us that while waiting for "free time" to put Christ back in Christmas, we're liable to miss it entirely. Jesus seeks us out in the place where we spend most of our time and energy. Simply acknowledging this possibility can alter our attitude toward the place, the job, the people who work with and for us. To incarnate the love of God in an ordinary workday takes no extra time, but it does take extraordinary attention. "Those who spend themselves in the search for 'transcendence' miss the transcendent in the ordinary."[1] Discovering the transcendent in the ordinary can be the real dawn of Christmas Day.

The Poets Respond:

A poet's relationship to the Gospel text is always interactive; she automatically "engages" the text with one or more strategies to make a familiar pericope momentarily strange. Sometimes a poet can assume the voice of one of the Gospel characters or personify one of the elements in the setting; he can interrogate or dialogue with the evangelist or with one of the principal actors in the Gospel drama. In the following poem Rainer Maria Rilke assumes the persona of the Christmas star and addresses the shepherds. (Of course, Rilke knows that it was to the Magi, not the shepherds, that the star appeared. The poet does not let such trivial discrepancies interrupt the flow of inspiration.) The star seems to know that the shepherds will hear and understand his words because they speak the same language: they "hear tongues everywhere." Yet, he tells them that "a new thing dawns today." Once earth and Paradise were two different worlds; now the fact of the Incarnation sacralizes all things earthly. This was the conventional theology of Rilke's day. But the poet goes beyond that to a vision which anticipates a contemporary incarnational theology, a perspective that abandons the medieval concept of man at the apex of an ontological hierarchy. From angel to thornbush to the heart of a shepherd and the womb of a virgin, Rilke insists, life is one and life is holy.

Annunciation to the Shepherds from Above

Look up you men, Men at the fire there, you
familiar with the skies unbounded ways,
star readers, hither! Look, I am a new
uprising star. My being is one blaze,
so filled with light the firmament is too
small now to hold me and my powerful rays,
for all its depth. Do let my splendor throw
its beams right into you: oh the dark sight,
the gloomy hearts, destinies black as night
that you're brim-full of. Shepherds, I am so
alone in you. Yet, now, there's room for me.
Weren't you astonished: the big bread-fruit tree
was casting shadow. Well, that shade *I* threw.
Oh you undaunted, if you only knew
how even now upon each gazing face
the future shines. Much will be taking place
in that clear light. To you I can speak out,
you have discretion; straight souls, free from doubt,
you hear tongues everywhere. Warmth speaks and rain,
wind, birds' flight, what you are; no one sound is
more than another, and no vanities
fatten themselves. You don't detain
things in that interval the breast, to be
tormented there. As his own ecstasy
streams through an angel, earthliness can make
its way through you. And should a thornbush take

fire suddenly, the Infinite could still
call to you from it; Cherubim would fill,
if any deigned to walk where your flocks graze,
those hearts of yours with no alarmed surprise:
you'd fall upon your faces and give praise,
and name this earth still and not Paradise.

But all this was. A new thing dawns today
For which the round earth seeks to grow more wide.
What is a thornbush now: God feels his way
into a virgin's womb. I am the ray
thrown by her inwardness, which is your guide.[2]

—*Rainer Maria Rilke*

Among modern poets inspired by the Gospels, another favorite interactive strategy is to invent a shocking alternative to the stark facts and gentle symbols of the first Christmas, contrasting the familiar Gospel imagery with harsh contemporary realities. Each year we can update topical references like Lawrence Ferlinghetti's images with even more relevant images of our own.

Christ Climbed Down

Christ climbed down
from His bare Tree
this year
and ran away to where
there were no rootless Christmas trees
hung with candycanes and breakable stars

. . .

hung with electric candles
and encircled by electric trains
and clever cornball relatives.

. . .

and where no Sears Roebuck creches
complete with plastic babe in manger
arrived by parcel post
the babe by special delivery.

. . .

Christ climbed down
from His bare Tree
this year
and softly stole away into
some anonymous Mary's womb again
where in the darkest night
of everybody's anonymous soul
He awaits again
an unimaginable
and impossibly
Immaculate Reconception
the very craziest
of Second Comings.[3]

—*Lawrence Ferlinghetti*

CHRISTMAS DAY

John 1:1-18

The Gospel Speaks:

Although, in general, I recommend a literary reading as only *one* of *many* approaches to a New Testament text, in the case of John's Prologue I do not hesitate to assert that the *only* way to engage these eighteen verses is to surrender to them as to poetry. In fact, I would go even further: all any commentator can do is facilitate an encounter with the pure poetry of John 1 on its own terms. These terms include submitting to the incremental effect of their repetitive power and *resisting the temptation* to interpret or paraphrase. A lifetime attachment to this Gospel has led me to this conviction, a conviction confirmed for me only recently by consulting respected Johannine scholars. At the risk of exposing an embarrassing level of naiveté, I summarize my experience briefly here.

During my childhood, John's Prologue was recited at the end of every Mass. Hence, "In the beginning was the Word" (John 1:1) was never the subject of a homily. But every practicing Catholic knew the verses by heart. With our solemn genuflection at the words "And the Word became flesh and lived among us" (John 1:14), we accepted a command to make the Word take flesh in our lives.

But although every other word in John's elemental vocabulary seemed self-explanatory, I was puzzled by one: the *Word*. What word? Throughout adulthood, experiences in prayer suggested different synonyms, but I never took a formal course in Scripture to answer the question definitively. One year I had the opportunity to spend a summer in a contemplative cloister. With me I took two cartons of theology books, but I never opened them. Each day my private prayer began with reading the words of John's Prologue, after which all books and questions seemed irrelevant. After a summer of meditating with no image for the Word, male or female, I felt that I knew God and myself as I had never known and been known before. A few months ago, when for the first time I read several works by the Johannine scholars

Raymond E. Brown and his student Sandra Schneiders, I understood the distinctive action of John's poetry in the soul of a receptive reader. Their descriptions echoed almost verbatim the "first-person" impact of this text in my own prayer.

Brown points out that John's "In the beginning was the Word" gestures firmly to its source in the Wisdom literature, "From the mouth of the Most High I came forth" (Sir 24:3), and that typically Divine Wisdom, personified as female, speaks in the first person.[1] Expanding on Brown, Schneiders goes on to stress the essentially reciprocal nature of revelation itself: "In John, revelation connotes a relationship, not a one-way communication of otherwise unavailable information" . . . but "an invitation . . . to participate in one's selfhood."[2] Further, she argues, this participation is facilitated by the distinctive literary structure of the work. Commenting on John's use of "staircase parallelism," for example, Schneiders notes: "The cyclical repetition in the Fourth Gospel is like a spiral staircase that takes the reader up higher, down deeper, passing again and again the same familiar points, giving an ever richer view of the One who stands in the center."[3] When we hand ourselves over, as preachers and as prayers, to the untranslatable action of the Word in John's poetry, we continue to receive "from his fullness . . . grace upon grace" (John 1:16) in the reciprocal revelation of who Jesus is and who we are in him. With the words "In the beginning," the Church greets us today, not with an ephemeral Christmas card, but with the mystery of ourselves and our world as a continually "new creation."[4]

The Poets Respond:

Although poetry can be a form of prayer, poets themselves are the first to agree with Vassar Miller that "the poet like the mouse will scuttle clean to the corner of the ineffable / then scurry back / with tidbits of the Vision."[5] As a young priest, Karol Wojtyla, John Paul II, wrote prayers in the form of poem-cycles. In one of these he assumes the persona of Mary, the mother of the Word Incarnate, after her Son has risen and left her. In these verses the poet allows Mary to be as puzzled and bereft as the rest of humankind. Wojtyla's vocabulary is simple, his ideas immediately accessible, almost prosaic. In his verb selection, however, we recognize the genius of the poet. Verbs do two important things here: (a) they embody the inner life of the poem, and (b) they create a pattern of movement that mirrors the movement of prayer. In the opening stanza, for example, "break," "falling," and "uplifted" set the pattern. You can almost see light "break" from the words, compel Mary to "fall" down in humility and / or sadness, then feel herself "uplifted" by a strength not her own. Is this not the rhythm of prayer inspired by contact with Jesus in the Scriptures?

Words which grow into me

Thought breaks from spoken words
and from the face, shadows falling from high walls.
People are uplifted: only yesterday
they had quiet conversations, summoning
echoes of changes far and near.

The first moment of amazement
which witnessed you, Son of my love,
shut me out.
This moment deepens still,
transforming my whole life,
and breaks, a drop of pure wax
before fading eyes.

This moment, a whole life experienced in the word
since it became my body, was nourished by my blood,
was carried in elation—
rising in my heart, as the New Man, quietly,
when thought was held in wonder and the daily toil of hands.
This high moment is fresh again
because it rediscovers you—
only the eyelashes, the drop
where once light from the eyes melted in cold air,
is no more.

Overwhelming exhaustion instead
has found its light and its meaning.[6]

—*Karol Wojtyla*

FEAST OF THE HOLY FAMILY

Matthew 2:13-15   Luke 2:22-40   Luke 2:41-52

The Gospel Speaks:

On the Sunday after Christmas, the Feast of the Holy Family, the Lectionary distributes over its three-year cycle all that the Synoptics have to say about Jesus' childhood. Matthew, the only one to mention the visit of the Magi, speculates that the costly impact of that visit was the family's exile to Egypt (Matt 2:13-15). Luke describes two bittersweet events in the temple: the encounter with Simeon (Luke 2:22-40) and the loss and finding of the boy Jesus (Luke 2:41-52). If, as Raymond Brown claims, each of the infancy narratives presents the Gospel message in miniature,[1] that message can scarcely be called Good News for any family. And those who expect poetry to idealize reality will scarcely call these snapshots of Jesus' childhood poetic. Only the most imaginative and determined commentators can wrest from these episodes the portrait of an ideal family—unless, of course, Christians are expected to accept disruption, sorrow, anxiety, misunderstanding, and frustration as "family values." However, those who appreciate the function of good poetry to undermine conventional priorities recognize how effectively these Gospels destabilize sentimental expectations. As parables of pedestrian holiness, all three texts offer Christian families comforting assurances as well as challenging questions.

Before commenting on these questions, however, let us ask: What is the "Gospel message" each scene dramatizes "in miniature"? I believe that in all three narratives the Holy Family acts out the message that the Incarnation embraces not only human nature but also human limitations, that the Word-made-flesh continues to reveal himself through families who share his vulnerability to pain, to evil, and to secular power. Mary and Joseph represent the rest of us, who, in parenting the presence of God in the human family today, must acknowledge the limitations of time, human understanding, and vulnerability, not as obstacles to holiness, but as the very locus for our encounter with divine mercy.

First of all, families that have been geographically uprooted can find in the Holy Family's exile in Egypt assurance that God's Son understands the suffering of aliens and refugees and seeks to be the stable presence in all forms of dislocation. A similar sense of displacement pervades neighborhoods where immigration has transformed familiar streets and shops into "foreign territory," and American families living there will feel emotional kinship with the exiled Holy Family. However, the story of the Egyptian exile warns us that God does not set a high value on physical and material security in this world, even and especially for the "best of families." Parents whose homes are models of comfort must have the courage to ask: Who or what threatens the spiritual life of my child? Who or what in our lifestyle threatens to slaughter innocence? And what am I willing to sacrifice to save it?

In the second scene, Luke's account of the presentation of the child in the temple includes Mary's bittersweet encounter with Simeon. Hailing the child as a "light for revelation to the Gentiles" (Luke 2:32), Simeon gives Jesus the title reverently mirrored in the para-liturgical blessing of candles on February 2. But Simeon does not allow us to enjoy the candle's romantic glow for long. This child is "destined for the falling and the rising of many," Simeon warns the mother, and "a sword will pierce your own soul too" (Luke 2:34-35). Has a child ever been born who does *not* eventually pierce the soul of his or her mother, either by success or failure, by maturity or immaturity, by excessive dependence or premature independence, by living too hard or dying too soon? Once celebrated as the Purification of Mary (until post-Vatican liturgical theology rejected the insulting redundancy of that title), this feast juxtaposes the warm glow of candlelight with the cold steel of the sword, twin reminders that all parenthood is a lifelong purification.

In the third episode, Luke seems to suggest that Jesus himself is eager to inflict the wound promised by Simeon. Apparently indifferent to the anguish he imposes on his parents, the twelve-year-old-enough to-know-better Jesus separates himself from Joseph and Mary for three days and then actually rebukes them for their frantic searching: "Did you not know that I must be in my Father's house?" (Luke 2:49). Mothers who find that Mary's virtuous silence usually defies emulation might be consoled by this scene where she seems to lose her temper—or at least her patience. Jesus should know that the kind of parents who turn to the Gospel for help need more encouragement than blame. So, is it possible to read his words as an act of kindness toward Mary and Joseph? Is Jesus trying to relieve his parents from all responsibility for a choice that is truly his own? Apparently the evangelist does not deem it blasphemous to suggest that they don't "get it," that the adolescent Jesus was as baffling to his parents as most adolescents are to theirs. Luke asserts that Mary and Joseph "did not understand what he said to them" (Luke 2:50).

After this scene Jesus disappears into silence until he leaves home. Don't all adolescents disappear from their parents as they begin their lonely search for identity? Is this not the time for parents to have faith that the soul of every child *is* the Father's house? For the rest of his time in Nazareth, we're told, Jesus was "obedient to them" (Luke 2:51). But the Gospel cannot say that he fulfilled their expectations. God's expectations of parents and children can be easier to fulfill than the goals we set for each other. And much holier.

The Poets Respond:

Poets inspired by the Gospels often focus on subordinate figures in the drama. The Lectionary selection from Matthew's narrative of the flight into Egypt stops short of the verses devoted to the infants that did not escape Herod's sword. The slaughter of these innocent children provides the first occasion in the liturgical year when we are forced to reflect on the mystery of God's passive complicity in evil. The mystery is exacerbated when God seems to intervene to save some and not others from the consequences of human freedom. Surely no crime cries to heaven more stridently than the excesses of a culture that has brought about the death, not of children, but of childhood. In Christopher Fitzgerald's sonnet, he uses the infant martyrs of Bethlehem to confront God the Father with questions that headlines provoke us to repeat almost daily.

> YOU DID NOT WILL that all those boys should die.
> And yet you let it happen, knew it would.
> Knew the heart of Herod, understood
> The certainty of swords, the anguished cry
> All Bethlehem would hurl against the sky.
> You could have intervened—not only could,
> But did, to save Your son, and that was good—
> And yet the march of evil You let by.
> You did not will it, did not want it, Lord,

But still, You let a wicked force prevail.
Thus human doubts our human minds assail:
What good is good when evil is ignored?
Forgive me, Lord, if I do struggle here;
You know my love's intact, as is my fear.[2]

—Christopher Fitzgerald

In these two poems inspired by Luke 2:22-40, the first poet plays with the paradoxes in the temple setting, in the person of Mary and in the words of Simeon. Taking the central image of light outdoors, the poet extends the arms of the newborn to embrace all of creation. Following this same movement, she then alternates between painting simple details of the temple scene and hinting at their larger significance in the Father' plan, between the sleepy oblivion of the child and the chilling shadow of the old man's prophecy.

presentation

sun creeps over mountain top
and bursts
into a million lights
against the temple wall
dropping bits of brightness
even into kidron's cavern

temple approaches temple
holiest of wombs
nears
holiest of places
bringing holiness
in her arms

moving through the temple courts
they bring turtledoves
for sacrifice
not dreaming of the greater sacrifice
now mewing at her breast
despite the prophet's words

what did he mean
a sign of contradiction
and a sword?

while the glory of his people
nestles deeper into sleep
smiling in his dream
safe
in his father's presence.

—*ruthann williams, o.p.*

Denise Levertov focuses on Simeon in the single moment where, standing at the threshold between the Old and the New Covenants, he rotates between faith and certitude, death and resurrection. This is the kind of spiritual event T. S. Eliot would describe as "Not the intense moment only / But a lifetime burning in every moment."[3]

Candlemas

With certitude
Simeon opened
ancient arms
to infant light.
Decades
before the cross, the tomb

and the new life
he knew
new life.
What depth of faith he drew on
turning illumined
towards deep night.[4]

—*Denise Levertov*

Surprisingly few poets have chosen to write about the episode of the lost boy Jesus. Yet, few emotions should elicit more sympathy than Mary's exasperation at losing something irreplaceable. This familiar emotion, rather than the Gospel story itself, inspired Poland's Nobel Laureate Wislawa Szymborska. She begins by painting a comic death-bed scene in which all the lost objects of a lifetime come flying home. Cumulatively, however, her subtle inference is serious: we waste lifetimes on things that do not matter. On the Feast of the Holy Family, this whimsical poem could trigger a reflection on what a family might be losing in its quest for material things.

Still Life with Toy Balloon

Instead of the return of memories
at the hour of death
I order up the return
of lost objects.

Through the windows, the doors—umbrellas,
a suitcase, gloves, a coat,
so I can say:
What use is all that to me?

Wherever you may be, key,
try to arrive on time,
so I can say:
It's all rust, my dear friend, rust.

A cloud of certificates will descend,
of passes and questionnaires,
so I can say:
The sun is setting.

O watch, swim out of the river,
Let me take your hand,
So I can say:
Don't still pretend to indicate the hour.

The toy balloon torn loose upon the wind
will also reappear,
so I can say:
There are no children here.

Fly off through the open window,
fly off into the wide world,
let someone cry out: Oh!
so I can weep.[5]

—*Wislawa Szymborska*

FEAST OF THE EPIPHANY

Isaiah 60:1-6   Ephesians 3:2-6   Matthew 2:1-12

The Gospel Speaks:

Most practicing Christians appreciate Matthew's Magi narrative as a *symbolic* enactment of Isaiah's prophecy as it is continually fulfilled in Jesus' spiritual manifestation to all nations. At a more intimate level, the wise men encourage us to brave our own quest for fulfillment. With envy for the certitude of a clearly recognizable star, modern Christians cultivate the light of conscience as its equivalent today.

In many respects, however, the legendary journey of the stargazers represents the triumph of poetry over scholarship. For example, throughout two millennia the story has sturdily resisted historical criticism, inspiring instead a quixotic quest for scientific affirmation of Scripture in astronomy. Furthermore, from the single phrase "wise men from the East" (Matt 2:1) imagination has extrapolated two richly robed Arabs and an Ethiopian, whom Hallmark artists depict balancing crowns on their heads as they steer their camels ("ships of the desert") over a misplaced snowscape. Finally, their fabled gifts of such dubious value to an infant that we question their reputed wisdom are responsible for the gift-giving industry that competes so strenuously with the true spirit of Christmas.

Despite such incongruities, the three kings and their mysterious star remain popular in Christian iconography. Perhaps the reason is as simple as the reason that the dragon dominates Chinese art: dragons, kings, and stars are visually beautiful. *And beauty communicates to the soul in a way that systematic theology does not.*

Keeping this fact in mind, we will never simply dismantle the inspired symbols. Instead, we will use them to segue into meditation. If, for example, we close our eyes and imagine the wisest person we know, we will conjure up the face of someone whose vision we envy and ask, "What do they see that others do not see? What seems to be the wisdom figure's *guiding star?* What does a wise person sacrifice to follow her star?" The preacher who allows silences long enough to address such questions will feel a palpable yearning begin to grow as each person begins to confront some simple paradoxes of faith: Only darkness reveals a star. Only those who have no baggage survive a desert journey. Those who reach out to the unfamiliar, unattractive *other* get to see God in this world.

When we embrace such paradoxes as the Magi did, with our bodies, our time, our security, we will feel Isaiah's poetry ignite our souls with an exuberance unspoken in Matthew's Gospel. "Then you shall see and be radiant; your heart shall thrill and rejoice" (Isa 60:5). Above all, we will hear how to fulfill our role in revelation: *spiritual joy is the radiance through which Jesus manifests his presence in the people of God today.* Assuredly, however, there are times when Christian joy can seem almost obscene. For example, recent American history has made it difficult to accept bearded men in turbans as representatives of the enlightened Gentiles whom the apostle Paul declares "fellow heirs, members of the same body, and sharers in the same promise in Christ Jesus" (Eph 3:6). Each day's headlines overshadow such assertions and provoke the question: How can those who perpetrate "crimes against humanity" reveal our Messiah to us? Every historic event, like every human life and every scientific discovery, forms part of the evolving revelation of God's love. Believing *that* is the real epiphany.

The Poets Respond:

The Magi story reminds us that, now and always, wisdom speaks through the natural sciences. Almost every day new advances in astrophysics bring us closer to the stars in knowledge and farther from them in time. Just as the earliest poets deduced theology from the revelations of the natural world, so many contemporary poets adopt scientific language in their search for new metaphors for religious experience. In its elemental diction and step-by-step rhythm, "Design" embodies an intellectual quest that begins with science and ends in faith.

From *Design*

"It is the dumb hunger, thrust upon the world."—*Robert Hass*

. . .

The astronomer with his telescope
measures receding starlight
far beyond our Milky Way
recording our cosmos
moving at a speed unspeakable.

Like a balloon expanding from within
emanating from a single point
it stretches into the hole of space
this universe
where nothing ends or is wasted

the way water crawls into ice
essence of water always
essence of water, but Oh
to walk across the frozen Tundra
is to bang into the mystery

and the fireball exploding across the Yukon
a meteor burning
in the earth's atmosphere
no larger than a tour bus
racing across the country

five billion years
it orbited the asteroid belt near Jupiter
then the fiery journey into time
and the rock that fell in northwest Canada
is even now transforming

to some altered state
which is to say
what matter was
is
star dust

scattered in our stones
seeded in our bones
it is the itch of memory
that calls us
to our Source.

—*Marion I. Goldstein*

Inspired by a similar reflection on science, the next poet hears the star of Bethlehem speak as a spiritual director who reduces the quests of science and psychology to a simple invitation to prayer.

What the Star Said

Before your eyes found me tonight
I blazed for centuries
and died light years ago
breathing my final word:
"The desire of the everlasting hills
desires you."

Now in your flesh
and in your brain
my fires burn anew
as you sift through
the warm debris
of cindered galaxies
searching for one spark
to re-ignite your universe.

Look no more to the skies
for signs of gods or destinies.
Astronomy is archeology.

True magi dare the steep descent
                         into the earth
                            and deeper.

Dig inward
        remove all gloves and claw
                through layered masks and myths
                        and buried stars.

Then kneel.
The Child is here.
Or nowhere.

                         —Elizabeth Michael Boyle, O.P.

NOTES

Chapter 1: Incarnation

[1] Geoffrey Hill, "Lachrimae Amantis," in *New and Collected Poems* (New York: Houghton Mifflin, 1994).

First Sunday of Advent

[1] Nuala O'Failan, "Close to the Madding Crowd," in *The New York Times Magazine* (April 1, 2001) 34–36.

[2] Thomas Merton, "Advent," in *A Man in a Divided Sea* (New York: New Directions, 1946).

[3] Merton, "The Victory," ibid.

[4] Denise Levertov, "Immersion," in *This Great Unknowing* (New York: New Directions, 2001).

Feast of the Immaculate Conception

[1] Stephen Mitchell, "The Annunciation," in *Parables and Portraits* (New York: Harper Collins, 1990).

[2] Simone Weil, *Seventy Letters* (London: Oxford, 1965), cited in Richard Rees, *Simone Weil: A Sketch for a Portrait* (Urbana, Ill.: Southern Illinois University Press) 140.

[3] Christopher Fitzgerald, "Sonnet 41," in *Sonnets to the Unseen* (Schiller Park, Ill.: World Library Publications, 2001).

[4] Luci Shaw, "Virgin," "The Overshadow," in *Writing the River* (Colorado Springs: Pinon Press, 1994).

[5] Cited in David Curzon, *The Gospels in Our Image: An Anthology of Twentieth Century Poetry Based on Biblical Texts* (New York: Harcourt Brace, 1995) 267, note on "The Mother of God."

[6] ". . . the bread of life . . . from the one table of the Word of God and the Body of Christ." Second Vatican Council, "Dogmatic Constitution on Divine Revelation," in *Vatican II: The Conciliar and Post-Conciliar Documents,* new rev. ed., ed. Austin Flannery, O.P. (Northport, N.Y.: Costello Publishing, 1998) no. 21.

[7] William Butler Yeats, in Curzon, *The Gospels in Our Image,* 12.

[8] Denise Levertov, "On the Mystery of the Incarnation," in *The Stream and the Sapphire* (New York: New Directions, 1997).

[9] Thomas Merton, "The Blessed Virgin Mary Compared to a Window," in *A Man in the Divided Sea* (New York: New Directions, 1946).

Second Sunday of Advent

[1] Carmen Bernos de Gasztold, *Prayers from the Ark and The Creatures Choir: The Voices of Animals Raised to God in Song,* trans. Rumer Godden (New York: Penguin Books, 1976).

[2] Donald Hill, *Richard Wilbur* (New York: Twayne Publishers, 1967) 57.

[3] T. S. Eliot, "Choruses from the Rock," in *The Complete Poems* (New York: Harcourt Brace, 1952).

[4] Carl Jung, "Answer to Job," in *Complete Works* 11, trans. F.C. Hull (Princeton: Princeton University Press, 1953–1978) 152.

[5] Sara Hong, "Hide and Seek," *Image: A Journal of the Arts and Religion* (Fall 2000).

[6] Richard Wilbur, in *Conversations with Richard Wilbur,* ed. William Butts (Jackson, Miss.: University of Mississippi Press, 1990) 52–53.

[7] Richard Wilbur, "Advice to a Prophet," in *Advice to a Prophet and Other Poems* (New York: Harcourt Brace, 1988).

[8] Mark Doty, "Messiah," in *Sweet Machine* (New York: Harper Perennial, 1999).

Third Sunday of Advent

[1] Pamela Smith, S.S.C.M., "The Cousin," in *Waymakers: Eyewitnesses to Christ* (Notre Dame: Ave Maria Press, 1982).

[2] Sister Maris Stella, C.S.C., "This One Heart Shaken," in *The Golden Book of Catholic Poetry,* ed. Alfred Noyes (New York: J. B. Lippincott, 1946).

Fourth Sunday of Advent

[1] For an in-depth treatment of all Luke's canticles, see Raymond E. Brown, S.S., *The Birth of the Messiah: A Commentary on the Infancy Narratives in Matthew and Luke* (Garden City, N.Y.: Doubleday, 1977) 346–392. For a summary of scholarship on these canticles, see *The Dictionary of Jesus and the Gospels,* ed. Joel Green and Scot McKnight (Leicester, Eng.: InterVarsity Press, 1992).

[2] In 1993 Mark Salzman, an agnostic novelist, met his first contemplative nun. After a six-year struggle with his own creative "dark night," he published *Lying Awake,* a lyric novel set in a modern Carmelite monastery. "Theirs is the most *useful* life I can imagine," he commented. Salzman's novel provoked hundreds of letters to the author as it went through eight printings in hardcover. The majority of these letters were from ex-Catholics, non-Christians, and agnostics who found themselves encouraged in a common struggle with Salzman's contemplative protagonist. (Personal interview with the author, New York, November 5, 2001).

[3] Thomas Merton, "The Quickening of John the Baptist," in *The Tears of the Blind Lions* (New York: New Directions, 1949).

[4] Pamela Smith, S.S.C.M., "The Carpenter of Nazareth," in *Waymakers: Eyewitnesses to Christ* (Notre Dame: Ave Maria Press, 1982).

Christmastime

[1] Raymond E. Brown, S.S., *The Birth of the Messiah: A Commentary on the Infancy Narratives in Matthew and Luke* (Garden City, N.Y.: Doubleday, 1977) 8. Italics added.

Christmas Eve

[1] W. H. Auden, "The Temptation of Joseph," in *W. H. Auden: The Collected Poems* (New York: Random House, 1972); Rainer Maria Rilke, "Joseph's Suspicion," in *Selected Works,* vol. 2: *Poetry,* trans. J. B. Leishman (New York: New Directions, 1967).

[2] John W. Lynch, S.J., *A Woman Wrapped in Silence* (New York: MacMillan, 1945) 24–25.

Christmas Midnight

[1] Raymond E. Brown, S.S., *The Birth of the Messiah: A Commentary on the Infancy Narratives in Matthew and Luke* (Garden City, N.Y.: Doubleday, 1977) 485.

[2] Rainer Maria Rilke, *Rilke's Book of Hours: Love Poems to God,* trans. Anita Barrows and Joanna Macy (New York: Riverhead Books, 1997).

[3] Christopher Fitzgerald, "Sonnet 54," in *Sonnets to the Unseen* (Schiller Park, Ill.: World Library Publications, 2001).

Christmas Dawn

[1] Mark Salzman, "The Transcendent in Contemporary Fiction," Auburn Theological School Lecture (New York, November 5, 2001).

[2] Rainer Maria Rilke, "Annunciation to the Shepherds from Above," in *Selected Works,* vol. 2: Poetry, trans. J. B. Leishman (New York: New Directions, 1967).

[3] Lawrence Ferlinghetti, "Christ Climbed Down," in *A Coney Island of the Mind* (New York: New Directions, 1958).

Christmas Day

[1] Raymond E. Brown, S.S., *A Retreat with John the Evangelist* (Cincinnati: St. Anthony Messenger Press, 1998) 20–22. Brown also identifies "Through him all things came to be" as John's allusion to Proverbs 8:22.

[2] Sandra M. Schneiders, *Written That You May Believe: Encountering Jesus in the Fourth Gospel* (New York: Crossroad, 1999) 48–49. Schneiders succeeds in her declared objective to open up the spiritual significance of literary structures. Peter Ellis, in *The Genius of John: A Composition-Critical Commentary on the Fourth Gospel* (Collegeville, Minn.: The Liturgical Press, 1984), demonstrates how "chiastic parallelism" controls the structure of the entire text.

[3] Schneiders, *Written That You May Believe,* 29.

[4] John's words are a deliberate parody on the opening words of the first creation narrative: Genesis 1:1.

[5] Vassar Miller, "Approaching Nada," in *If I Had Wheels or Love* (Dallas: Southern Methodist University Press, 1991).

[6] Karol Wojtyla, "Words Which Grow Into Me," in *Collected Poems,* trans. Jerzy Peterkiewicz (New York: Random House, 1979).

Feast of the Holy Family

[1] Raymond E. Brown, S.S., *The Birth of the Messiah: A Commentary on the Infancy Narratives in Matthew and Luke* (Garden City, N.Y.: Doubleday, 1977) 8.

[2] Christopher Fitzgerald, "Sonnet 66," in *Sonnets to the Unseen* (Schiller Park, Ill.: World Library Publications, 2001).

[3] T. S. Eliot, "East Coker," in *The Complete Poems and Plays* (New York: Harcourt Brace, 1952).

[4] Denise Levertov, "Candlemas," in *The Stream and the Sapphire* (New York: New Directions, 1997).

[5] Wislawa Szymborska, "Still Life with Toy Balloon," in *Sounds, Feelings, and Thoughts: Seventy Poems by Wislawa Szymborska* (Princeton: Princeton University Press, 1981).

Chapter 2

REDEMPTION
Ash Wednesday Through Holy Week

The Season of Lent

The first season of the liturgical year opened with a warning that time is short; the season of Lent, with its ancient penitential associations, suggests that time can also be long. Whether time feels long or short depends on whom we spend it with. Forty days move swiftly when every day promises a rendezvous with someone who loves us. Commitment to a daily five-minute appointment with Love itself could have a dramatic impact on the rest of our schedules.

Despite the softening of Lenten discipline since the sixties, many of us continue to regard Lent as spiritual motivation for the diet we abandoned shortly after the New Year. In fact, however, for the past four decades the Church has invited us to concentrate instead on spiritual *nourishment*. In the Constitution on the Sacred Liturgy, the Second Vatican Council redefined Lent as a "period of closer attention to the Word of God."[1] Our daily Lenten tryst could consist of simply reading a short passage of Scripture, listening for the voice of one who loves us, and silently uttering a single-sentence response. Those who habitually begin the day with a prayerful reading of the day's Scripture find themselves paying closer attention to the voice of God in nature, in human events, and in the affection and needs of others. Listening to these voices constitutes the habit of poetry, even for those who never write a verse.

One of the things attentive reading of Scripture has revealed is that, like poetry, like everything in nature, Scripture speaks through rhythmic repetition. Something in human psychology responds positively to rhythm. The Lenten period of forty days honors one of the richest repetitive patterns in the Bible. Every year we are reminded that Lent imitates Jesus' forty-day retreat in the desert and that he himself was fulfilling a symbolic pattern recurrent throughout the Hebrew Scriptures. This pattern begins with the forty days and nights of the deluge that cleansed the earth of human corruption, after which the Creator offered the human race a "second chance." The pattern continues with forty-day episodes in the stories of Elijah, Jonah, and Moses and culminates in the forty-year journey of God's chosen people through the desert to the promised land.[2] In each of these stories, the recurring theme of a second chance sings an attractive perennial reassurance for the ordinary Christian, who always needs at least one more chance to "start over and get it right." At the beginning of every Lent, we pray with the poet John Berryman:

> "Under new management, Your Majesty, Thine.
> . . . confusions and afflictions followed my days.
> . . . Bankrupt I closed my doors. You pierced the roof
> Twice and again. Finally you opened my eyes."[3]

Each Old Testament forty-day episode also dramatizes one or more of the elements of an ideal Lent: journey, conversion or renewal, intimate conversation with God, a new outpouring of God's mercy. At the end of Lent, the readings for the Easter Vigil highlight this continuum throughout the history of God's chosen people.[4] "This inner movement from one reality to another becomes then a divine pedagogy introducing us to the mystery."[5] Surrendering to the rhythms of Scripture, we ride wave after wave onto the shores of divine mercy. Such a Lenten program substitutes feasting for fasting and amply repays whatever time we have invested. Practically speaking, of course, spending even a little extra time a day reading the Scriptures will involve giving up something else. Lent might well begin with an honest assessment of our daily schedules to find one activity from which we could "fast" to make room for the nourishing Word.

ASH WEDNESDAY

Joel 2:12-18   Matthew 6:1-6, 6-18

The Gospel Speaks:

Before September 11, 2001, few Americans snapped to attention when the preacher explained that the prophet Joel's proclamation of corporate penance was delivered at a time of national disaster. Specifically, a plague of locusts afflicted the Hebrew nation, and locusts sleep for years in our midst before they break out in a life-threatening swarm. The analogy between this plague and terrorism will certainly compel attention now, at least until the locusts go back to sleep.

Regrettably, personal or national disaster often seems like God's only means of getting our attention. But God does not stage human catastrophe to promote church attendance or punish indifference. As Simone Weil has observed, *affliction* is the spike driven into the human heart through which God gains access to our inmost being.[1] Into the human heart hollowed out by affliction God pours abundant love. Through the entire first reading, God and Joel speak in two antithetical voices, contrasting human misery and guilt with divine kindness and mercy. But true affliction is never of our own choosing. Lent is a time of choice, a voluntary emptying of cluttered minds and hearts to make room for a God eager to pour into our lives the light and freedom that rewards reordered priorities. "Long have I waited for your coming home to me and living deeply our new life."[2]

This promise of a deeper, happier life also pervades Matthew's Gospel for today, a continuation of the more familiar verses of the Sermon on the Mount (Matt 5). Whoever wrote this Gospel understood how rhythm, repetition, and grammatical parallelism guarantee that a message will be remembered. Hence each beatitude's "Blessed are they" anticipates its own rhythmically rendered reward. Today's passage follows a similar design as Jesus sets down the conditions for a happiness the world cannot give. Jesus distinguishes true holiness from hypocrisy in an insight later paraphrased by T. S. Eliot: "The last temptation is the greatest treason: / to do the right deed for the wrong reason."[3] Jesus' test of authentic holiness is *interiority.*

Matthew drives home this message by repeating three devices of emphasis: *antithesis, hyperbole,* and *refrain.* In each stanza Jesus contrasts the hollow glare of publicity with the intimate gaze of "the Father who sees in secret" (Matt 6:1-4, 16-17). At the time the Gospels were written, hyperbole was a commonly understood mode of emphasis. When we read these hyperbolic exhortations aloud in church today, however, some unintended comic ironies can also result. An instruction like "But whenever you pray, go into your room and shut the door" (Matt 6:6) will amuse people who are expected to be at Mass every Sunday. (Besides, in American culture, only teenagers are permitted to shut themselves up in their rooms, and when they do so, it is rarely to conceal virtue.) "Do not let your left hand know what your right hand is doing" (Matt 6:3) will elicit few donors for the capital campaign. Yet the refrain is neither archaic nor ambiguous; it encapsulates the point of all Lenten practice: "your Father who sees in secret will reward you" (Matt 6:16-17). Whether we fast from food or from some more subtle form of self-indulgence; whether we pray by sharing Scripture with friends or by simply shutting off the cell phone during our morning commute; whether we give our money to strangers or share our time and our deepest selves with those we love, getting closer to our God is Lent's ultimate reward.

The Poets Respond:

A close reading of Jesus' Lenten program of "interiority" demands replacing our habit of harsh judgment with the assumption that deep desire accompanies failed intentions. The first two poems, each inspired by repeated failure, urge us to compassion rather than to judgment, even and especially of those we love.

In The Desert

Yellow boxes bloomed at Lent in my house,
Decorated with the familiar cross-stitch.
Whitman Sampler chocolates were prayer beads
for my father's annual Novena for abstinence.

They were off limits to us;
my mother fearful that, running out,
he'd have an excuse to cheat,
as if he ever needed one.

The first few luscious pounds took him from
Ash Wednesday to his Sunday dispensation
(Lent has 40 days not counting Sundays),
but there was no subtraction for the craving.

Monday he woke with a hangover
he could only treat with chewy nougats,
not hair of the dog that bit him
though he burned with need.

By mid-week he gave up his good intentions
instead of alcohol, leaving the candy to us,
the victory—bittersweet.
What chance did we have to make him stop,
if God was not enough?

—Keven Bellows

THAT I HAVE SINNED, O Lord, You know too well,
For you were there each time I fell from grace,
However much I tried to flee Your face.
Before each tempting moment, You could tell
My predilection for a taste of hell.
You knew my mind and manner. You could trace
The grim particularities of place
And time and opportunity and all
The trappings of the senses—all in league
To lead me from the grayness of Your law
To splendid danger. I was held in awe
Of my own self-importance, self-intrigue.
O Lord, I am not worthy, nor will be.[4]

—Christopher Fitzgerald

The reward of "closer attention to the Word" is to discover the eyes of the God who sees in secret seeing you—as you are—and loving you. Again and again Scripture assures those who feel God's absence more than his presence that God's attention has never wavered, especially toward those whose relationship to God must be hidden. The following poem, written the year after the collapse of atheistic communism in Russia, celebrates the survival of the Christian faith in secret during three-quarters of a century of political suppression. Unfortunately, there are places on almost every continent where religious practice must go underground. Faith faces an even greater challenge in places where the historic collapse of institutional credibility leads many to murmur, "Nothing is as it used to be."

Moscow's Secret

"Nevah's steel-grey waters no longer reflect the sun,"
The weary elders said.
"Peter's palette of bold colors
Has faded and chipped beyond reconstruction.
On the embankments, twin-headed eagles
Rust into wrought-iron silence
And fold their wings.
Over in the Field of Mars
Giant dandelions give birth
To lying gypsies
And nothing is as it used to be."

But quietly, in the chilled museum-churches
The smoldering icons flare.
Children, warming their hands by the fire
Hear the icons speak:
"Seventy-five years of darkened
Altars are no more
Than the brief hour between
Midnight and morning in
Russia's eternal white night.

"Look now! The Savior Cathedral's plump towers—
Bright balloons of gold and circus stripes—
Are tugging at their launching ropes.
Come with us to the bridges
And watch them lift off
And soar."[5]

—*Elizabeth Michael Boyle, O.P.*

FIRST SUNDAY OF LENT

Matthew 4:1-11   Mark 1:12-15   Luke 4:1-13

The Gospel Speaks:

Visualizing the mountaintop confrontation between Jesus and Satan feels a little like watching an Olympic competition on videotape hours after its decisive outcome. Knowing already who will win, we still delight in the champion's superior power and style. Today we follow Satan's athletic leaps from sand to pinnacle to mountain peak as he repeatedly raises the stakes and the danger. Then we applaud as Jesus' quiet retorts expose and flatten the tempter's flimsy value system. What the text does not record is the expression in Jesus' eyes as he answers. My imagination sees in Jesus' look neither contempt nor triumph, but genuine pity. However, the Gospel offers more than an instant replay of Jesus' testing; it vividly previews our own. The symbolic narrative testifies to Jesus' divinity;[1] at the same time, it dramatizes instruction for the daily struggle with our greatest temptation: the fear of trusting a God who does not share our values.

Jesus' opening words embody the first desired outcome from our Lenten diet: a spirit nourished by the Word (Luke 4:4). The image of the angels ministering to Jesus after his triumph embodies the second benefit: a will empowered through trial (Matt 4:11). First, Jesus urges us to reject all instant gratification and deepen our spiritual hunger. "One does not live by bread alone, but by every word that comes from the mouth of God" (Matt 4:4). And second, Jesus invites us to re-evaluate the positive function of temptation in our lives. "The Holy One tests a man in order to exalt him," says a rabbinic aphorism based on a pun between the Hebrew words for "test" and "exalt." The Temptation pericope acts out this reversal neatly in three brief scenes, but as we listen, we acknowledge that our less spectacular temptations endure over lifetimes.

The contest in the desert begins literally as an intellectual game in which opponents trade quotations from the Old Testament.[2] The compelling repartee between Jesus and his adversary should not persuade us that life's problems can be solved either by verbal cleverness or by a literal reading of the Bible. As Shakespeare has famously noted, the devil quotes Scripture for his own purposes. "*Every* word that comes from the mouth of God" should be interpreted as a subtle condemnation of that *selective* reading of God's word that embraces only passages that console us and condemn others, but avoids those that challenge us to change. Searching the Scriptures for spiritual guidance, we always find what we are looking for. If we seek a *way out*, we're sure to find one. But when we seek the *way*, we allow the Word to *search us*. If we can survive this scrutiny, we truly begin to be nourished by God's divine hunger for us and to worship by serving God only.

Jesus doesn't need to prove his authenticity but we do. We are the Body of Christ on trial. Our test involves choices less dramatic but even more dangerous than hurling ourselves off a cliff. Is not humanity itself poised on such a decisive precipice at nuclear test-sites in our deserts? And does not imitating Jesus' disdain for secular kingdoms demand a brave reassessment of lifestyle, both for individuals and for the Church? "If you are the Son of God," begins Jesus' temptation. "If you love the Son of God," begins ours. If you love the Son of God, turn stones like "minimum wage" into the bread of economic justice. If you love the Son of God, resist corporate exploitation with corporate honesty and responsibility. If you love the Son of God, support his Church, not just by writing checks, but by speaking the truth to each other. Living by every word from the mouth of God means doing the one thing the Gospel leaves out: looking Jesus in the eye.

The Poets Respond:

Ruthann Williams exposes a hidden stream of symbolism flowing beneath the desert landscape of the Temptation. Dispensing with the evangelists' wordplay, she intensifies the theological focus by giving the Son of Man a choice paralleling the first disastrous choice in the Garden of Eden. Also, by imposing on nature the tone of gloom and menace we associate with clinical depression, she adds a psychological dimension. Cumulatively, the images build to the precipice of despair. Reading this poem, I found myself asking, "Could giving time to lonely and difficult people be a more strenuous form of almsgiving than writing a check for recipients at a safe distance?"

mount of temptation

stark rocky heights
jab against the sky
yellow, dun
hard glow in desert sunlight

sharp, relentless

stained teeth
biting at the empty air
tearing at the atmosphere
to make a meal of solitude
a feast of loneliness

the rocks are hard and hot
on bare and dusty feet

beasts lurk
and captured echoes of laughter

while madness mocks the shimmering air
taunts you to the precipice
cries
    jump and i will save you
    jump and i will hold you
    jump and . . .

skin aches for touching
sweat leaves a salty residue
tears creep from hidden sorrow
and the taste of fear
is bitter bile

even the sky is torment

a snake slides
into the darkness of a cleft

waits there

waits

this is a place of hunger
and carrion birds
slow-moving shadows
seeking death for food

hunger rises, grows, takes form
command these rocks to turn to bread
then eat
or wait

wait
and become the breath of life
creation trembles.

—ruthann williams, o.p.

Mark's addition of wild beasts to the Temptation landscape (Mark 1:13) vividly exemplifies allusion, a poetic shorthand that evokes whole worlds in a few words. The picture of Jesus surrounded by both beasts and angels is clearly an allusion both to the harmony and interdependence that human choice destroyed at the dawn of creation and to the "peaceable kingdom" whose restoration is promised as one of the signs of the eschaton (Isa 11:1-10). Lent might be a good time to ask: Could my conscientious use of water and other natural resources be an appropriate form of fasting that can help to atone for the many violations of nature my lifestyle demands? On the other hand, those who already suffer from an excessive sense of guilt will welcome Wislawa Szymborska's light touch as she suggests a refreshing way to take responsibilities seriously and ourselves lightly.

In Praise of Self-Deprecation

The buzzard has nothing to fault himself with.
Scruples are alien to the black panther.
Piranhas do not doubt the rightness of their actions.
The rattlesnake approves of himself without reservations.

The self-critical jackal does not exist.
The locust, alligator, trichina, horsefly
Live as they live and are glad of it.

The killer whale's heart weighs one hundred kilos
But in other respects it is light.

There is nothing more animal-like
Than a clear conscience
On the third planet of the Sun.[3]

—*Wislawa Szymborska*

SECOND SUNDAY OF LENT

Matthew 17:1-9   Mark 9:2-10   Luke 9:28-36

The Gospel Speaks:

Poetry is more memorable than prose; its evocative visual and aural imagery lingers in memory like music. Ideally, Transfiguration imagery will accompany us throughout Lent, with the refrain "This is my Son, my Chosen; listen to him!" (Luke 9:36). The Transfiguration narrative translates the Synoptics' post-resurrection understanding of *who Jesus is and who we are in him* into a complex metaphor for a wordless "vision" that can be communicated only in contemplative prayer.[1] We receive hints of who we are in God in intense moments (rarely in church on Sunday) when time ceases and we feel our ordinary selves transfigured for an instant, connected to all the beauty of creation. The Transfiguration Gospel affirms experiences like that and, more importantly, validates prayer as a continuing source of revelation for God's Church.[2] Hence, although this episode held a special theological-historical significance for early Christians, it holds no less significance for you and me.

When the Gospel authors tried to translate into human language how the disciples "saw" Jesus' divinity, it seems that they chose allusive scriptural imagery that would render the disciples' spiritual vision accessible to a Jewish audience. Luke's account includes all the following details. On a mountaintop Jesus appears with his face burning like the sun, reminiscent of Moses on Sinai. He is clothed in white, the sum of all color, a biblical sign associated with the Divine Presence. Moses and Elijah join him briefly. Then these representatives of the Law and the Prophets, respectively, fade from view, leaving the figure of Jesus alone. A filmmaker might render this scene with the cinematic device of a *dissolve,* suggesting that all God had promised their ancestors is now embodied in Jesus. Then a voice from the cloud trumpets the musical climax: "This is my Son, my Chosen; listen to him!" (Luke 9:36). In that instant, it is as if the disciples intuit an inexpressible, instantaneous sense of connectedness, not only with Jesus but with their entire history as God's chosen people.

Today, Transfiguration imagery symbolizes how Jesus continues to reveal himself to our hearts through prayer. Going up to a mountaintop represents visually the first effect of contemplative prayer: our ascent to a higher level of consciousness. In this state, however momentary, we glimpse the full force of Jesus' identity and our own in him. "I pierce the universe / God pierces me / I do not think / I am thought / I do not know / I am known."[3] Simultaneously, we recognize in Jesus what Teilhard de Chardin has called the "omega point of human evolution,"[4] and we yearn toward the summit of our own transformation through grace.

But does everyone have the stamina for mountain climbing? We will find out by taking one step at a time. For the fearful, here's a simple suggestion. Every morning for the rest of Lent, awake listening for God to say, "You are my beloved, my chosen one." Then set aside one quiet time of each day to enter the cloud of deeper awareness just long enough to hear those words again. Next, try looking at or picturing the one you love, or better, someone you find hard to love. Repeat your refrain. Punctuate your day with split-second prayers like that, and step by step you will enter a higher level of consciousness that transfigures your perception, not only of yourself and of all your relationships but also of time, work, play, sexual union, and all the other metaphors for God's love. Gradually you will discover that prayer, like all "committed relationships," demands an investment of quality time. You will find intimacy with God worth whatever it costs to give that time. The poetry of the Transfiguration encourages you to keep climbing.

The Poets Respond:

Our reflection on the Transfiguration experience suggested that intimacy with God can transform our human relationships. Some of our best secular writers describe sexual union in language that is indistinguishable from the language of the mystics when they describe union with God. The novels of D. H. Lawrence and Graham Greene, among others, contain outstanding examples of "secular mysticism." Teilhard de Chardin includes such a level of consciousness in his evolutionary theory: ". . . an ascent of consciousness . . . implies essentially the consciousness of finding oneself in actual relationship with a spiritual and transcendent pole of universal convergence."[5] The following fragment from the German poet Goethe expresses sexual ecstasy in terms the mystics use to express the phenomenon of simultaneous self-immolation and self-fulfillment in union with the Other.

From *The Holy Longing*

> I praise what is truly alive
> What longs to be burned to death!
>
> In the calm water of the love-nights,
> Where you were begotten,
> Where you have begotten,
> A strange feeling comes over you,
>
> . . .
> No distance makes you falter.
> Now, arriving in magic, flying,
> And finally, insane for the light,
> You are the moth, and you are gone.
>
> And so long as you have not experienced this:
> To die and so to grow,
> You are only a troubled guest
> On the dark earth.[6]
>
> —*Johann Wolfgang von Goethe*

In contemplative prayer we see anew and "all-at-once" the meaning of all that has gone before. In Ruthann Williams' poem, the Tabor event includes and illuminates Jesus' entire ministry. As the poem unfolds, it reveals a design of transformative relationships arranged in an order ascending from earthbound concerns like hunger and hospitality, to healing miracles, to the elevation of flesh to sacrament. Each stanza mirrors the design of the whole by transforming into poetry the elements the Incarnate Word used to minister to basic human needs. The final stanza affirms the transformative power of art.

mount tabor

transfigured . . .
homespun brushed to gold
your hair in maple glory
and eyes a sacrament
our joy was such
we could not turn aside
but longed to hold the moment still

can this be
the carpenter's son?

transfigured . . .
loaves in abundance
and fish to share
five thousand fed
and more besides
from this small offering
this single loaf, these tiny fish

what sort
of man is this one?

transfigured . . .
water turned to cana wine
the law of love unfolds
to moisten bridal lips
to thrust between the letters
searching out the spirit
pouring from unaccustomed urns

why have you
saved the best till now?

transfigured . . .
twisted limbs are straightened
blind eyes leap at sunlight
death peels away like useless skin
ears start to the sound of birds
and laughter following
joyful laughter following him

are you he
who is to come?

transfigured . . .
demons flung aside
a woman's hair unbound
wipes tears away from dusty feet
and in that single moment
with repentance
comes the certainty of love

who is this man
that he even forgives sins?

transfigured . . .
wine to blood and bread to flesh
flesh and blood to sacrifice
blood and flesh to sacred meal
take, eat, and drink
who he is, how he loves
who we may become

what wrong
is this man guilty of?

transfigured . . .
my song
rushing from the mountaintop
to where the galilean sea
glitters in the fertile valley
waiting for each fragile note
to near forgotten melody.

surely this man was
the son of God?

—*ruthann williams, o.p.*

The ascent to the unifying vision of Tabor can be the struggle of a lifetime, a struggle for authenticity and unselfish love in which being "all one" inevitably involves the capacity to be alone.

Climb

It is not the ruin
but the view from the ruin
that is worth the long climb
and the risk of a fall.

It is not the temple
but the myth that built the temple
that survives
earthquake, erosion, murder, betrayal
and the lightning bolt in the heart.

Day after day in the August sun
we ascend and descend
and ascend again
chilled to the bone in our separate solitudes:
ruins wandering the ruins
islands adrift among islands
stones communing with stones.

But it is not the ruin
but the view from the ruin
that will have been worth both climb and fall
when, back to back at the summit,
we pluck the last flower piercing the rubble
and disappear into the view.

—*Elizabeth Michael Boyle, O.P.*

THIRD SUNDAY OF LENT

John 4:5-31, 39-42

The Gospel Speaks:

Poets and biblical commentators avoid the phrase, "just a symbol," for symbolism always connotes more, not less, than realism. In the encounter between Jesus and the Samaritan woman, the evangelist demonstrates this fact by showing how Jesus leads her faith from literalism through symbolism to a radiant reality exceeding her messianic expectations. Because this story is told so convincingly, we are surprised to learn from other New Testament passages that Jesus never preached in Samaria.[1] Hence we discover that this unforgettable woman, the site for her meeting with Jesus, and the design of their dialogue are all "typical" in symbolic biblical literature.

The woman's story follows a familiar literary form: a conversation between a wisdom figure and a stranger whose naïve questions elicit profound theological instruction. The scene takes place at the well where Jacob met his future spouse. So we are told, when Jesus breaks the rules of ritual propriety to ask the woman for a drink, a Jewish audience expects to be entertained by a typical drama of forbidden romance. But symbolically, the protagonists in this male / female encounter represent a divine / human covenant that shatters all stereotypes and transcends all earthly romance.

Moreover, the conversation at the heart of the action is unique, not only in what it says but more importantly in what it *does*. What do the words of the Samaritan woman *do*? First of all, without a single adjective, her "voice" paints a self-portrait so real that we can imagine her visually and experience her whole personality. We see her tall, graceful figure sitting erect, searching Jesus with unflinching eyes.[2] We watch her bold facial expression rebuff a stranger's transgressive request,[3] assume an ironically superior attitude as she tests his theological credentials, then gradually move from curiosity to humility to wonder. And what do the words of Jesus do? First, in a single symbolic sentence, they lay bare the woman's whole life of misdirected passion. But at the same time, Christ exposes the authentic thirst that drives that passion and reaches out to introduce her to the Messiah who alone will satisfy it (John 4:26).

We who feel, perhaps, no need to be convinced of who the Christ is can still find repeated challenge in the dialogue that led to this dramatic climax. A closer look at the sequence of questions and answers, and of the symbols that echo them, will reward us by drawing us into an intimacy both symbolic and real. First of all, Jesus' request for a drink demolishes the distance between Jew and Samaritan, preparing the way for his new law of love, which excludes no one. Next, Jesus clearly signals the sacramental symbolism of the whole exchange by offering the woman "living water" that will become an internal "spring . . . gushing up to eternal life" (John 4:10-13). Once again, however, the woman's literalism misses the point. "Sir, you have no bucket. . . . Are you greater than our ancestor Jacob?" (John 4:11). And when, finally, she asks for access to his inexhaustible spring, it is only to save her the trouble of coming daily to the well (John 4:15).

Jesus seizes the reference to Jacob to segue to a different approach, introducing the Old Testament matrimonial metaphor for God's covenant with Israel. "Go, call your husband, and come back." "I have no husband" (John 4:16-17). Jesus agrees: "You have had five husbands, and the one you have now is not your husband" (John 4:18).[4] Now, because Jesus tells her who she is, she dares to hope who he might be. Knowing and accepting the truth about herself opens the way to union with truth itself. This in turn emboldens her to ask for her people the crucial question: Where is the "right place" for worship? (John 4:20).[5]

Paradoxically, Jesus' twofold response both restrains and releases her. Lest the ecumenical import of his next statement be mistranslated as "one religion is as good or as bad as another," Jesus calls the Samaritan woman unequivocally back to her "true husband." "You worship what you do not know; we worship what we know, for salvation is from the Jews" (John 4:22).[6] But that salvation is not trapped in any geography, in any architecture, or even in one exclusive liturgy: "Woman, believe me, the hour is coming when you will worship the Father neither on this mountain nor in Jerusalem. . . . God is spirit, and those who worship him must worship in spirit and in truth" (John 4:21, 24). With clarity and authority these words fall like rain on her own parched spirit. Can this be the awaited Messiah? Jesus confirms her hope: "I am he, the one who is speaking to you" (John 4:26). Almost afraid now to take him literally, the woman rushes off to find corroborating witnesses. Her whole person persuades those she meets to seek out the source of her transformation. And after two days with Jesus, the other Samaritans declare their faith with unambiguous conviction: "We know that this is truly the Savior of the world" (John 4:42).

Once we accept the fact that the Samaritan woman cannot be taken literally, we cannot escape the fact that she must be taken seriously, because *she is in us and among us in our individual selves and in our communities.* Most obviously, she is among us in those whom we try to keep at a distance. She is among us demanding that we defy petty distinctions and trivial taboos to embrace the alien and the alienated, even and especially those who rebuff our good intentions.

But our identification with the Samaritan woman goes deeper than that. She is in us, male and female, in all our multiform infidelities. She challenges us to admit that we also are married to too many husbands. Which of us is not "married to an idea"—perhaps to an idea of God that sets a limit on divine mercy? Who among us has not been so "married to a job" that we neglect human relationships and other opportunities for spiritual growth? The woman shows us her people in our world, torn and terrorized by religious dissent, struggling over half a century for possession of Jerusalem and other shrines, wherever religiously motivated violence drowns out Jesus' simple message: "God is spirit, and those who worship him must worship him in spirit" (John 4:24). She exposes our collective guilt for incipient forms of false worship, like the subtle idolatry in an economic system that subordinates all other values, including reverence for the earth and for the inherent dignity of the unskilled laborer. She begs our culture and our Church to listen to Jesus in the voices of our poets crying: "Let me in! Let me in! / I have been born many times, a false Messiah, / But let me be born again / Into something true."[7]

Fortunately, the woman of Samaria is not only in us—she invites us to get inside her, inside her thirst for spirit and truth. To explain a symbol reduces it, drains it of its essence, which is mystery. But if we inhabit the symbol, we experience its meaning from the inside, and no explanation is necessary. Inhabit the thirst of the Samaritan woman; carry it with you throughout Lent as you journey with those preparing for baptism; bring your thirst with you to the Easter Vigil. Then, with the woman at the well and the newly baptized, drink afresh at "the fountain of living water" and taste it for the first time.

The Poets Respond:

"Transparent": the single word expresses both theme and style of
the nine-poem sequence in which Karol Wotjyla assumes the persona
of the Samaritan woman and accompanies her in prayer.

From *Song of the Brightness of the Water*

. . .

His recognition was different. He hardly raised his eyes.
He was a great gathering of perception—
like the well blowing the brightness of water
into a face.
He had a mirror—like the well—shining deep,
For him no need to come out of himself or raise his eyes to guess.
He saw me in himself, possessed me in himself.
He suffused me with ease,
Burst my shame in me and the thoughts
I'd suppressed for so long
As if he—touching a rhythm in my temples—
all of a sudden
carried that great exhaustion
in me, with such care.

. . .

He was whole in my sin and my secret.

. . .

Such a shortcut, such goodness of perception!
And You did not even raise your eyes
You talked to me only with those eyes
Which the well re-created
in its deep brightness.

. . .

It joined us together, the well;
the well led me into you.
No one between us but light
deep in the well, the pupil of the eye
set in an orbit of stones.

Within your eyes, I,
drawn by the well,
am enclosed.

. . .
. . . I can never take all of you
into me. Stay then as a mirror in the well.
Leaves and flowers remain, and each astonished gaze
brings them down
to my eyes transfixed more by light
than by sorrow.[8]

—Karol Wojtyla

The Samaritan woman begins by questioning Jesus' infraction of
the rules, and ultimately questions her own religious tradition. Significantly, it is not recorded that she stopped questioning. Into a few rapid
steps, her symbolic narrative collapses the journey of a lifetime, a journey that includes questioning the cultural encrustations of our tradition and even struggling with theological doubt. Nor does baptism
end doubt. Ultimately, as the poets of the "dark night" attest again
and again, doubt deepens faith. For contemporary Christians, scientific advancements often initiate or exacerbate religious doubt. But
for some poets, science is another form of revelation, as difficult and
mysterious as Scripture. The imagery throughout Marion Goldstein's
poem suggests that nature itself mirrors the elusive face of the God of
nature.

Uncertainty Principle

"In the subatomic realm it is impossible to know velocity and location
of an object simultaneously. We can know one condition or the other
but not both."—*Heisenberg*

I

Faith is not
to know.
It is the iridescent scrim
of a pickerel
fin.
It weighs heavily

and it weighs nothing
slipping through your fingers
like froth on a mountain stream.

It is jealous of the crocus
anchored to the earth
and yearns for proof
reliable as tides
careening between continents.

It doubles back and plants itself
like a tree
gazing at galaxies.
It meditates on infinity
and takes pleasure in measuring.
    . . .

It leaves no trace
which is to say cannot be measured
the way loss enters a body

Tom's wife
is still
in the casket.
Her stone hands will never again
stir the soup
or brush back hair
to better kiss a child's forehead
and her laugh, so light, will never ever
fulfill
every cell in his body
infused with pain so exquisite
it is crushing him under its weight.
And yet
it weighs nothing.

II

I have been to Lourdes.
I have counted crutches
hanging onto the grotto walls
I have dipped my fingers in the spring
pouring from the living stones.

I have read the book of miracles
and doubted.

We are all pilgrims
grasping each other by the hand
locked in each others' eyes
and in "every language known on earth"
we long for the harmonies
over and over
and 350 miles over the earth
the Explorer satellite hears
the cosmic whisper

the smoldering ash
of the birth of time.

—Marion I. Goldstein

FOURTH SUNDAY OF LENT

John 9:1-41　　　　　　John 3:14-21　　　　　　Luke 15:1-3

The Gospel Speaks:

In a famous essay, "The Music of Poetry," T. S. Eliot offers a key to decoding his own puzzling verse—and also Scripture. Image by image, Eliot explains, a poet develops theme and counter-theme as a composer uses different instruments to explore the same melody in music.[1] Once we apprehend Eliot's method, stanzas that at first appear unrelated begin to mirror and explicate each other with incremental clarity.

Applying the poet's insight to the New Testament, we can see the evangelists "performing" the same theological theme on different literary instruments. All three Gospels selected for this Sunday, for example, reinforce and illuminate the theme and counter-theme of light and darkness. In John's account of the man born blind (John 9:1-41), the instrument is a tightly constructed miracle play. In Jesus' midnight dialogue with Nicodemus (John 3:14-21), John uses the literary device of double meaning as an instrument to define "rebirth" as access to the light through baptism. The third instrument, the well-loved and easily understood parable of the Prodigal Son (Luke 15:1-3), appears to have nothing in common with the other two texts—no darkness, no water, no climactic "I am."

But a closer reading exposes the nexus uniting the parable to the other texts. Does not the father's embrace enact one answer to Nicodemus's question: "How can anyone be born after having grown old?" (John 3:4). And does not the returning son enter a second time the womb of love from which he was born? (Luke 15:24). The sin of clinging to darkness, the counter-theme identified vaguely in the instruction to Nicodemus, rings out clearly through the strident instrument of the elder son, who refuses to celebrate his brother's return (Luke 15:28). That same counter-theme echoes in the cacophony of the Pharisees who excommunicate the man born blind. Analysis of these literary instruments can bring about a contact with Scripture deeper than music.

I believe that we can best hear the music of each Gospel by *becoming* its instrument, by *inhabiting* its central symbol, or letting that symbol *breathe through* us. When we let the man born blind get inside us, we see what he sees; but we also see through the prism of our own personalities. Some of us will simply imagine his first joy in color or in the play of light on the waters of the healing pool. Others, appreciating the symbolism of spiritual vision, will silently thank God for their gift of faith. Emotional response can be enough, or at some point in life, all that we can manage. When we are stronger, this Gospel might challenge us to develop the honesty to see into our own blindness, to keep looking until we wince, recognizing in ourselves the critics who attack a new, unorthodox vision because it threatens us with unnerving moral responsibilities. Or perhaps we will be granted the vision to admit that a sinner, an "oddball," or even someone excommunicated for following his or her conscience could become an instrument of grace for others. Seeing with the new eyes of the blind man will have consequences for us and for the Church. Not all of us are equipped with courage equal to these consequences. But all of us can sit quietly, handing over all our personal darkness and confusion as we pray for the gift of sight. It is not too much to pray that the Light of the World will shine on one person or one problem in that part of the world or in that part of the Church that God has given us eyes to see.

From both a literary and a pastoral perspective, few Gospels are more fascinating than the healing of the man born blind, so it deserves extended attention.[2] Here the theme of light embodied in the miracle contrasts sharply with the counter-theme of spiritual blindness embodied in the Pharisees' perversity. Changing circumstances will dictate which theme is more appealing or appropriate each time we re-read this story—Jesus' power over darkness or the limits of his power—for clearly he finds it easier to restore sight to the blind than to convert those who are attached to their own blurred vision. Those involved in preparation for baptism and / or those whose faith seems dimmed by psychic or historic events will be drawn into the tender interaction between the blind man and the Light of the World and find in it a metaphor for reanimated faith. In the theological heart of our own communion, we hear "I am the Light" echo Jesus' personal epiphany to the Samaritan woman (John 9:37; 4:26).

However, John devotes his greatest skill to exposing spiritual blindness, and circumstances might inspire a bold preacher to draw attention to the less comforting message for the "righteous" in this text. The evangelist wisely frames Jesus' attack on elitism in a compelling literary form: a brief drama with all the dramatic and situational irony of Greek theater. The carefully crafted ironies of the narrative carry the disturbing message that there are forms of willful blindness no miracle can cure. Biblical metaphor often equates blindness with "hardness of heart,"[3] suggesting that spiritual blindness is the *choice* of those who judge and exclude others.

John dramatizes rash judgment and God's reaction to it in a series of ironic reversals. First, the Pharisees' question "Whose sin has made this man blind?" morphs perversely to "Whose sin has restored his sight?" (John 9:1-16). Dramatic irony intensifies throughout the scene as the Pharisees set out to "convict" the person the audience knows is the fulfillment of the Law. And when the Pharisees demand, "Give glory to God!" (John 9:24), they use a rabbinical expression synonymous with "Confess your sin."[4] Then, precisely for refusing to call the miracle a sin, they expel the man from the synagogue. The entire prosecution has focused myopically on a violation of the Sabbath, a day set aside for worship. When the man born blind falls on his knees before Jesus in an act of worship (John 9:38), he delivers an ironic visual rebuttal to this charge. Finally, standing beside the man rejected by the Establishment, the criminal indicts the prosecution: "If you were blind, you would not have sin. But now that you say, 'We see,' your sin remains" (John 9:41). Thus Jesus reverses the initial question of moral responsibility for the man's blindness. The Pharisees remain imprisoned in the blindness of false certainty, while the man who knows he does not know is liberated into the vision of faith.

Counterpoint to the Pharisees' descent into darkness runs the blind man's gradual ascent into light: ". . . he was born blind so that God's works might be revealed in him" (John 9:3). The steps in the healing action open up that process for us. First of all, Jesus prefaces the healing ritual with the words "I am the light of the world" (John 9:5). The power behind the "I am" formula alone could have dispelled the man's darkness. But Jesus chooses to make a salve of mud to smear on the blind eyes. With symbolism reminiscent of the creation of the first human being in Genesis (Gen 2:7), Jesus signals his intention not only to restore sight but to empower a whole new person. Then, in a clear allusion to baptismal waters, he commands the man's active co-operation: "Go, wash in the pool of Siloam" (John 9:7). Obeying the command of an invisible stranger, the blind man personifies the highest form of faith, believing without seeing (John 20:29).[5]

The Poets Respond:

Getting inside the blind man, a poet explores the time before and after the miracle, when the cured man assesses its impact.

The Price

To be born blind is to be born without:
    to believe without icons
    to worship without idols
    to reflect without mirrors
    to live without "living up to"
    any image, especially your own.

I had no idea of darkness
until I saw the light.

Bathing in the pool of Siloah
I didn't have the sense
to search its clear bright waters
for a glimpse of my own face.

And so it was that his kind eyes
were the first to meet my own.
"So, this is what we look like,
And this is what it feels like to be seen."
If only sight had stopped there.

For then I yearned to show my parents
but their eyes flinched and failed to hide
other faces—judging, staring, bruising
fearing him, fearing me.

I had no idea of darkness
until I saw the light.

              —Elizabeth Michael Boyle, O.P.

Christ opens the eyes of one "born blind," not once or twice, but repeatedly throughout the lifetimes of individuals and of cultures. Enlightenment seems to alternate between opening our eyes to truths and graces to which we had been blind, on one hand, and opening our eyes to unacknowledged guilt and responsibilities on the other. Sometimes, a historic event opens our eyes collectively, either to beauty or to danger or to human possibility—or to all these at once. On September 11, 2001, such an event opened America's eyes to its hidden strengths and vulnerabilities and, however briefly, replaced celebrity with heroism, complacency with soul-searching. The event inspired thousands of poems and revived thousands of others with fresh meaning. In Pamela Smith's poem, written twenty years before 9/11/01, the man born blind utters words of prophetic irony, and by the final lines, seems to speak for the soul of a nation.

The Unblinding

What I have seen today
I could never have seen with my eyes anyway.
Nothing that is mere man,
nothing that looks like trees;
I have seen spirit awakening,
the future in the making, liberty.
Though I gaze and now know
that the sun is yellow, the sky blue,
that his eyes are even warmer

than the voice I felt to my fingertips,
to the startlement of my heart,
I have seen beyond all looking.
I have seen a prophet who sees through me.
I have been unblinded frighteningly,
and I welcome it—revel, rejoice—
yet dread that I am on the edge of terror and mystery;
for I sense that he is the undoing of all that I was.
I have seen the breaking in half of history.[6] (John 9:1-41)

—*Pamela Smith, S.S.C.M.*

Nicodemus's secret meeting with Jesus follows a model John uses frequently to create an opportunity for Jesus to explain a theological concept. A conversation begins with a misunderstanding of language and proceeds to a monologue. The text selected for the Fourth Sunday of Lent retains only the monologue and eliminates Nicodemus altogether. Although Nicodemus did eventually become a disciple, tradition and poetry continue to define him by his fear. And perhaps it is his conspicuous lack of heroism, his doubts and qualms that account for his enduring appeal.

Nicodemus

A fraidy-cat in spite of my Pharisee propriety, my pomp
A sucker for esteem among the Sanhedrin,
And wanting only good gossip,
I slunk like a stealthy prowler to see him by night.
It was, if it matters, a Wednesday.
Wrapped in my solitude as in the prayer shawl
Weeks later, I keep trying to decipher it.
If only I could read him
As one pores over the lines of the law . . .
I still do not understand about the water.
I wonder about the wind.
How to be born again? In what womb?
I wrack these runes like a myopic scribe.
In the terrors of my sleep,
When I am drowning,
When the wind blows me away,
When I cannot gulp a breath of air
Or catch hold of the limb of the tree,
It is always he who rescues me[7] (John 3).

—*Pamela Smith, S.S.C.M.*

Almost all poetic and artistic treatment of the parable of the Prodigal Son has focused on the father's limitless love and forgiveness; the wayward son has served to convince those who have given up on themselves that it is never too late to return to God. The following poem suggests that the prodigal is not the one most in need of conversion.

Question

It's all about the homecoming:
the fatted calf, the robe, the ring
the hugs, hilarity, and partying.
Who wouldn't want to rush right home
to all of that?

But what I'd like to know is this:
What drove the nameless, shameless boy
into distant countries in the first place?
Was it greed or recklessness or boredom,
or that tired old cliché, "to find himself"?

Or did he need to get as far as he could run
From his righteous elder brother?
Ah, could that be why the sinful son departed
and why, to tell the truth, their prodigal father
did go a little wild when he returned? (Luke 15:1-3)

—*Elizabeth Michael Boyle, O.P.*

FIFTH SUNDAY OF LENT

John 11:1-45   John 12:20-33   John 8:1-11

The Gospel Speaks:

As we enter the final weeks of Lent, John's account of the raising of Lazarus from the dead (John 11:1-45) offers a stunning reality for our celebration and contemplation. Celebration and contemplation, according to Nobel Laureate Octavio Paz, express the dual nature of "poetic experience," an experience familiar to those who immerse themselves in the realities of faith through Scripture.[1] Paz defines celebration as "participation or communion" in and with an event.[2]

Standing in communion with Martha and Mary outside the tomb of their loved one, is it not really our own pain and loss we feel? And do we not yearn to share their grief's transformation into joy? No matter how many times we hear the story, our blood throbs a silent cheer when Jesus commands Lazarus to emerge from the tomb and the dead man obeys. Does not our psychic participation in the event reach its climax when the image of Lazarus stumbling out into the arms of Martha and Mary grants our hearts a moment of communion, however brief, with our own departed loved ones? That form of communion can propel us into contemplation, "a silent dialog with the universe and with ourselves."[3] No matter how frozen our spirits have been throughout the long winter, springtime surrounds us with resurrection imagery so powerful that nature itself calls us out of the tomb of self-absorption into creation's universal chorus of hope.

When we contemplate the Gospel text closely, we notice the meticulous steps leading up to the resurrection miracle, and in Jesus' strategy we discover seeds of hope for ourselves and for our world. Jesus took great pains to assure that Lazarus was truly dead. He deliberately delayed arriving in Bethany until after his friend had been buried and lingered to elicit separate acts of faith from Martha and from Mary. Then he also made sure that there were hostile witnesses who did not share that faith. He even used Martha's reluctance to expose a rotting corpse to underscore that Lazarus was "too far gone" to be restored to life. Jesus did all this to send a message to you and me: no one is too far gone to be called back from the dead.

To experience this Gospel in relation to the living, I suggest that you close your eyes and summon the face of the deadest person you know: a husband, wife, child, sibling, or friend buried for years in the living death of addiction, denial, abuse, depression, self-absorption. Picture the face of someone who seems separated from the living, from God, from himself or herself. Speak to Jesus Christ with confidence, making the words of this Gospel your own: "Lord, he whom you love is ill" (John 11:3). Believe Jesus when he answers: "This illness does not lead to death; rather it is for God's glory, so that the Son of God may be glorified through it" (John 11:4). Understand that the one you love will be sicker still, appear to die, perhaps, before he or she obeys the divine command to come out of the tomb into new life. But do not despair. Jesus could easily have prevented the death of his friend. But the story of Lazarus assures us that God is more glorified by a return from death than by its prevention. Hold your loved one in your heart as you hear Jesus address these words to you: "I am the resurrection and the life. Those who believe in me, even though they die, will live. . . . Do you believe this?" (John 11:25). Mean it when you answer: "I believe that you are . . . the Son of God, the one coming into the world" (John 11:27). Not the one who came once. The one who is still coming. Believe it.

The Poets Respond:

In general, poets expand and enhance our vision of the Gospels, but among the many poems inspired by the raising of Lazarus, there seems to run a perverse instinct to minimize the miracle and mock its imagined aftermath, not by denying that Jesus raised Lazarus from the dead, but by suggesting that the dead man would have preferred to be left alone. In David Curzon's anthology, for example, of the four selections on the Lazarus theme, not one celebrates the event.[4] Agnes Nemas Nagy compares awakening after being buried for four days to having the gauze ripped off a healing wound.[5] Nicanor Parra actually pleads, "don't do it old friend don't do it," and reminds Lazarus that the self he couldn't stand when he was alive will be just as cranky when he comes back from the dead.[6] William Butler Yeats plays with the paradoxes of love and death by creating a rebellious Lazarus who waits on the road to Calvary to take Christ's place and be restored to death because "Alive, I could never escape your love."[7]

Thus, it is with a sense of grateful relief that we come to May Sarton's treatment, which, although beginning with a fairly bleak vision, works its way to hope. Sarton, inspired by an eleventh-century statue, appropriates the Lazarus theme as a metaphor for rebirth through art. First, the sculptor brings Lazarus to life in stone; then the poet endows him with twentieth-century angst. Finally, she experiences an artistic "breakthrough," hears Lazarus calling her back to life, and begins to create new music out of the old life she has resumed. Sarton's poem suggests that the resurrection miracle is accessible to all of us, not in spectacular physical comebacks, but in the perennial renewal of ordinary lives through creativity.

From *Lazarus: Anglo-Saxon, A.D. 1000 Chichester Cathedral*

> From the rock and from the deep
> The sculptor lifts him out aware.
> This is the dead man's waking stare.
> This is a man carved out of sleep.
> The grave is hard, the walls are steep.
> . . .
> Lazarus lifts huge hands in prayer
> He turns the world round in his stare.
>
> He sees his late death everywhere.
> It hurts his eyes, he has to care.
>
> Now broken from the rock of sleep,
> He comes towards us from the deep.
>
> To face once more the morning star,
> To see us desperate as we are.
>
> And Lazarus relearns despair.
> His look is grave; his gaze is deep
> Upon us, men carved out of sleep
> Who wish to pray but have no prayer.

2

A weightless traveler, I too come back
From miles of air, from distant and strange lands,
Put on my house again, my work, my lack,
And looking down at my own clumsy hands,
Feel courage crack.

. . .

How can I answer all these needs at once?

. . .

How lift my smothered flame up to the day?
Have I come back depleted of desire,
To tire and fray?

At last I hear the silence in the room:
That buried self is breaking through to be,
And Lazarus is calling me by name.
At last I slowly lift the poem free,
One-pointed flame.

. . .

Detached from all except the living beat,
I dance my way into complex design
On weightless feet.[8]

—*May Sarton*

The forgiveness of the adulterous woman (John 8:1-11) parallels the raising of Lazarus from the dead. Traditional commentary has focused on contrasting human judgment with divine mercy. In recent years feminist criticism has shifted attention to the issue of female victimization. Though speculation on the question "What did Jesus write in the dust?" is ultimately futile, we may entertain ourselves with the suggestion that he was writing a new version of the law that punishes the male adulterer.

Poets, like the rest of us, have been fascinated by the question, especially since, as one of them has pointed out, this is the only incident on record where Jesus writes something. The poet-playwright Tadeuz Rozewicz dismisses the content of Jesus' scribbling as irrelevant. For him, what's significant is that the Incarnate Word did not wish his words to be recorded permanently: "When / Matthew, Mark, Luke and John / approached him / he covered the letters / and erased them / forever."[9] Since Jesus himself was so careless in preserving his own words, the act of erasing implicitly condemns those who live and judge by the exact words of the Bible.

For Miguel de Unamuno, Jesus did not write on the earth once; he is always writing there, inscribing powerful lessons we cannot afford to ignore. Unamuno's gentle vision assumes sharper edges in new contexts. Phrases like "the earth, your open book, alive and sacred" become ironic when framed by nuclear proliferation, deforestation, and frightening forms of agricultural engineering. Having died in 1936, decades before modern technology had deracinated so many landscapes, Unamuno himself could scarcely have predicted the stinging relevance of his plea: "In the insubstantial dust / let us read the lesson of conscience."

Forefinger of the Right Hand

The forefinger of your right hand
from the wooden cross directs us
to what is written in the eternal book
of life. Only once, on earth,
did you write, Jesus, You, the Word,
on dust tread by men of mud,
without ink or reed but with finger bare,
gently touching the lids of the blind,
and healing. It was morning.
Doing it, humbling yourself, you bent
over the earth. The inscribing finger
was God's, was yours when you cast out
those demons.

In the insubstantial dust
let us read the lesson of conscience
traced by your finger as you bent over
the earth, your open book,
alive and sacred. In writing on her
you showed the humility of your ministry.

The adulteress, her gaze upon that dust, veiled eyes,
tears of sighs, was going, alone,
arms across her chest,

guarding there the pledge of your forgiveness,
a mother embracing her new babe.

O, may my pen reborn
write upon the earth of my homeland
the lesson of the pardon you have left us![10]

—*Miguel de Unamuno*

PALM SUNDAY

Matthew 21:1-11   Mark 11:1-10   Luke 19:21-40

The Gospel Speaks:

For those who love a parade, the account of Jesus' triumphal entry into Jerusalem ranks as one of the most neglected texts in the Lectionary. Because Palm Sunday's liturgy includes both the pre-procession reading and Matthew's Passion, homilists usually confine their comments to condemning the fickle crowd. In a few days, we are routinely reminded, the same voices that sang "Hosanna" will shriek "Crucify him!" (John 19:6).

Before the inevitable onset of the crowd's disillusion and betrayal, fairness to them dictates that we pause to appreciate their nobler instincts. The best feature of this scene differentiates it from any parade we're likely to see. Police and politicians are conspicuously absent. Neither T-shirt vendors nor video cameras are on hand to commodify the crowd's deepest emotions. Their hero arrives on a beast of burden, with neither pope-mobile nor motorcycle escort to protect him from all the unpredictable hazards of popular enthusiasm and hostility. For a moment this crowd celebrates the very lowliness and vulnerability of their savior. Of course, they are swept up in the moment, but is this not a moment of grace?

The response of the crowd is a religious response. Tearing branches from the trees, they obey the psalmist's joyous command for the Feast of Tabernacles: "Inaugurate the ceremony with branches in your hands up to the horns of the altar" (Ps 118:27).[1] In this outdoor ceremony Jesus himself is the altar, and the fact that in a few days he will be the sacrificial victim does not taint the congregation's sincerity. In fact, all their words and gestures are taken from the same psalm, a magnificent hymn praising God for his steadfast love, which will rescue his chosen people from all evil. Their cheer is also a prayer: "Hosanna," originally a cry for help, then an expression of messianic hope, and finally a cry of homage (Matt 21:9; Mark 11:9-11).[2]

Next, the people throw down their clothes to be trampled on by the donkey. They are not cleaning out overcrowded closets like ours; one cloak is all most of them own. Providing the biblical version of red-carpet treatment costs them something. Today, a few minutes after our rather lackluster procession with palms, the congregation will participate in a dramatic reading of Matthew's Passion narrative. Our assigned role will be the voice of the crowd. The salutary exercise of hearing "Crucify him!" issue from our own throats will force us to confront our tacit complicity in the myriad mundane crucifixions of the innocent recorded in our daily press. However, if we readily accept the guilt of the fickle mob, we should consider redeeming ourselves by imitating their virtue. Theirs is the legendary generosity of Third World peasants who, having nothing, insist on giving half away. Before entering into the suffering of Jesus next Friday, we might think of a way to join in the joyous abandon of Palm Sunday by doing something extravagant to celebrate the triumph of love over caution.

On the first Palm Sunday, the crowd was following a script for welcoming the Messiah, the script set down by Zechariah. "Rejoice greatly. . . . Lo, your king comes to you, triumphant and victorious . . . humble and riding on a donkey" (Zech 9:9). Jesus was following the same script when he gave his disciples instructions about where to find the requisite donkey (Matt 21:2-3). Following a script does not preclude authentic emotion. On the contrary, those who cherish family rituals and sacred liturgies appreciate how each re-enactment deepens emotion and elicits both nostalgia and new insight. In meticulously acting out Zechariah's description of the Messiah's arrival, Jesus uses vivid visual language to remind the Jews that the Messiah promised to them by the prophets will be distinguished, not by might, but by meekness, that his kingdom will be spread, not by military violence, but by compassion. Why did the Jews need to be reminded? Why, after hearing so often their prophets' imagery of a suffering servant, did they still hope for a king with worldly power? The better question is: Why do Christians need reminding? Why do we listen Sunday after Sunday to Jesus' demand for a counterculture and then go home to invest our hopes and our lives in things God does not value? Why are we repeatedly shocked to discover that money does not save us even from ourselves? We who place our security in cultivating "the right people" need to be reminded of whom the Son of God designated the right people: the poor in spirit, the meek, the merciful, the clean of heart, the non-violent, those who sacrifice comfort for justice. On Palm Sunday Jesus invites us to "join the right crowd": that joyous, generous, slightly crazy crowd who made good their Hosannas by forgetting all other security and just giving God the shirts off their backs.

The Poets Respond:

In poetry and prose, in serious apologetics and in whimsical fiction and verse, G. K. Chesterton never failed to employ the New Testament's favorite literary device, paradox. The voice in Chesterton's Palm Sunday poem is not that of an animal-rights activist, but the voice of the jackass itself. Through this humble beast the poet reminds us that the Son of God chooses vehicles of contradiction and failure more often than success to ride into history and into our lives.

The Donkey

When fishes flew and forests walked
And figs grew upon thorn,
Some moment when the moon was blood,
Then surely I was born.
   With monstrous head and sickening cry
   And ears like errant wings,
   The devil's living parody
   On all four-footed things.
The tattered outlaw of the earth,
Of ancient, crooked will.
Mock, scourge, deride me: I am dumb,
I keep my secret still
   Fools! For I also had my hour,
   One far, fierce, hour and sweet.
   There was a shout about my ears
   And palms before my feet![3]

—*G. K. Chesterton*

THURSDAY OF THE LORD'S SUPPER

Luke 4:16-22   John 13:1-15   1 Cor 11:23-26

The Gospel Speaks:

The Lectionary readings for the Easter Triduum are rich in parallelism between and within Old and New Testament texts. Although literary critics have devoted gallons of scholarly ink to *forms* of parallelism,[1] relatively few ounces of that ink demonstrate how parallelism *functions* in relation to meaning. Literary parallelism in the readings for Holy Thursday and Good Friday can have theological, pastoral, and personal implications, for ultimately the function of literary parallelism is to encourage us to live lives that parallel the Gospel.

Every attentive listener will notice immediately that in the readings that open Thursday's Liturgy of the Word, the instructions for the first Passover feast in Exodus parallel Paul's description of the first Eucharist.[2] Jesus and his friends were obeying the instructions for a liturgical meal given by God to the captive Israelites. The Christian Churches have always used this parallel to designate the Gospel of the Lord's Supper as both a "fulfillment text" and a "proclamation narrative." Jesus formally initiates the new covenant by offering himself as the Lamb whose blood saves us from the angel of death and whose love leads us out of bondage to sin, just as God led the Israelites out of bondage to Egypt.

In the past, homilies stressing the fulfillment of the Scriptures and the institution of the Eucharist tended toward a triumphant tone; now, however, since Holy Thursday is always celebrated on or near Passover, sensitive preachers use the occasion to remind Christians of their Jewish roots and to encourage us to unite in prayer with the people with whom Jesus himself annually observed these sacred rites. Is it not time to go a little further and reflect together on the conclusion of modern biblical scholars that "never in New Testament sources is Jesus represented as inaugurating a separatist movement."[3] For the first function of parallelism between Old and New Testament texts is *ecumenical:* it highlights the bonds between Christians and Jews and reminds us that the best Christians are those who strengthen those bonds by study, dialogue, and fellowship, and by uniting with our Jewish brothers and sisters who are conspicuously committed to the struggle for justice and peace.

But parallels internal to New Testament texts suggest *theological* and *pastoral* responsibilities more challenging than ecumenical ties. Some of that challenge has been obscured, in my judgment, because traditional theology construes part of the scene literally and the other symbolically. Close attention to parallelism among the evangelists restores the full kerygmatic power of the event. The text on which the Catholic Church bases its eucharistic theology concludes with the words "Do this in remembrance of me" (Luke 22:19).[4] Tradition has interpreted these sacred words as a command for the first priests to initiate a sacrament that, like baptism, would be a distinguishing feature of the new covenant. Officially, "Do this" has been taken to mean exclusively: "Consecrate bread into my Body and wine into my Blood so that I can nourish you with my own life."

And indeed, that is one meaning the words will always have for many Christians, including me. The average Catholic never hears these words explicated with theological and pastoral implications that embrace the "non-ordained." Yet, when we look at the parallel texts in Luke's and John's Gospel, we must conclude that Jesus' words are addressed to all "priestly people." John, alone among the evangelists, interrupts the ceremonial supper to have Jesus perform the foot-washing. The Fourth Gospel, which omits the consecration of bread and wine, pictures an essential part of the first Mass. John uses synonymous parallelism to reiterate what Jesus considers *the point* of the bathing: "So if I, your Lord and Teacher, have washed your feet, you also ought to wash one another's feet. For I have set you an example, that you also should do as I have done to you" (John 13:14-15), an obvious parallel to "In remembrance of me, do what I have done."

Yet, since the first century, no Church has ever limited Jesus' command to mean literally that we imitate him best with water and a towel. Nor has any Church decreed that since there were no women at the Lord's Supper, the most menial ministries should be reserved for the ordained clergy. Even scriptural fundamentalists have refrained from suggesting that since Jesus identified himself as "Teacher" in this scene, we should build bathing facilities instead of seminaries and universities. At a minimum, however, the foot-washing paradigm certainly does demand that educational facilities built in Jesus' name graduate students who have learned how to put their degrees in business, economics, psychology, and sociology to work finding effective ways to serve humanity's basic needs. Without elaborate exegesis, ordinary people instantly "get the message": Jesus' symbolic action is an instruction to all, priests and faithful, to roll up their sleeves and do whatever is necessary to bring God's love to bear on fundamental human needs.

The foot-washing pericope has always been given the broadest application in practical works of charity. By contrast, the other "Do this in remembrance" text has been narrowly confined to liturgical premises in the ritual consecration of bread and wine. I believe that Jesus' parallel language communicates a wider mandate, and perhaps, a more inclusive priesthood. Is the eucharistic mandate ever really completed in church? Should not the whole community of believers hear Jesus saying something like this: "In remembrance of me, feed the hungry as I have fed you. In remembrance of me, replace the minimum wage with a living wage, at least for those you employ. In remembrance of me, feed deeper hungers in your spouse, your children, your friends and colleagues. In remembrance of me, when you ask, 'What will you have to drink?' invite your guest to share a thirst for truth, for dignity and equality; for peace based on justice. Lift a glass to each other's thirst for beauty and toast your abiding thirst for 'something more.'"

Here's the something more. Jesus said not only "Eat this bread and drink this cup"; he said "my body . . . is given for you"; "my blood . . . is poured out for many" (Luke 22:19; Mark 14:24). We who eat this bread and drink this cup become a eucharistic people when we imitate the text in its entirety. Pouring out our life's energy in remembrance of Jesus' total self-giving is not something we can accomplish by attending Mass on Sunday. Although it probably begins with hearing God's word and receiving God's strength in the sacrament, our Eucharist does not end there. In fact, only our own lives can write the final parallel text to the Holy Thursday readings. "For as often as you eat this bread and drink the cup, you proclaim the Lord's death until he comes" (1 Cor 11:26). As often as we both share and feed humanity's deepest hungers with all our material and spiritual resources, as often as we share and heal humanity's wounds, we proclaim Jesus' redeeming death. It is to this constantly new and unpredictable sacrament that Jesus invites us. Only through you and me can this Scripture be fulfilled: "Having loved his own who were in the world, he loved them to the end" (John 13:1).

The Poets Respond:

Poets like to appropriate to themselves the biblical exclamation "See, I am making all things new" (Rev 21:5). Today, when Jesus and his message seem to suffer from overexposure, poets can assist in revitalizing the Gospels.[5] They have many ways of achieving what playwright Bertolt Brecht called the "alienation effect," that is, any device in text or stagecraft that renders the familiar "strange." During the final quarter of the twentieth century, the feminist movement created the alienation effect by forcing us to look at almost everything too familiar in our patriarchal culture through the eyes of a woman. How many things does the poet make us re-think by claiming that the too familiar words of sacramental consecration were spoken first, and perhaps most appropriately, by a woman?

Communion

Who spoke the words
now repeated by the priest,
words at the breaking of bread,
ascribed to the Lord of the Feast?
Good friends and wine and food,
yet still his heart was sore.

And she who had swept the floor
and, after the making of bread,
had set the board,
did she listen behind the door
to the words many say he said?

Did sorrow pierce her to the bone
for all that lay ahead
causing those tears to flood?
The words are a woman's own
who for her child has borne and bled.[6]

—*Virginia Hamilton Adair*

After the sordid exposés of sin and sickness among the Catholic clergy in 2002, no priest needs to be reminded of his humanity. But the danger might be for a good priest to lower his standard in examining his conscience from "imitation of Christ" to innocence from high crimes and misdemeanors. Daniel Berrigan holds the priest to the standard of the foot-washing. "In Memoriam II" was inspired by the death of a priest-professor whose only crime seems to have been that he "passed from unawareness to light" without "suffering (what) marks man . . . saved." The memorial reads more like an indictment than a eulogy. In Berrigan's view, his brother priest "never conveyed a man, Christ or himself," and even though he lived near a ghetto, he never heard the Gospel its poor preached to him. Hence the poet sets out to rectify in the afterlife the deficits from which his brother suffered here on earth.

In Memoriam II

Heaven is everything earth has withheld.
I wish you, priest, for herald angel
a phthisic old man
beating a tin can with a mutton bone—
behold he comes!

For savior
unsavory men
a wino's dime
a Coxey's army, a Bowery 2 a.m.
For beatific vision
an end to books, book ends, unbending minds,
tasteless fodder, restrictive order.

For eternal joy
Veins casting off, in a moment's
burning transfiguration
the waste and sludge of unrealized time.

Christ make most of you!
Stitch you through
the needle's eye, the grudging gate.

Crawl through
that crotch of being;
new eyes, new heart, the runner's burning start.[7]

—Daniel Berrigan

GOOD FRIDAY OF THE LORD'S PASSION

Isaiah 52:13–53:12   Hebrews 4:14-16; 5:7-9   John 18:1-19, 42

The Gospel Speaks:

Poems about Jesus' passion and death are innumerable, eloquent, clever, ironic, heartbreaking, powerful—and ultimately superfluous. The crucifixion itself is the Incarnate Word's supreme poem comprehended without explication in every language by thousands who understand no other theology. The crucifix is one of those "poems that tremble with human presence, that put the suffering of a single human being squarely in front of you (with) . . . the power to disturb and even shame."[1] At the same time, in the passion narratives, as nowhere else, the Jesus of history and the Jesus of faith unite.[2] We can contemplate and preach the crucifixion without fear that contemporary scholarship is poised to unmask a "myth."

As a literary genre, passion accounts are the only New Testament material we recognize as "narrative," that is, linear, chronological reports of connected events.[3] Verifiable facts affirm the imagery's raw realities, yet the verbal and non-verbal language evangelists employ to communicate the significance of these facts offers a paradigm of poetic power and a virtual compendium of poetic devices. If no other evidence of his existence survived, history would accord Jesus Christ the title "poet" on the basis of the passion narratives alone. Although crucifixion, as a particularly ignominious form of execution, was used by the Romans primarily as a "deterrent," Jesus seems to have recognized kerygmatic values in this particular form of death. We recognize these values through three poetic devices.

The first of these devices is visual, symbolic imagery. Jesus knew that his public execution, his supreme act of love, witnessed by both the highest and the lowest strata of humanity, would burn forever into human consciousness the symbol of the invisible reality he had come to proclaim: his relationship to the Father and his power to unite us to redemptive love: "When you have lifted up the Son of Man, then you will realize that I am he, and that I do nothing on my own, but I speak these things as the Father instructed me. . . . And I, when I am lifted up from the earth, will draw all people to myself" (John 8:28; 12:32).[4] Lines like these are the work of a poet who loved wordplay, especially the double meaning of puns. The phrase "lifted up" refers to elevation both on the cross and beyond it. Jesus embraces his public death as one way of assuring belief in his resurrection. "So must the Son of Man be lifted up that whoever believes in him may have eternal life" (John 3:14-15).[5]

The first to preach the Good News were men and women who had seen the same body crucified and resurrected. But more than that, as the first believers grew in understanding, they experienced the exaltation of the Crucified and his resurrected life in the community of believers.[6] Isaiah prefaces the litany of insults and abuse that the liturgy has appropriated for Good Friday with these words: "The Lord has given me the tongue of a *teacher* that I may know how to sustain the weary with a word" (Isa 50:4). For the next two chapters Isaiah details the image of a *silent* sufferer who consoles the grief-stricken and the desperate, sustains victims, and rebukes perpetrators of all forms of abuse and violence. Biblical imagery, mirrored in the crucifix, gives us a vulnerable God, scarred beyond recognition. This image is the "tongue" God gave Jesus the Teacher, and no spoken text surpasses its power to communicate to the soul. Other teachers can do no better than to be as compassionately present to all in whom truth or love or justice is crucified.

In every room or church where an image of the wounded body of the Crucified hangs, the crucifix also speaks by way of juxtaposition; Jesus' suffering creates a silent commentary on whatever we may be doing, thinking, or suffering near it. Besides offering a consoling presence, the body of the Crucified can either enlarge and transform or expose and trivialize our solitary suffering with a glance. Throughout the centuries celebrants, after reciting a Latin Mass, commonly observed one or more communicants lingering before the crucifix, which at that time occupied a central position above or near the altar. Even after the people of God began to hear the Word proclaimed in their own languages, they continued to look to the crucifix for compassion and guidance. For the people, regardless of what language the priest spoke, the crucifix always *listened* in the "vernacular." Yet, during the liturgical renewal following the Second Vatican Council, liturgists exiled the image of Christ Crucified from new and renovated sacred spaces and replaced it with images of Christ Risen. Their theology is sound, of course; Jesus has triumphed over death once and for all, but evidence of that triumph dominates neither our personal lives nor our culture. And, to date, academic theology seems not to have supplanted either basic human psychology or the power of the crucifix to penetrate places where formal theology stands outside and knocks. Because the crucifix, more than any other sacramental artifact, seems to make God "relevant," it is "creeping back," not only into reactionary parishes but also into contemporary liturgical design. I suggest that we be willing to learn something from this experience.[7]

Poets use symbols both to reveal and conceal realities beyond sensible expression. The crucifix demonstrates how symbols communicate, not by being explained, but by being experienced, *intact*. For a few hours the Son of God concealed his divine beauty beneath disfiguring torture; for over two centuries the symbol of his death, replicated in both crude and gorgeous artifacts and venerated with wordless understanding, has revealed the fullness of compassion. Regardless of its artistic merit, the symbol communicates to eyes and lips and fingers a love beyond words. On the cross Jesus was unrecognizable because he was so ugly; a few days later, the Risen Jesus was unrecognizable because he was so beautiful. Through events both real and symbolic, the Word Incarnate is trying to tell us to search for him and serve him where his presence is most *unrecognizable*.

Like poetry, the crucifix draws us into paradox and silence. As a "sign of contradiction," the cross provides, simultaneously, the focus of our faith and the test of Jesus' own. His paradoxical cry "My God, my God, why have you forsaken me?"[8] both baffles and consoles us. Though he can never be separated from the Father, Jesus knows what God's absence feels like; and he feels it most keenly when he is in the very act of fulfilling his mission.

We need to believe that, especially now. At no time in history have devout Roman Catholics understood Jesus' anguished cry with such strange and excruciating immediacy as on Good Friday 2002, when the community of the faithful felt betrayed and abandoned by men they had been taught to revere as "other Christs." Yet, when scandal struck the shepherds, the flock did not, by and large, scatter.[9] Perhaps that is because Catholic laity are no longer sheep. At the dawn of the third millennium, an educated and courageous laity gives reason to hope that the very bruises in the Body of Christ will heal it (Isa 53:5).

Meantime, we can pray that history will record the humiliating *kenosis* of Good Friday 2002 as the inauguration of the greatest ecclesiastical cleansing since the Reformation, that the cult of clerical privilege will finally be exorcised, that the simplicity, humility, and openness of the first Christian communities will be restored. Until that transformation becomes as visible as the tragedies that provoked it, the crucifix will resume its ironically appropriate position at the center of Catholic iconography.

The Poets Respond:

The first two poets below begin with observed fact, then extrapolate imagined consequences. Levertov begins with a painting, Williams with observations in her healing ministry. Both then extrapolate psychological consequences for the Son of Man. Williams expresses these consequences structurally: the spaces and single-word lines mirror the isolation and focus of personal pain. Yet, the words "everywhere / pain is / he begins the awful death" erase isolation and self-absorption.

Salvator Mundi: Via Crucis

Maybe He looked indeed
much as Rembrandt envisioned Him
in those small heads that seem in fact
portraits of more than a model.
A dark, still young, very intelligent face,
a soul-mirror gaze of deep understanding, unjudging.
That face, in extremis, would have clenched its teeth
in a grimace not shown in even the great crucifixions.
The burden of humanness (I begin to see) exacted from Him
that He taste also the humiliation of dread,
cold sweat of wanting to let the whole thing go,
like any mortal hero out of His depth,
like anyone who has taken a step too far
and wants herself back.
The painters, even the greatest, don't show how,
in the midnight Garden,

or staggering uphill under the weight of the Cross,
He went through with even the human longing
to simply cease, not to be.
Not torture of body,
not the hideous betrayals humans commit
nor the faithless weakness of friends, and surely
not the anticipation of death (not even then, in agony's grip)
was Incarnation's heaviest weight,
but this sickened desire to renege,
to step back from what He, Who was God,
had promised Himself, and had entered
time and flesh to enact.
Sublime acceptance, to be absolute, had to have welled
up from those depths where purpose
drifted for mortal moments.[10]

—Denise Levertov

From *"the sorrow"*

he dies

pain is
and is everywhere
there is nothing to ease the dying
the torture
nails
thorns
lash
hands
feet
head
everywhere
pain is

he begins

the awful death

no longer certain
what is real

except the pain

. . .

father!

he listens to his frantic heart
where there is no answer
but desperation
no cry of son
no voice of love
and so he thirsts
unquenched

my God! my God!
why have you forsaken me?

time
measured out in torment

then

it is finished

his final breath
a sigh of blood
death closes over him

the spirit
sobbing
rends the temple veil.

—*ruthann williams, o.p.*

Gabriela Mistral, the Chilean lay Franciscan who won the Nobel Prize for Literature in 1945, envisions here an imaginative relationship with the tree of the cross, beginning with the human body itself and proceeding through a series of dreamlike segues where the poet seems to speak sometimes for herself, sometimes for humanity, and sometimes with a consciousness melded with that of the Crucified. Mistral's "correspondences," a combination of Franciscan spirituality and Latin American magic realism, seem to anticipate the doctrine of human-nonhuman interdependence that now unites environmental scientists and "creation theologians" in a common cause.

Final Tree

This solitary fretwork
they gave me at birth
that goes from side
to fiery side,

that runs from my forehead
to my hot feet
this island of my blood
this minuteness of kingdom

I return it fulfilled.
With arms outstretched I give it
to the last of my trees,
to tamarinth or cedar.

In case in the second life
they will not give again what has been given
and I should miss this solace
of freshness and silence,

and if I should pass through the world
in dream, running or flying,
instead of thresholds of houses
I shall want a tree to rest under.

I bequeath it all I had
of ash and firmament,
my flank of speech,
my flank of silence.

Loneliness I gave myself,
Loneliness they gave me,
The small tithe I paid the lightning
of my God, sweet and tremendous.

My play of give and take
with clouds and with the winds
and what I knew, trembling,
of secret springs.

Ay! Tremulous shelter
of my true Archangel,
ahead on every road
with branch and balsam.

Perhaps it is already born
and I lack the grace to know it
or it was that nameless tree
I carried like a blind son.

At times a dampness falls
around my shoulders, a soft breeze,
and I see about me
the girdle of my tree.

Perhaps its foliage
already clothes my dreams
and in death I sing beneath it
without knowing it.[11]

—*Gabriela Mistral*

EASTER VIGIL

Matthew 28:1-10   Mark 16:1-8   Luke 2:1-12   Romans 6:3-11

The Gospel Speaks:

The Lectionary readings for the Triduum liturgies contain the seeds of a magnificent celebration of both verbal and non-verbal poetry. Based on all four evangelists' assurances that Jesus was buried,[1] earlier liturgical practice translated the sense of God's absence into a full day of symbolically cold, empty churches that almost belied our confidence that Jesus can never die again. However, those of us who have lived through the second half of the twentieth century need nothing to provoke a sense of God's absence. And the deeper our understanding of that absence, the more profound will be our resurrection experience.

Modern Christians know keenly what it is like to be in the historical and emotional locus one philosopher has designated as "the time between the no longer and the not yet."[2] For contemporary Christians, basic mysteries simply "taken on faith," Scriptural texts with a single, literal interpretation, and moral questions with clear unequivocal answers are *no longer*. But theologically sound, emotionally satisfying alternatives are *not yet*, or at least not yet universally accepted. Intellectually and psychologically, many feel as if they live in the same place occupied by Jesus' closest friends between the first Good Friday night and Easter Sunday morning. For some terminally disaffected Christians, the tomb is not empty: it is jam-packed with the corpses of childhood certitudes and sanctities. Many of these sad people entertain more resentment than nostalgia, resentment of both their traditional teachers and of the new iconoclasts who have displaced them.

The silence in the darkened church can speak eloquently to and for all these, and with nuanced eloquence to those who have benefited from a post-Vatican theological education. A presider who trusts the symbolic poetry of darkness long enough to make his congregation nervous, to allow each adult to face the interior darkness from which the Risen Savior liberates us, again and again, will need no homily. The beautiful words that accompany the blessing of the new fire, the lighting and sharing of the paschal flame, the singing of the *Exsultet* proclamation, and the sacramental rites of initiation—all incorporate theology into genuine prayer.[3] The Liturgy of the Word, when it comes, confirms the elemental poetry that has already accessed the deepest desires of those present. As more than one mystic has expressed it, prayer is simply an act of attention.[4] Let fire and water speak for themselves. The Easter Vigil defies paraphrase.

The Poets Respond:

The Easter Season brings a unique emotion to those who have recently buried the dead, an emotion that can be described only with oxymorons like "painful joy" or "fearful hope." For those in grief, more than others, perhaps, belief in the resurrection of the body becomes both an intellectual challenge and an emotional imperative. The two poets below, one a nineteenth-century visionary, the other a plain-spoken twenty-first-century realist, deal with these emotions very differently. In the imagery of the first poem, which begins with Mary the night after her son's death, Rainer Maria Rilke seems to capture the shifting emotions, not only of the Mother of God but also of us, her other children. In the second poem, a contemporary poet muses on the possibility of meeting in the afterlife someone he has met only in prayer.

O Lacrymosa

I

Oh tear-filled figure who, like a sky held back,
grows heavy above the landscape of her sorrow
And when she weeps, the gentle raindrops fall,
slanting upon the sand-bed of her heart.

Oh heavy with weeping. Scale to weigh all tears,
Who felt herself not sky, since she was shining
and sky exists only for clouds to form in.

How clear it is, how close, your land of sorrow,
beneath the stern sky's oneness, Like a face
that lies there, slowly waking up and thinking
horizontally, into endless depths.

II

It is nothing but a breath, the void.
And that green fulfillment
of blossoming trees: a breath.
We, who are still the breathed-upon,
today still the breathed upon, count
this slow breathing of earth,
whose hurry we are.

III

Ah, but the winters! The earth's mysterious
turning within. Where around the dead
in the pure receding of sap,
boldness is gathered,
the boldness of future springtimes
Where imagination occurs
beneath what is rigid, where all the green
worn thin by the vast summers
again turns into a new
insight and the mirror of intuition;
where the flowers' color
wholly forgets that lingering of our eyes.[5]

—*Rainer Maria Rilke*

A Meal Now and Then

We almost sat at table once,
but the cards could not be dealt.
A storm arose, or a plane was missed,
something.

So we never knew if we'd be friends;
having a friend in common is
of course no guarantee.

When she learned the diagnosis,
she asked my prayers and so
for the last years I prayed
for someone I might never meet.

The case is settled now.
The disposition is clear,
as definitive as the body
brought down from the cross.
What did the friends think,
having left Jesus wrapped
in cloth away from their eyes
forever, they thought, in the tomb?

Never again to see,
never again to hear the voice
of one they loved.

I have known this silent stone,
rolled over the mouth of death.
I have seen the lid sealed
Over the remains of father, grandparents,
friends. I have awaited the day
of my children, when they will arise
in the embrace of their ancestors.

For what are we waiting, my loved ones,
here on the edge of this world
that to us does not seem a horizon?

The horizon is always beyond us.
There the sun rises, the moon too.
There the sun sinks
Yet we wait,
expecting the Last Day, here

which to the Holy Fire that is coming
is the edge of a darkness
that will be transformed.

We wait, the long trial of waiting,
the sentence is incomplete.

Will we be filled with the fire?
What will be the banquet
when horizons cease?
Will we find ourselves
at the same table at last?[6]

—Leo Luke Marcello

NOTES

Redemption

[1] "Constitution on the Sacred Liturgy" (1963), in *Vatican II: The Conciliar and Post Conciliar Documents,* new rev. ed., ed. Austin Flannery, O.P. (Northport, N.Y.: Costello Publishing, 1998) no. 109.

[2] For an in-depth study of this pattern and its significance in Christian spirituality, see Roger Poelman, *Times of Grace: The Sign of Forty in the Bible* (New York: Herder and Herder, 1964).

[3] John Berryman, "Eleven Addresses to the Lord," in *Love & Fame* (New York: Farrar Straus, and Giroux, 1970).

[4] Poelman, *Times of Grace,* 72.

[5] Ibid., 73.

Ash Wednesday

[1] Simone Weil, *Waiting for God,* trans. Emma Crauford (New York: Harper Torchbooks, 1973) 134–135.

[2] Gregory Norbet, O.S.B., "Hosea," The Benedictine Foundation of Vermont, Inc.

[3] T. S. Eliot, "Murder in the Cathedral," in *The Complete Poems and Plays* (New York: Harcourt Brace, 1952) 196.

[4] Christopher Fitzgerald, "Sonnet #31," from *Sonnets to the Unseen* (Schiller Park, Ill.: World Library Publications, 2001).

[5] The Nevah River runs through St. Petersburg, named after Peter the Great, who painted the buildings in bold colors. In the Russian Orthodox calendar, two hundred days are "fast days." During the "white nights" of August, the sun shines through the night, often leaving only an hour between midnight and dawn. Although a few synagogues and churches remained open during the reign of atheistic communism, those who worshiped in them were excluded from jobs, housing, education, and other material benefits.

First Sunday of Lent

[1] Liturgically, the Temptation occurs between the Baptism and the Transfiguration episodes, in each of which the Father is heard to say: "This is my Son, the Beloved, with whom I am well pleased." The Transfiguration statement adds: "Listen to him." Some scholars discern in the Temptation pericope a dramatic version of the Father's witness: a theological testimony followed by instruction to which those who acknowledge Christ's divinity should listen.

[2] *Jesus:* Deut 8:3; 6:16; 6:13. *Satan:* Ps 91:11-12. Satan stops short of the lines in this psalm that refer to crushing the serpent.

[3] Wislawa Szymborska, "In Praise of Self Deprecation," in *Sounds, Feelings, and Thoughts: Seventy Poems by Wislawa Szymborska.* (Princeton: Princeton University Press, 1981).

Second Sunday of Lent

[1] "The narrative must rest on a mystical experience of the disciples." John McKenzie, S.J., *The Jerome Biblical Commentary,* 43:119. Luke's account specifies that Peter, James, and John saw Jesus' appearance change "while he was at prayer." Moreover, Peter declares that there are no words for their experience. Jung, among others, teaches that what we cannot put into words we recognize and express in images.

[2] That the Church endorses this form of revelation is evident every time Rome accords the title "Doctor of the Church" to a mystical theologian. For the first women to receive this title, Catherine of Siena, Teresa of Avila, and Thérèse of Lisieux, mystical experience was a *primary* source of revelation. Moreover, the hyperactive life of Catherine, who never lived in a convent, attests that engagement with "the world" does not preclude mystical experience. When the Church belatedly acknowledged these women as theologians, I believe that, although the politics of the feminist movement played no small part in the decision, the Church was also consciously honoring not only women but also a *way of knowing* that the laudable rigor of academic theology today necessarily neglects.

[3] Mark Salzman, *Lying Awake,* (New York: Alfred A. Knopf, 2000) 116. These words of the novel's Carmelite protagonist, like all her other descriptions of contemplative prayer, represent the author's distillation of his six-year research on the texts of classical mysticism and on numerous unpublished writings by contemporary contemplative women.

[4] Teilhard de Chardin, *The Phenomenon of Man* (New York: Harper Torchbooks, 1959) 298.

[5] Ibid.

[6] Johann Wolfgang von Goethe, "The Holy Longing," trans. Robert Bly. [www.favoritepoem.org/poems/goethe/index.html]

Third Sunday of Lent

[1] Matt 10:5; Luke 9:52-53. Obviously, one of the objectives of this Fourth Gospel post-Resurrection pericope was to correct the exclusion of Samaritans from the apostolic mission recorded in the Synoptics.

[2] Some feminist critics, drawing elaborate inferences from the five husbands, have pictured her as seductive, ravaged by serial adultery, etc. Sandra Schneiders rejects such speculation because it deflects focus from the theological significance of her person and her questioning. Sandra M. Schneiders, *Written That You May Believe: Encountering Jesus in the Fourth Gospel* (New York: Crossroad, 1999) 138.

[3] Both the woman and her cup are off limits to an observant Jew.

[4] Deliberate misunderstanding is one of the distinctive literary devices the author of the Fourth Gospel uses to prepare for a Christological revelation. Among other examples, the formula occurs in the Lenten Gospels John 3:5; 4:15; 11:6. Peter F. Ellis, *The Genius of John: A Composition-Critical Commentary on the Fourth Gospel* (Collegeville, Minn.: The Liturgical Press, 1984) 53.

[5] John 4:16-17. The poetic skill of the evangelist is especially evident in this section: the setting at Jacob's well (Gen 29:1-20) suggests the word "husband,"

which in turn evokes the poetry of the prophetic tradition in which marriage is a metaphor for the covenant relationship between Yahweh and the Jewish people. Jesus is the bridegroom who consummates that covenant. To interpret "husband" literally here or to treat any bridal metaphor literally diminishes not only the poetry but also the theology of biblical literature. Jesus refers to that theology in John 3:27-30. "Jesus' declaration that Samaria has no husband is a classic prophetic denunciation of false worship (Hos 2:2)." Cited in Schneiders, *Written That You May Believe*, 138.

⁶ This is actually the question on which Samaritanism, a form of Judaism, was founded. Over centuries of political strife, the issue eventually crystallized around the issue of Jerusalem. In fact, the Samaritan version of the Decalogue adds an eleventh commandment to build an altar on Mount Gerizim. See "Samaritans," in *The Anchor Bible Dictionary*, ed. David Noel Freedman (New York: Doubleday, 1992) E4.

⁷ Anne Sexton, "Jesus the Actor Plays the Holy Ghost," in *The Awful Rowing Toward God* (Boston: Houghton Mifflin, 1975).

⁸ Karol Wotjyla, "Song of the Brightness of the Water," in *Collected Poems* (New York: Random House, 1982) 34–39.

Fourth Sunday of Lent

¹ T. S. Eliot, "The Music of Poetry," in *On Poetry and Poets* (New York: Farrar, Straus and Cudahy, 1957) 32. The musical analogy helps to penetrate Eliot's own *Four Quartets*, which juxtaposes seemingly unrelated symbolic landscapes, metaphysical lyrics, philosophical prose, and multilingual citations.

² Nicodemus and the Prodigal Son are treated below in the poetry section, pp. 105–106.

³ Rudolf Schnackenburg, *The Gospel According to St. John* (New York: Doubleday, 1979) 2:270–274.

⁴ Ibid., 251.

⁵ In both the Old and the New Testaments, verbs of *seeing* are associated with *believing,* and *believing* in turn with *salvation.* See Exod 14:13; Ps 50:23; 91:16; 119:123; Isa 40:5; 42:16-17; 59:11; John 4:29, 39-42.

⁶ Pamela Smith, S.S.C.M., "The Unblinding," in *Waymakers: Eyewitnesses to Christ* (Notre Dame: Ave Maria Press, 1982).

⁷ Smith, "Nicodemus," ibid.

Fifth Sunday of Lent

¹ Octavio Paz, *The Other Voice: Essays on Modern Poetry* (New York: Harcourt Brace Jovanovich, 1991) 142–143.

² Ibid., 143.

³ Ibid.

⁴ David Curzon, ed., *The Gospels in Our Image: An Anthology of Twentieth Century Poetry Based on Biblical Texts* (New York: Harcourt Brace, 1995) 151–155.

⁵ "Lazarus" in Curzon, *The Gospels in Our Image*, 155.

⁶ "The Anti-Lazarus," ibid., 154.

⁷ "Calvary," ibid., 152.

[8] May Sarton, "Lazarus," in *Collected Poems 1930–93* (New York: W. W. Norton, 1966).

[9] Tadeuz Rozewicz, "Unknown Letter," in *Unease* (Minneapolis: New Rivers Press, 1981).

[10] Miguel de Unamuno, "The Forefinger of the Right Hand," from "The Christ of Velasquez," in *The Last Poems of Miguel de Unamuno* (Madison, N.J.: Fairleigh Dickinson University Press, 1974).

Palm Sunday

[1] Literal translation, *The New Jerusalem Bible* (Garden City, N.Y.: Doubleday, 1985) note *h*.

[2] What began literally as "Save us, we pray" survives now in both Judaic and Christian liturgies exclusively as a prayer of homage. *The Jerome Biblical Commentary*, 42:67.8; 43:142.9.

[3] G. K. Chesterton, "The Donkey," in *The Collected Poems* (New York: Doubleday, 1932).

Thursday of the Lord's Supper

[1] I use the term "parallelism" here, not as confined to lines of Hebrew verse, but as it is used in structural analysis of both prose and poetry in the Old and New Testaments.

[2] Exod 12:1-8; 1 Cor 11:23-26 based on Luke 22:14-20.

[3] "Jesus voluntarily pours out his life for the community of Israel, and in so doing inaugurates a new covenant for a covenant community, already in being, that believed itself to be true heirs of the promises of Abraham." W. F. Albright and C. S. Mann, *Matthew: A New Translation with Notes,* The Anchor Bible (Garden City, N.Y.: Doubleday, 1971) 26:323.

[4] Also, 1 Cor 11:26: "For as often as you eat this bread and drink the cup, you proclaim the Lord's death until he comes."

[5] This is the thesis of Peggy Rosenthal's excellent *Praying the Gospels Through Poetry: Lent to Easter* (Cincinnati: St. Anthony Messenger Press, 2002) Preface.

[6] Virginia Hamilton Adair, "Communion," in *Beliefs and Blasphemies: A Collection of Poems* (New York: Random House, 1998).

[7] Daniel Berrigan, "In Memoriam II," in *Selected and New Poems* (New York: Doubleday, 1973).

Good Friday of the Lord's Passion

[1] Edward Hirsch, "Poet's Choice," in *The Washington Post Book World* (April 4, 2002) BW12.

[2] Even Bishop Spong, whose years with the Jesus Seminar led him to characterize everything else in the Gospels as "fiction," concludes that Jesus Christ's death by crucifixion is indisputably history. John Shelby Spong, *Liberating the Gospels: Reading the Gospels with Jewish Eyes: Freeing Jesus from 2,000 Years of Misunderstanding* (San Francisco: Harper, 1997).

³ Joseph A. Fitzmyer, *The Gospel According to Luke,* The Anchor Bible (Garden City, N.Y.: Doubleday, 1981–1985) 28–28A:1359ff. Fitzmyer notes, however, that the passion narratives cannot be reduced to "solely factual" material, for they also include theological and apologetic motifs.

⁴ Though he fulfills the will of the Father, Jesus does not die in obedience to a deity who demands human sacrifice. As Old Testament scholar Carol Dempsey, O.P., explains, the Abraham/Isaac story embodies Yahweh's *rejection* of the ritual of human sacrifice, which was practiced during Abraham's time. The image of God communicated through Abraham and the first monotheists is not that of a petulant monarch demanding human sacrifice but of a loving father who rewards the obedience of his servant by choosing life for him. (Personal interview, February 14, 2001).

⁵ Also John 8:28; 12:31; Matt 26:31. At the Last Supper, Jesus indicates both the inevitability of his death and the certitude of the resurrection: ". . . it is written, 'I will strike the shepherd, and the sheep of the flock will be scattered.' But after I am raised up, I will go ahead of you to Galilee."

⁶ Joseph Fitzmyer defines "lifted up" as "exaltation," "passage from death on the cross to a heavenly existence with the Father in glory." *A Christological Catechism: New Testament Answers* (Ramsey, N.J.: Paulist Press, 1982) 91. Sandra Schneiders goes so far as to say that the resurrection of Jesus' body was unnecessary, for his glorification was complete on the cross. *Written That You May Believe: Encountering Jesus in the Fourth Gospel* (New York: Crossroad, 1999) 56ff.

⁷ "The symbol of the cross has 'staying power' because it captures the place where the terror of history and the mystery of God meet." Wayne G. Rollins, *Jung and the Bible* (Atlanta: John Knox Press, 1983) 89. "The symbol must emerge in the depths of the artistic experience in the larger community. . . . The pressing desire to recapture an experience of meaning in resurrection language should not tempt one to short-circuit the reflective process or to hurry the gestation of new images. . . . Such a quick route to relevance is often attempted by theologians, but there is always danger of self-delusion." Pheme Perkins, *Resurrection: New Testament Witness and Contemporary Reflection* (Garden City, N.J.: Doubleday, 1984) 396–397.

⁸ Matt 27:46; Mark 15:34; Luke 23:46; Ps 22:1.

⁹ "I will strike the shepherd, and the sheep of the flock will be scattered." Matt 26:31; Mark 14:21.

¹⁰ Denise Levertov, "St. Thomas Didymus," in *The Stream and the Sapphire* (New York: New Directions, 1997).

¹¹ Gabriela Mistral, "The Final Tree," in *Selected Poems of Gabriela Mistral,* trans. Doris Dana (Baltimore: Johns Hopkins University Press, 1971).

Easter Vigil

¹ Matt 27:57-61; Mark 15:42-47; Luke 23:50-56; John 19:38-42.

² Martin Heidegger, *Poetry, Language,Thought,* trans. Albert Hofstader (New York: Harper and Row, 1971) 184.

[3] When the void is filled with constant movement, the silence destroyed by choir practice, and the total darkness compromised by dim lights, a yawning congregation misses the profound impact of the *Lumen Christi.*

[4] Simone Weil, Abraham Heschel, and others.

[5] Rainer Maria Rilke, "O Lacrymosa," in *The Selected Poetry of Rainer Maria Rilke,* trans. Stephen Mitchell (New York: Vintage Press, 1989).

[6] Leo Luke Marcello, "A Meal Now and Then," in *Nothing Grows in One Place Forever* (New York: Time Being Books, 1998).

Chapter 3

RESURRECTION
The Sundays of Easter

Eastertide, the season between the lighting of the paschal candle and its symbolic extinguishing, is neither so frenzied as Advent, so abruptly anti-climactic as Christmas, nor so challenging as Lent. Unlike the commemoration of Jesus' nativity, the celebration of his far more astonishing resurrection has escaped commercial commodification. For this very reason, we have the leisure for a truly spiritual Easter, free of mandatory shopping, decorating, and partying, leisure to meditate not only on the Easter event itself but on the newness of life in all its manifestations.

Nature cooperates with the kind of reanimated landscape that tempts us to abandon routine for a day or more. No serious Christian should resist this temptation. To put aside whatever is deadening—workaholic rituals, soporific entertainment, compulsive pessimism—can "roll away the stone" from our own hearts. While society pressures us to celebrate Christmas with conspicuous consumption, it permits us to celebrate Easter at no cost at all, except, of course, a modest investment in time and imagination. To replace life-denying habits with *anything* done simply to express the joy of being alive constitutes an appropriate "Alleluia!"

Those whose Lenten schedule has included spending time with the Scriptures will cheat themselves of its dividends if they stop now when the Gospels focus on the dogma of Christian faith that "doubles the return" on every other belief. As we peruse our favorite texts, our Easter-faith acts like a Rosetta stone, providing the essential clue to the meaning of Jesus' most mysterious statements, but it also points up

141

the need for more prayerful study. "The Christian claim concerning the Resurrection of Jesus is not that he picked up his old manner of life, but rather that he entered an entirely new form of existence . . . sharing in Jesus' new life through the power of the Holy Spirit is an essential dimension of the Resurrection."[1] Perhaps this is the ideal time to begin nibbling at the insights of contemporary scriptural theologians to discover what this "entirely new form of existence" means. So too, the speculations of the poets, playful and profound, can liberate our minds and hearts from mere literalism.

Whatever we decide to do, a spirit of genuine joy should permeate our activity. While anyone who goes through the whole of Eastertide without reassessing his or her priorities in light of Christ's triumph over death should feel guilty, anyone who cannot claim at least one imaginative extravagance with *time,* either alone or with loved ones, should feel even guiltier. A Christian who truly values time knows how and when to "waste" it. The Easter Season, more urgently than any other, invites us to indulge in an act of gratitude for the sacrament of the present moment. All Christians should share the ambition of the poet Mary Oliver: "When it's over, I want to say: all my life I was a bride married to amazement."[2]

THE EASTER SUNDAY GOSPELS[1]

| Matthew 28:1-10 | John 20:1-23 | Luke 24:1-49 |

The Gospel Speaks:

Every time we bury a loved one, our minds grapple with questions of life after death, and our hearts re-enact the drama of Easter morning. Then, like detectives investigating a crime, we search those readings that assemble "the case" for the "resurrection of the body." Though we note the absence of a single eyewitness to the moment when Jesus arose, we take heart as a series of "corroborating witnesses" attest to the appearances of his risen body. Reading Acts and the Epistles, we savor certitudes like "If there is no resurrection of the dead . . . then your faith has been in vain" (1 Cor 15:13-14).

But much as we cherish the hope of reunion with familiar bodies, we find the concept of a mass resuscitation at the end of time too grotesque to contemplate.[2] Hence we need to find in the Resurrection narratives something more than proof texts and condolences for the bereaved. Our affirmation of fundamental belief in a basic New Testament proclamation must include discovering its meaning in *this life,* not only in the hereafter. With this in mind, both those who use the Scriptures for personal prayer and those who preach will benefit from a sense of the poetic *structure* of Resurrection narratives as a whole before reflecting individually on each post-Resurrection appearance on the discrete Sundays to which the Lectionary assigns them.

Each evangelist values slightly different details, but all "appearance scenes" follow the same design: during each appearance pericope, the protagonist(s) move from proof of physical presence to an understanding and/or mission related to the deeper significance of Jesus' presence among the living. Matthew's version is the most dramatic and, perhaps, the most self-consciously poetic. As we have observed before, evangelists usually leave description to our imagination, but in this scene, where the angel announces the unimaginable, Matthew chooses to use vivid description, not to present a videotape of a phenomenon, but to compress into a few symbolic phrases the historic significance of this event. The appeal of his account derives from his skillful use of three poetic devices: symbolic description, antithesis, and paradox. "And suddenly there was a great earthquake; for an angel of the Lord, descending from heaven, came and rolled back the stone and sat on it" (Matt 28:2). Matthew's opening description involves all four elements: earth, air, water, fire, suggesting that creation itself was the first to know that its Lord had risen. Matthew employs the traditional spatial metaphors familiar to his audience. The earth erupts in astonishment as the angel descends from above to deliver the heavenly message. He speaks first in sign language. He rolls back the stone separating the living from the dead, and—just to be sure we know who's in control here—he sits on it. The angel's calm assurance contrasts with the chaos of the earthquake and the terror of the guards. Matthew then moves his camera in for a close-up of the angel: "His appearance was like lightning, and his clothing white as snow" (Matt 28:3).

It is possible to translate this dazzling image as the author's attempt to articulate the impact of the Easter annunciation on the women at the empty tomb: a revelation as astonishing as lightning married to snow. T. S. Eliot, in his symbolist poem on the mystical life, employs similar imagery to express the instant of the soul's illumination, imagery that juxtaposes extremes of time, temperature, and texture:

> Suspended in time, between pole and tropic.
> When the short day is brightest, with frost and fire,
> The brief sun flames the ice. . . .
> . . . This is the spring time
> But not in time's covenant. Now the hedgerow
> Is blanched for an hour with transitory blossom
> Of snow. . . .[3]

In Matthew's angel, as in Eliot's landscape, the elements, in their impossible fusion, embody the paradoxical nature of God's compassion and power, made manifest in the paschal mysteries of life-in-death: the awesome, destructive power of lightning melds with the gentle cleansing of snow.

Matthew continues to build his narrative on a series of contrasts, this time, I suspect, with tongue-in-cheek. The women act quickly, moving from fear of believing news too good to be true to spreading that news with "fear and great joy." By contrast, the men guarding the stone are themselves "petrified" (Matt 28:4-8). The Risen Jesus rewards the women's faith by appearing to them in person even before they have completed their mission, but the cowardly soldiers are left to guard an empty tomb.

Matthew contrasts heavenly and earthly testimony with a comic coda mocking false "witnesses." Although he obviously intended the tale of the guards to strengthen the credibility of the women, his final statement provides one of the rare examples of comedy in the New Testament. According to Matthew, the chief priests first hired the guards to prevent deception, and then bribed them to propagate a deception, that is, that while they were sleeping, the friends of Jesus stole his body away. Readers are left free to decide whose naivete the story illustrates—that of the priests or that of an audience easy to convince that sleeping men make reliable eyewitnesses.

The design of Matthew's account of the holy women at the tomb varies only slightly from the pattern we will see in the four Resurrection narratives in John and the two in Luke. Each of these episodes involves a testing of faith, an affirmation of belief, a command to let go of the physical presence of the Risen One (or his own sudden departure), and a commission to communicate the Resurrection experience to others. Luke's account of the holy women's visit to the tomb differs in detail, but not in design (Luke 24:1-12). Two men in dazzling clothes add to the news a reminder that Jesus is fulfilling his promise to rise from the dead. The women, who had at first reacted with fear, leave the empty tomb and go to tell the "eleven" (Luke 24:9). Luke also contrasts the prompt faith of the women with the disbelief of the men, two of whom rush off to see with their own eyes.

Luke's Emmaus episode follows a similar pattern. It begins with the disappointed disciples mourning the loss of their messianic hopes, moves through their gradual recognition of the truth, and concludes with their spreading of the Good News (Luke 24:13-35). While the disciples are discussing the Emmaus report, Jesus appears among them, confirms their faith by physical contact, continues the Emmaus instruction, and commissions them to spread the Good News to others (Luke 24:36-49). In John's Gospel this design functions consistently through three Easter Sunday events: the race to the tomb, the appearance to

Mary Magdalene, the evening appearance to the disciples. Again, each event involves a testing of belief, a confirmation of belief, followed by transformation and/or commissioning (John 20:1-31).[4]

The insistent repetition of this design throughout the Resurrection narratives holds hermeneutical imperatives for those struggling to keep faith alive in a "post-Christian" culture. Collectively, these texts achieve an incremental intensity. First of all, each Resurrection episode compresses into a tightly structured dramatic poem the imperative to seek the Risen Lord among the living and in the act of living. Jesus' firm rejection of Mary Magdalene's restraining gesture embodies that imperative. (Karl Rahner explains how that gesture was recently replicated when the renovation of liturgical spaces de-centralized the tabernacles in an attempt to reinstate those "elements of the . . . New Testament experience of resurrection" that had come "to be expressed in the piety of the Catholic West as devotion to the presence of Christ in the Blessed Sacrament.")[5] Secondly, each episode offers the assurance that faith can be strengthened as well as threatened by challenges to faith. Each scene acts out the tensions of faith in an age that worships scientific "truth," the tension between the visible and the invisible, between logic and mystery, between what we want to believe and what we're afraid to believe, between the literalism we cling to and the deeper meanings which that literalism obstructs.

A closer look at some of the details common to Jesus' Easter appearances will reward us with a deeper alternative to literalism. The details make one thing immediately certain: Jesus' bodily resurrection is not the same as the resuscitation of Lazarus or that of the widow's son. The glorified body of Jesus is so different that even Mary Magdalene fails to recognize him. Although the evangelists repeatedly offer evidence that the glorified Jesus is the same *person* who was crucified, they also emphasize that his *body* is different.[6] Jesus himself makes both points whenever he appears. Having passed easily through locked doors, Jesus invites his closest friends to touch his wounds and be reassured that he is not a ghost. On the other hand, he scarcely allows them to enjoy his presence, for he speaks immediately of returning to the Father and of their responsibility to act in his place. Clearly, the Risen Jesus uses his body as an instrument for communicating the fact that there is life after death, and just as clearly he is intent on communicating that this body is not the only or primary *locus* for life after death. And we should be grateful that this is so. The physical bodies to which we are so attached are also the source of our chief limitations. Jesus uses his risen body to point to a greater reality: death demolishes all these limitations.

But human beings are more comfortable with human limits than with freedom from them. "Do not hold on to me," Jesus says firmly to Magdalene (John 20:17). Like too many misguided religious zealots, Mary wants to localize her God, to nail him down to a specific historical spot on earth. Jesus directs her to the deeper, wider meaning of the Resurrection. She has looked for his body to embalm it; he is not there. She has found him alive right in front of her, but he refuses to be confined there. He sends her to where he wants to be found from now on: in the body of the Church and in the invisible but very real kingdom which that Church will build on earth. She is the first one commissioned to tell his disciples what Jesus himself will repeat when he directs them also to go where he can be found on earth even after he returns to the Father.

The physical body of Jesus is the revelatory sign of life after death.[7] But what, physically, does that mean for us? No one alive knows the answer to that question. When we recite the Creed, we declare that "we believe in the resurrection of the body," not knowing exactly how that resurrection will be accomplished. Despite the many popular films and television shows that appeal to our desire to see our beloved dead again, we must accept that though they are "embedded by death in the silent, secret ground of our own existence . . . they can only appear, as *we* are, not as *they* are."[8] Meantime, we can assert our belief in something more immediate and more wonderful than a physical reunion with our own bodies and those of our loved ones: we can affirm our participation in the risen life of Jesus *wherever he is*. So, where are my beloved dead? And where will I be after I die? *The dead are in God, which means, wherever God is.* "I will come again and will take you to myself, so that where I am, there you may be also" (John 14:3). No wonder we feel their presence in the beauty of places where they have never been, in the spiritual vitality of people whom they have never known, in the illumination of books they have never read. No wonder we feel a shock when they enter a room as quietly as light, or more shockingly, enter *us* during our thanksgiving after Holy Communion. No wonder Eastertide urges us to drop everything and indulge in a day of holy communion with everyone we've ever loved who is risen and with us *wherever God is*.

The Poets Respond:

We have no idea exactly what the weather was like during the first Easter season, but poets have always imagined springtime as Easter's perennial symbol. John Lynch follows this tradition in these lines from his book-length poem that has been called "The Gospel According to Mary."

From *A Woman Wrapped in Silence*

This wonder and this clear, unyielding joy
Uncaptive, free, and new upon the tears
Of loss, still sounds in all the triumph bells
We ring, and in the peal of trumpet lilies
That we gather up to stand among
Our songs. This still is shouting in our Spring.
We have not lost His accent of return.
We listen yet and hear the quivered air
Take up the sounding of His voice to carry
It in limpid waves along the far
Receiving skies until the whole of air
Is new and silvered in the breath of Him.
This dawn that cannot be, and is, still lights
For us. We have not grown too gross with years,
Nor dull with other deaths to keep this day
And trace again the first fresh news of it.[9]

—*John W. Lynch, S.J.*

When a perfect spring day issues an irresistible temptation to make "wasting time" an act of worship, a favorite nature poem helps to provoke and prolong alleluias. Gerard Manley Hopkins found the predictable elegance of iambic pentameter too tame to contain the energy of nature and the fierceness of his protest against the abuse of God's creation, so he invented the clashing cymbals of his own "sprung rhythm."

God's Grandeur

The world is charged with the grandeur of God.
    It will flame out, like shining from shook foil.
    It gathers to a greatness, like the ooze of oil
Crushed. Why do men then now not reck his rod?
Generations have trod, have trod, have trod;
    And all is seared with trade; bleared, smeared with toil;
    And wears man's smudge and shares man's smell; the soil
Is bare now, nor can foot feel, being shod.

And for all this, nature is never spent;
    There lives the dearest freshness deep down things;
And though the last lights off the black West went
    Oh, morning, at the brown brink eastward, springs—
Because the Holy Ghost over the bent
    World broods with warm breast and with ah! bright wings.[10]

                —*Gerard Manley Hopkins, S.J.*

"Nothing has life except the incomplete," says William Butler Yeats. Perhaps one of the sources for the Gospels' inexhaustible literary life is their incompleteness. Into the spaces and silences created by the evangelists' reticence enters the poet's imagination. One of the New Testament's most tantalizing silences is the absence of a Resurrection appearance to Mary. Lynch first speculates that such a meeting was unnecessary and then invents a scene anyway.

From *A Woman Wrapped in Silence*

                            Or is
       It truer thought of her she found no need
       To search? And better said that she had known
       Within, they'd not discover Him again
       Among the dead? . . .
       We have no word of this sweet certainty
       That hides in her . . .
       This is hers. We are not told of this,
       This quaking instant, this return, this Light

Beyond the tryst of dawn when she first lifted
Up her eyes, and quiet, unamazed,
saw he was near. This is her own, this moment
When He came . . .

. . .

But this was not the old ways come
Again. She knew that. He had not returned.
His presence might be here, or there. They'd see
Him. He was living. He was on the earth
And real, and He had moved again to plans
And to directions. He would speak to them
And touch them out of sorrow and defeat
Their grief

. . .

He had not been given back to her,
Nor ever would be. Time was past her now.

. . .

The wounds were on him, sealed
And shining. She had seen Him. He had come
Again, and fire was running on the earth,
He was alive, but he was not returned

. . .

He was beyond the hold of any hearth
Or need or place or time. He was her own.
That was still true. But He was not returned.[11]

—*John W. Lynch, S.J.*

In Rainer Maria Rilke's version of the post-resurrection reunion
of Jesus and Mary, as in all the scenes of his imagined "Life of Mary,"
the poet manages to create as many silences as he fills.

Mary at Peace with the Risen Lord

What they experienced then: is it not
beyond all secrets sweet,
and all still terrestrial;
when he, a little pale still from the grave,
disburdened came to her:
in all parts resurrected.

Oh, to her first. How they were both then
inexpressibly healing.
Yes, healing, just that. They did not require
to touch at all strongly.
He laid for a bare second,
his soon to become
eternal hand on her woman's shoulder.
And they had started,
quietly as trees in springtime,
immensely together,
this season of their
farthest-reaching communion.[12]

—*Rainer Maria Rilke*

"We meet the living dead," says Karl Rahner, "when we open our hearts to the silent calm of God himself in which they live."[13] In the three decades since my mother's death, though I have never been able to conjure her image, not even in dreams, I have frequently experienced her unobtrusive presence when I pray.

Easter to Pentecost

This is the bittersweet season
when everything dead
leaps back into life
and my mother lies dying.

Between us and the shore
of that far country
she rides the buoyant Eastertide
speeding her homeward
leaving me homeless.

Into her room each morning
I carry my offering of flowers:
daffodils, pansies, and tulips
a single, just-opening rosebud
wet with fresh tears.

Today she awakes to a bowl
of violets floating in crystal.
Their tiny fists unfurl, then clench
then reach green fingers out and down
like errant roots in liquid soil.

Breakfast trays and bureau tops
become white-linened altars where
I lay my fragrant, futile bribes.
Nothing wilting, stained, decayed
allowed: I whisk them away before fading

pretending that this ritual can
hold the "hound of heaven" at bay.
One branch of stolen dogwood
its wounded blossoms spent
she will not let me move.

"Not yet. Not that one.
All night long its shadows
throw patterns on my wall.
I've grown attached
to that dark forest."

Now throughout one timeless season
wherever branches splinter sunlight
on wood or water, stone or linen
softly, surely we are one
deep in her forest's radiant dark.

—*Elizabeth Michael Boyle, O.P.*

SECOND SUNDAY OF EASTER

John 20:19-31

The Gospel Speaks:

"Form is never more than a revelation of content."[1] Ideally, in a Gospel story, as in a poem, structure mirrors emotional movement and supports thematic subtext. The design of the Easter Sunday appearances of Jesus fulfills this function by operating at three levels: the journalistic, the emotional, and the kerygmatic. The evidentiary buildup of the "case" for the Resurrection is mirrored in the emotional buildup and faith response in the Christian community. In each episode we see the community move gradually from mourning, through blindness and fear, to recognition and conversion, to uncontainable joy and commitment to the future. The Gospel for the Sunday after Easter climaxes this pattern: it completes the evidentiary buildup in the confrontation between the Risen Christ and the quintessential "doubter" Thomas; then it crowns the doubter's emotionally charged theological witness with Jesus' address to the Church of the future. "Blessed are those who have not seen and yet have come to believe" (John 20:29). Today Jesus blesses us and directs us to determine how better to deserve that blessing.

Actually, we always feel secretly blessed to have a Thomas among us. He's the one who blurts out the questions we are too embarrassed to ask. Earlier in John's Gospel he appears as a reasonable man who insists on knowing "the game plan" (John 14:5), but who, once convinced, puts his body squarely on the line for what he believes. Few of us remember that a while ago this same Thomas urged his companions to go with Jesus "that we may die with him" (John 11:16). But Jesus remembers. He knows that a man whose commitment is equal to his skepticism can become an eloquent, credible witness to generations of cynics like ours.

Jesus' procedure in the Easter Gospels yields psychological as well as theological insight. With Thomas, as with Mary Magdalene, Jesus exhibits profound respect for the human personality. He gives Thomas the proof his temperament needs, just as he gave Mary the one-on-one attention her nature craved. But Jesus does something more: he extends his hands and tells Thomas—and you and me and everyone else who is looking for God in this world—where to find him. "If you feel that you have lost me, touch my wounds," says Jesus. After touching Jesus' wounded humanity, Thomas utters the strongest possible testimony to his divinity: "My Lord and my God!" (John 20:28).

Thomas's experience dramatizes one of the great paradoxes of Christian life: logically, the closer we are to human suffering, the harder it is to believe in a loving, compassionate God. But missionaries and others who work closely with the economically poor, the terminally ill, and those enduring extremes of injustice and pain testify that the opposite is so. Those afflicted with "all five wounds of Christ guaranteed not to heal"[2] preach of God's love more powerfully than any homily. Grief, loss, pain, disappointment in ourselves and others, devastation —our own or that of the world around us—these bring us solidly into the presence of the Incarnate Son of God. When we reach out our hands to humanity's wounds, we touch the Body of Christ. Sending a check does not usually transform the donor, but touching the wounds *in person* does. When we recognize our unrecognizable God among us in this way, the perception can change us. The Easter appearances dramatize where to find Jesus now; they also dramatize how the Risen Jesus empowers the Christian community. "Christ has risen. / Whoever believes that should not behave as we do."[3]

The Poets Respond:

In my reflection above I referred to situations that both challenge and strengthen belief in a merciful God. I received a most striking example of this thirty years ago when, shortly after the martyrdom of American missionaries in El Salvador, a Maryknoll sister addressed our retreat group. She acknowledged that after serving among the desperately poor in Central America for a number of years, she completely stopped believing in God's mercy. Still, she remained at her mission because she loved the people and could not abandon them as God (if one existed) had abandoned them. By an irony she could not explain, the brutal martyrdom of her fellow missionaries restored her faith in God and gave her a new vision of her vocation. Suddenly she felt herself and her people united in the wounded Body of Christ.

During this same time period, the poet Denise Levertov, an agnostic during most of her adult life, was received into the Catholic Church as a direct result of working alongside activist priests and nuns and of writing "El Salvador: Requiem and Invocation." In the following poem, she assumes the persona of Thomas the doubter, also called "Didymus," meaning "twin." Regrettably, there are few cities in our world where the scene described in the poem is not in some way being duplicated.

Saint Thomas Didymus

In the hot street at noon I saw him

> a small man

>> gray but vivid, standing forth

> beyond the crowd's buzzing

holding in desperate grip his shaking

> teethgnashing son,

and thought him my brother.

I heard him cry out, weeping, and speak

> those words,

Lord, I believe, help thou

>> mine unbelief,

and knew him

> my twin:

a man whose entire being

> had knotted itself

into the one tightdrawn question,

>> Why,

why has this child lost his childhood in suffering,

>> why is this child who will soon be a man

tormented, torn, twisted?
                              Why is he cruelly punished
who has done nothing except be born?

The twin of my birth
                              was not so close
as that man I heard
                              say what my heart
sighed with each beat, my breath silently
                                             cried in and out,
in and out.

After the healing,
                              he, with his wondering
newly peaceful boy, receded;
                              no one
dwells on the gratitude, the astonished joy,
                                             the swift
acceptance and forgetting.
                              I did not follow
to see their changed lives.
                              What I retained
was the flash of kinship.
                              Despite
all that I witnessed,
                              his question remained
my question, throbbed like a stealthy cancer,
                                             known
only to doctor and patient. To others
                              I seemed well enough.[4]

                                             —*Denise Levertov*

Levertov's poem responds to the mystery of suffering embodied in a child, a stranger. More frequently, faith is tried by the suffering of a loved one. Although tragedy in our own lives often tests our faith more deeply than the suffering of strangers, happily, long after we have given up believing in God's goodness, we may be given evidence that God has not given up believing in ours.

Quid Pro Quo

Just after my wife's miscarriage (her second
in four months), I was sitting in an empty
classroom exchanging notes with my friend,
a budding Joyce scholar with steelrimmed
glasses, when, lapsed Irish Catholic that he was,
he surprised me by asking what I thought now
of God's ways towards man. It was spring,

such spring as came to the flintbacked Chenango
Valley thirty years ago, the full force of Siberia
Behind each blast of wind. Once more my poor wife
was in the local four-room hospital, recovering.
The sun was going down, the room's pinewood panels
all but swallowing the gelid light, when, suddenly,
I surprised not only myself but my colleague
by raising my middle finger up to heaven, *quid
pro quo*, the hardly grand defiant gesture a variant
on Varmi Fucci figs, shocking not only my friend
but in truth the gesture's perpetrator too. I was 24,
and, in spite of having poured over *The Confessions*
and that Catholic tractate called *The Summa*, was sure
I'd seen enough of God's erstwhile ways toward man.

That summer, under a pulsing sky
shimmering with Van Gogh stars, in a creaking,
cedarscented cabin off Lake George, having lied
to the gentrified owner of the boy's camp
that indeed I knew wilderness & lakes and could,
if need be, lead a whole fleet of canoes down
the turbulent whitewater passages of the Fulton Chain

(I who had last been in a rowboat with my parents
At the age of six), my wife and I made love, trying
not to disturb whosoever headboard and waterglass
lay just beyond the paperthin partition at our feet.
In the great black Adirondack stillness, as we lay
there on our sagging mattress, my wife & I gazed out
through the broken roof into a sky that seemed

somehow to look back down on us, and in that place,
that holy place, she must have conceived again,
for nine months later in a New York hospital she
brought forth a son, a little buddha-bellied
rumplestiltskin runt of a man who burned
to face the sun, the fact of his being there
both terrifying & lifting me at once, this son,

this gift, whom I still look upon with joy & awe.
      Worst,
best, just last year, this same son, grown
to manhood now, knelt before a marble altar to vow
everything he had to the same God I had had my own
erstwhile dealings with. How does one bargain
with a God like this, who, *quid pro quo,* ups
the ante each time He answers one sign with another?[5]

—*Paul Mariani*

THIRD SUNDAY OF EASTER

Acts 2:42-47   Acts 4:32-35   Acts 5:12-16
              Luke 24:13-25   John 21:1-19

The Gospel Speaks:

Poet Francis Thompson liked to show how metaphor can reverse conventional values. ". . . two child-eyes have dimmed a firmament for me," for example, suggests that comparing someone's eyes to stars really flatters the stars.[1] Recently I listened to a less innocuous reversal in a very well-planned homily equating each step in the Emmaus narrative with a corresponding part of the eucharistic celebration: the entrance procession repeats the journey; the Liturgy of the Word replicates Jesus' exposition of the Scriptures; the Liturgy of the Eucharist re-enacts the breaking and sharing of the bread, etc. Everything fit so tidily into the metaphor that one could infer that Catholics who go to Mass on Sunday can have the whole Emmaus experience in an hour.

However, for me at least, this perfect analogy reversed the whole point of the Gospel. Moreover, it also seemed to reverse the forty-year effort initiated by the Second Vatican Council to effect an historic paradigm shift from *orthodoxy* to *orthopraxy,* from teaching dogma to promoting action. The interpretation suggests that the journey to Emmaus ends in church, but for me the Emmaus itinerary moves in just the opposite direction: Eucharist occurs today in the journey *from* Emmaus, when we leave church to bring the Risen Christ into our world. For this reason, the Easter Gospels cannot be fully interpreted without the readings from Acts that the Lectionary assigns for the three Sundays after Easter. These selections from Acts show the *effects* of the Resurrection in the lives of the first Christians. Today's Christians can read in these scenes three conditions for experiencing the Easter event fully in our lives now: placing God at the center of daily life, sharing material resources, linking Scripture to "current events."

First of all, we read that the first Christians "broke bread at home" (Acts 2:46). We become an Easter people when Eucharist really happens "where we live." Secondly, when the first Christians "devoted themselves to the apostles' teaching and fellowship," something revolutionary happened: "they would sell their possessions . . . and distribute the proceeds to all as any had need" (Acts 2:42, 45). As a result, "the whole group were of one heart and soul . . . and great grace was upon them all. There was not a needy person among them" (Acts 4:32-34).

In a capitalist culture, economic justice is not accomplished so simply, but the experience of the first Christian community confirms what we acknowledge too late, namely, that material prosperity does not make people happy, that letting go can be more life-giving than "keeping up," and that liberation from a lifestyle dominated by material values benefits both the haves and the have-nots. Even now, those who have the courage to liberate themselves, like their first-century counterparts, will eat "their food with glad and generous hearts" (Acts 2:46). Acts also shows how individual conversion impacts on the larger society. "Now many signs and wonders were done among the people" (Acts 5:12), notably the curing of the sick and "those tormented by unclean spirits" (Acts 5:16). And in his last dramatic appearance to his disciples, Jesus used a miraculous catch of fish to show them how conversion of life empowered them before he commissioned them to bring that life to others (Acts 5:12-16; John 21:1-19). From how many sicknesses and unclean spirits would our society be freed if more of us were truly liberated from the obsessive demands of a materialistic lifestyle?

Finally, both in the Emmaus Gospel and in the first Christian community, the extraordinary joy of the early disciples was linked to the study of Scripture: "They said to each other, 'Were not our hearts burning within us while he was talking to us on the road, while he was opening the Scriptures to us?'" (Luke 24:32). Don't you wish the disciples had taped that discourse? Isn't it exasperating that the evangelist records only a single sentence from Jesus' interpretation of his entire life in light of the Scriptures? Luke leaves us only an image, an image of Jesus interpreting Scripture in the light of current events and current events in the light of Scripture.[2] Moreover, the story shows us the image of the disciples being instructed by a stranger, a stranger who is in fact their Redeemer. They brought to that stranger the remnants of their shattered hopes, exposed to him their deepest disappointments in the events of the day. And Jesus "opened the Scriptures to them" in the light of their existential situation; above all, he illuminated for them the meaning and power of his suffering.

I once had the privilege of traveling with a group of American Christians to Mexico, where "our hearts burned within us" as we listened to a factory worker tell the story of how biblical study had transformed his life. He had been jailed for publishing a human rights leaflet that simply juxtaposed the words of Jesus with the words of the labor code. From this uneducated man we learned that orthopraxy results when we honestly juxtapose our personal and professional lifestyles alongside the New Testament.

For twenty-first century Christians, the journey at issue is not the road to Emmaus but rather the road *from* Emmaus, from sacramental communion with Jesus to communion with the human family through communal study and communal action. We travel the road from Emmaus whenever we enroll in an adult course in theology or volunteer to participate in an RCIA or Scripture-sharing program where we open our hearts to one another and share our deepest theological questions and convictions. We also participate in a Liturgy of the Word when we study together economics or law or social analysis for the sake of liberating the powerless from systems that exploit them. When Jesus companioned the disciples on their journey, he deliberately withheld his identity from them, as he does from us.[3] On our road from Emmaus, only when we share our physical and spiritual resources with those in whom our God is totally unrecognizable will we begin to know Jesus Christ as we have never known him before.

The Poets Respond:

Gabriela Mistral, a professional educator, addresses her harsh pedagogy, not to children, but to adults.

The House

The table, son, is laid
with the quiet whiteness of cream,
and on four walls ceramics
gleam blue, glint light.

Here is the salt, here the oil,
in the center, bread that almost speaks.
Gold more lovely than gold of bread
is not in broom plant or fruit,
and its scent of wheat and oven
gives unfailing joy.
We break bread, little son, together
with our hard fingers, our soft palms,
while you stare in astonishment
that black earth brings forth a white flower.

Lower your hand that reaches for food
as your mother also lowers hers.
Wheat, my son, is of air,
of sunlight and hoe;
but this bread, called "the face of God,"
is not set on every table.
And if other children do not have it,
better, my son, that you not touch it,
better that you do not take it
with ashamed hands.

My son, Hunger, with his grimaced face
in eddies circles the unthrashed wheat
they search and never find each other,
bread and hunchbacked Hunger.
So that he find it if he should enter now,
we'll leave the bread until tomorrow.
Let the blazing fire mark the door
that Quechuan Indian never closed,
and we will watch Hunger eat
to sleep with body and soul.[4]

—*Gabriela Mistral*

While some poets imagine the missing details in a Gospel, others, like Sandra Duguid, warn of how much of its message we miss—even with our eyes wide open.

Road to Emmaus

There have been crucifixions, too,
in our town—innocents
gunned down in their doorways
or in school halls; or radiation's
black outlines, three crosses
marked a sister's chest: no wonder
we walk in quiet rage, musing

And who, on this road, will join us
seeming unaware
of the worst news in the neighborhood,
but spelling out the history of the prophets
and a future:
> Ought not Christ to have suffered these things
> and to enter into his glory?
Could our hearts still burn within us?

Will we ask the stranger to stay?
Break bread? And how
Will our well-hammered and nailed
kitchens and bedrooms appear to us
when we understand who he is
just as he steals away?

—*Sandra Duguid*

FOURTH SUNDAY OF EASTER

John 10:1-10   John 10:11-18   John 10:27-30

The Gospel Speaks:

In the parable of the Good Shepherd, as in no other, Jesus himself assumes the role of protagonist. At the time the New Testament was written, this instruction, "less than an allegory and more than a parable,"[1] appealed directly to an audience on whose economic landscape sheep and shepherds were familiar and essential figures. Furthermore, in their biblical literary tradition, the pastoral genre featured shepherd heroes like David and Moses. For this reason Jesus invoked the pastoral tradition when he called Peter to leadership saying, "Feed my lambs" (John 21:15-17).[2]

Our post-industrial society is likely to regard shepherds merely as figures in a Christmas tableau, and most of us encounter lambs only in the antiseptic pastures of Toys R Us. Moreover, as members of an educated, democratic society, we scorn the term "sheep." However, despite many mixed connotations,[3] we keep the model of the Good Shepherd alive in the titles "pastor" and "pastoral minister," and the lost sheep remains among Christianity's most consoling metaphors (Matt 18:12-24; Luke 15:4-7). Throughout the ages, the relevance of the Good Shepherd parable endures, for its imagery defines the relationship of the Risen Christ with the individual soul and with the Church.

Here, in one of thirty occasions in the Fourth Gospel where Jesus uses the powerful "I am" formula, the Gospel expands the self-defining title into a concrete extended metaphor.[4] As a discourse on God's love and our dependence on it, this deceptively simple trope offers a comforting image in times of personal crisis. More importantly, the symbol presents a model for the relationship between ecclesiastical shepherds and their flocks.

Jesus first announces this theme in a somewhat awkward sentence: "I am the gate for the sheep" (John 10:7). Although "gate" appropriately denotes access to an outdoor venue, for most of us the term "door" has more positive connotations.[5] Perhaps our feelings about a gate depend on how we relate to the gatekeeper: Does he keep us in or out? Once in, do we feel "safe" or "trapped"? A "doorman," on the other hand, welcomes people in and usually greets each one by name.

The parable then builds its image of the model shepherd by contrasting him with hirelings and thieves. The "good-guy / bad-guy" language here seems to encourage a certain religious elitism. Since that sentiment generates so much violence in our age, it would perhaps be best to interpret Jesus' condemnation of the hirelings and bandits more as a warning against predatory forces *within* our culture rather than as an endorsement of an exclusionary religious stance. What seems unambiguously significant is that the sheep, once recognized by the keeper, are trusted to move freely as they choose. Their intimate relationship with the guardian of the sheepfold is the basis not only of safety but also of freedom. "I am the gate. Whoever enters by me will be saved, and will *come in and go out* and find pasture" (John 10:9). The phrase "Whoever enters by me" provides the segue from a well-guarded place to an intimate interior. When the gatekeeper assumes his unambiguous identity as the shepherd, "he calls his own sheep by name and . . . the sheep follow him because they know his voice" (John 10:3, 4). Their following represents, not mindless subservience, but a reciprocal relationship deeper than any they have ever known. Following the voice of the Good Shepherd leads to something within themselves and beyond their imagining.

Like a wise homilist, Jesus gets his points across with verbs; the Good Shepherd *is* what he *does*. He knows, calls, and leads his own; he does not drive them. He opens the way to freedom, nourishment, and perhaps adventure. All the Good Shepherd's actions implicitly await a response: he *calls, opens, leads, freely lays down his life* that his own may have life more abundantly. Simply cataloging these verbs becomes an invitation to greater intimacy. Reflecting on this intimacy, we are reminded of that exquisite moment Easter morning when Jesus addresses Mary Magdalene by name. In his voice she recognizes not only Jesus' transformed life but also her own. At the sound of her name, she also hears the ultimate answer to her search for his body and her need to be with him after he goes away again. From now on she will be closer to Jesus in her own soul, in her ministry of the Word, and in prayerful union with the God of eternal love than she had ever been with Jesus in his brief physical presence (John 20:11-18).

For the three weeks following Easter, the subject of the readings is the physical presence of the Risen Christ. As the Easter Season moves toward Pentecost, the Lectionary begins to focus on the presence of the Risen Christ in his Mystical Body, the Church.[6] One cannot meditate on the mystery of the Church at this point in its history without confronting the unpleasant fact that the most visible symbol of the Good Shepherd, the bishop's crosier, has become for many "a sign of contradiction." Perhaps our moment in history demands nothing less than a symbolic corporate "death of the shepherd" before Christ's risen life can be made manifest again in its official representatives. It is not coincidental that the ultimate test of the Good Shepherd—his willingness to die for his flock—includes reference to power: "The good shepherd lays down his life for the sheep. . . . For this reason the Father loves me, because I lay down my life in order to take it up again. . . . I have power to lay it down, and I have power to take it up again" (John 10:11, 17-18). Only when shepherds have the courage to lay down their power, not by capitulating to an enemy, but by sharing responsibility with a flock whose loyalty has proved stronger than its disillusion, will that power again symbolize visibly the reality of the Resurrection. Only then will we realize in the very guts of the Mystical Body the true meaning of Christ's redemptive death: "a piece of the world, real to the core, but occupied by the . . . dispassionate freedom of Christ . . . surrendered in the total self-mastery which can be achieved by fallen man only in the act of death."[7]

Meantime, however, the Good Shepherd calls us to embody—and enjoy—the "kinder, gentler" aspects of a relationship grounded in reciprocal knowledge and trust. At minimum, the Roman Catholic credibility crisis is calling its hierarchy to replace the current desiderata for appointing ecclesiastical administrators with one Good Shepherd criterion: "I know my own and my own know me" (John 10:14). To give Church leaders time to listen and learn from their people would require a revolutionary restructuring of responsibilities and priorities. With encouragement from an articulate and patient community of believers, real leadership will seize the opportunity to say, "I lay it down of my own accord. I have power to lay it down, and I have power to take it up again. I have received this command from my Father" (John 10:18). Then the "princes of the Church" will rejoice to lay down a great burden as they take up a more abundant life for themselves and for their churches.

The Poets Respond:

Perhaps nowhere in English literature is the presence of the Risen Christ in this world expressed more vibrantly than in the lyrics of Gerard Manley Hopkins. Hopkins hears the Good Shepherd of all creation "call his own by their name" with profound respect for individuality in all its forms, an individuality mirrored in the sonnet's "instress" of idiocyncratic syntax and diction. The second poem moves from meditation to a prayer of pure praise.

As *kingfishers catch fire,* dragonflies draw flame;
As tumbled over rim in roundy wells
Stones ring; like each tucked string tells, each hung bell's
Bow swing finds tongue to fling out broad its name;
Each mortal thing does one thing and the same:
Deals out that being indoors each one dwells;
Selves—goes itself; *myself* it speaks and spells,
Crying *What I do is me; for that I came.*

I say more: the just man justices;
Keeps grace: that keeps all his goings graces;
Acts in God's eye what in God's eye he is—
Christ—for Christ plays in ten thousand places,
Lovely in limbs, and lovely in eyes not his
To the Father through the features of men's faces.

Pied Beauty

Glory be to God for dappled things—
    For skies of couple-colour as a brinded cow;
        For rose moles all in stipple upon trout that swim;
Fresh-firecoal chestnut-falls; finches wings;
    Landscape plotted and pieced—fold, fallow, and plough;
        And all trades, their gear and tackle and trim.
All things counter, original, spare, strange;
    Whatever is fickle, freckled (who knows how?)
        With swift, slow; sweet, sour; adazzle, dim;
He fathers forth whose beauty is past change:
                Praise him.[8]

—Gerard Manley Hopkins

FIFTH SUNDAY OF EASTER

John 14:1-12   John 15:1-8   John 13:31-35

The Gospel Speaks:

Faith and imagination support each other; both proceed from the known to the unknown. But the Gospel stories for the weeks immediately after Easter challenge imagination because we can't *know emotionally* what it is like to see, embrace, share a meal with someone who has come back from the dead. For us it is easier to imagine life *without* a departed loved one. So let us enter this Gospel by imagining what it was like when Jesus' disciples knew they would never see him again.

Picture them now, his closest friends, seated together around a beach fire on the shores of Tiberias, murmuring reminiscences like mourners at an Irish wake. We can hear them repeating: "Remember the first time—the last time—the best times?" Finally, we see Peter get up, take a stick, and stir the embers of the fire. A shower of sparks flies up against the night sky and dies. A chill settles over the group, and we hear someone say quietly, "Remember how he spoke the night before he died?" Now they relive that night of special intimacy with the little group who lingered after Judas had left the room. They recall how lovingly Jesus had looked at them, how, they realize now, he was trying to prepare them for sudden trauma followed by long loneliness.

Then one by one each friend brings forth a sentence or two of Jesus' long, soft-spoken monologue. Certain phrases recur like the waves lapping against the shore: "Fear not," "I am," "I will not leave you," "Love as I have loved." Through them all the word "Father" sounds like a refrain. As they repeat his words, Jesus seems to become present among them. Sitting a little removed from the group, we see the one called the Beloved Disciple silently listening. He is thinking of you and me and how we too will need to bring Jesus into our human love and loss and loneliness by recreating the spell of his last words. Half a century later, the Beloved Disciple gathers up all these fragments, arranging and rearranging the sounds and images until they find their perfect hypnotic form. Then he writes it all down, Jesus' final discourse, a long incantatory poem that comprises almost three chapters of the Fourth Gospel.

Every year on these Sundays after Easter, the Lectionary revives that poem for us as the readings concentrate less on what Jesus *did* and more on who Jesus *is* and what he *does in* and *through us*. The Gospels circle back to the time just before Jesus' death when, through his last discourse, he is leading his disciples over the bridge from the Jesus of history to the Jesus of faith. Jesus' last message cannot be "explained," any more than a good marriage between two totally opposite temperaments can be explained. The poetry and power of these Gospels can be experienced only in an act of prayer. All that a preacher can do is indicate how to enter into prayer by cooperating with the literary device that the author of the Fourth Gospel invented to lead us there. That device is called "cyclical repetition," and anyone who listens attentively can hear it. Those of us who have read the monologue over and over without trying to explicate it can affirm the accuracy of one Scripture scholar's description (previously cited p. 57):

> The cyclical repetition in the Fourth Gospel is like a spiral staircase that takes the reader up higher, down deeper, passing again and again the same familiar points, giving an ever clearer and richer view of the One who stands at the center . . . the reader is . . . always standing contemplatively before the figure of Jesus. . . . This is a text that the writer intends the reader to read, re-read, and read again. And each time the work will be new because the reader is being educated by the text, initiated into a mystery that deepens as one participates in it.[1]

The phrase that helps us meet Jesus on this spiral staircase, though familiar to us, was quite shocking to the first Christians, for Jesus appropriates the very words used by God to Moses. The recurrent phrase is the formula "I am." Like all good poets, the author of the Fourth Gospel recognizes that metaphor is always stronger than simile. Because he is God, Jesus is not "like" anything: he simply *is*.[2] Sometimes it is enough to tread John's spiral staircase to access a state of contemplative rest. At other times, either life's exigencies or our own temperaments won't let us rest. But even in such circumstances, when we repeat the "I am" metaphors over and over, they begin to generate a personal dialogue:

Are you feeling lost, literally don't know which way to turn? "I am the way"—*trust me.* "I am the good shepherd"—*I'll find you* (John 14:6; 10:11).

Are you fed up with the multiple pretenses of a lifestyle that's robbing you of a life? "I am the truth"—*The truth about you is who you are, not what you earn* (John 14:6).

Are you desolated by the loss of a loved one, through death or one of the multiple forms of loss worse than death? "I am the resurrection and the life" (John 11:25).

Do you feel rootless and disconnected? "I am the vine, you are the branches. Those who abide in me and I in them bear much fruit" (John 15:5).

Are you overwhelmed with a sense that you have no real control over anything that matters? "Apart from me you can do nothing."—*Don't even try!* (John 15:5).

But "If you abide in me, and my words abide in you, ask for whatever you wish, and it will be done for you" (John 15:7).

Inevitably, prayer intensifies our involvement in and concern for the life of the world and its people, for in prayer we know ourselves loved, and "just as I have loved you, you also should love one another" (John 13:34). There are times when God's love can be brutal, when we feel the pruning shears more than the love that motivates the pruning (John 15:8). Loving as Jesus loves can inflict severe pain. It helps to discover that Jesus uttered his strongest pledge of abiding presence in the hours surrounding betrayal and denial by his closest friends and those to whom he had entrusted his mission. It was precisely at the moment that Judas went out to hand him over to be crucified that Jesus said, "Now the Son of Man has been glorified, and God has been glorified in him" (John 13:31).

Inevitably, prayer leads in and out of the Gospels, and what we read there emboldens us to pray for more. "If you abide in me, and my words abide in you, ask for whatever you wish, and it will be done for you" (John 15:7). When we really believe Jesus and take him at his word, we will have confidence to pray: Dear God, whatever the pruning process, we welcome it. Give us the grace to go down in history as Christians privileged to live in "the ages of faith."

The Poets Respond:

"Corresponding images are a kind of non-aural rhyme."[3] In "Accepting," the images of the cross and the vine rhyme in a way that implies a command from Christ the vine to us his branches: Do these two things with me: Be rooted in the earth and participate redemptively in human suffering.

Accepting

Lord, serene on your symbol,
You plant your flag
on pain's last outpost.

Your arms span its horizons,
your feet explore it,
your eyes are its seas.

You, pioneer in pain,
reclaim its wastes,
and so you prove it.

No more an alien planet,
only our earth
whose soil stains your fingers.

Against your side woe's wildness
strings its red vine
and shadows your face.

Then name this holy ground
firm underfoot
home, however homely.[4]

—*Vassar Miller*

SIXTH SUNDAY OF EASTER

John 14:15-21   John 15:9-17   John 14:23-29   1 John 4:7-10

The Gospel Speaks:

On this Sunday before Ascension Thursday, the Lectionary continues to nourish us with selections from Jesus' farewell discourse. In the
poignant words introducing the monologue, the evangelist sums up the
theme of the discourse and the motivation for Jesus' whole life: "Having loved his own who were in the world, he loved them to the end"
(John 13:1).[1] We could stop right there and meditate on those words
for the rest of our lives: "loved to the end." The end of what? The end
of his life? Our lives? The end of time? The end of divine patience and
endurance? In the context of the Eternal Word, such parameters are
meaningless. God is "the beginning who is still there when *we* end."[2]

No, Jesus loved to the end of love, that is, not to love's limit but to
love's ultimate consummation in joy. "I have said these things to you so
that my joy may be in you, and that your joy may be complete" (John
15:11). As usual, Jesus travels to clarity by way of paradox: "I am going
away, and I am coming to you" (John 14:28). To understand what that
means, we can do no better than to read, again and again, the long,
rhythmically repetitive poem that the Beloved Disciple invented to
communicate the emotional inscape of the event. The farewell discourse offers a superb example of what poets call "organic form," that is,
poetry in which "content and form are in a state of dynamic interaction," in which each unit of perception elicits an emotional response.[3]

For five chapters Jesus reiterates crucial themes that revolve like
spokes around one central axis, his enduring love. Gradually these
themes penetrate our consciousness in a spiral movement that seems
to go in two directions. First, the voice of a gentle speaker bores down
into our littleness and reams out our pettiness. Then suddenly love reverses direction, lifting us up into the wide embrace of creative love.
Finally, the wings of the Spirit carry the soul into something bigger
than the self, the life of the Church.

Propelling this movement are two revolving themes: a new commandment and a new power. The new commandment sets the terms for the reciprocal relationship: "Love one another *as I have loved you*" (John 15:12). Fidelity to the terms of Jesus' new covenant not only demonstrates and intensifies our love but also draws us into Jesus' relationship with the Father. "Those who love me will keep my word, and my Father will love them, and we will come to them and make our home with them" (John 14:23). Each reiteration of the theme carries with it an increment of intimacy and promise: "I will . . . reveal myself to them" (John 14:21). "I have called you friends" (John 15:15). "I will ask the Father, and he will give you another Advocate, to be with you forever" (John 14:16); "The Father will give you whatever you ask him" (John 15:16). The new relationship accesses the generosity of a Father eager to share spiritual power with the friends for whom the Son lays down his life (John 15:13).

What are these new powers that the Son of God now shares with us? Vision and life. "The world will no longer see me, but you will see me; because I live, you also will live" (John 14:19). Those who love as Jesus loves, with "a love that breaks all rocks," see him not only in ideal circumstances but in the very times and places where those who make headlines obscure and desecrate his face. We will find there "a saviour / Rarer than radium, / Commoner than water, crueler than truth."[4] This power awaits those who let the Holy Spirit "ride through the doors of our unentered house."[5]

The Poets Respond:

The following poem refers to a series of biblical texts, among which are several from the final discourse: "Knock, and the door will be opened for you" (Matt 7:7); "I will not leave you orphaned" (John 14:18); "The Father will give you whatever you ask him" (John 15:17). Here the poet suggests that we need not even say prayers; the unspoken prayer of a radically simple life is, in itself, an answer to prayer.

Knock with Your Little Fist

Knock with your little fist—I will open.
I always opened the door to you.
I am beyond the high mountain now,
Beyond the desert, beyond the wind and the heart,
But I will never abandon you . . .
I didn't hear your groans,
You never asked me for bread.
Bring me a twig from the apple tree
Or simply a little green grass,
As you did last spring.
Bring me in your cupped palms
Some of your cool, pure, Neva water,
And I will wash the bloody traces
From your golden hair.[6]

—Anna Akhmatova

The spiral staircase of the farewell discourse is reversed in Francis Thompson's classic, "The Hound of Heaven," where he pictures the soul as fleeing from Jesus rather than meeting him. The poem begins: "I fled Him down the labyrinthine ways of my own mind." Commenting on these lines, Robert Waldron identifies the labyrinth as a "resonant metaphor for modern life . . . the maze of confusion, anxiety, and fear."[7] Though Thompson himself lived and died in a state of destitution, many of his lines could easily be addressed by Jesus to modern Christians afflicted with a strange sense of emptiness that accompanies affluence: "Naught contents thee who contents not me." The poem concludes with Jesus uttering words of both compassion and challenge:

From *The Hound of Heaven*

All which I took from thee I did but take,
Not for thy harms,
But just that thou might'st seek it in My arms.
All which thy child's mistake
Fancies as lost, I have stored for thee at home:
Rise, clasp my hand, and come!

Halts by me that footfall:
Is my gloom, after all,
Shade of His hand, outstretched caressingly?
'Ah, fondest, blindest, weakest,
I am He whom thou seekest!
Thou dravest love from thee, who dravest Me.[8]

—*Francis Thompson*

SEVENTH SUNDAY OF EASTER

Acts 1:12-14   John 17:1-26

The Gospel Speaks:

Approaching the feast of Pentecost, the Lectionary highlights the culminating verses of the farewell discourse, where Jesus suddenly segues from exhortation to his disciples into prayer addressed to the Father. In that prayer Jesus stipulates his legacy, which the Spirit will execute after the Resurrection. The following reflection, suggestive rather than exhaustive, will focus on only two facets of this exceptionally rich text: the farewell discourse as an instruction on prayer and as a spiritual legacy.

As we ponder and internalize Jesus' farewell testament, we discover that his words model both contemplative and intercessory prayer. All forms of prayer lean on the limits of language, both verbal and non-verbal, and the language of the Word Incarnate is no exception. So, first of all, when Jesus addresses God as "Father," his beautiful metaphor initiates a contemplative action that leads inevitably to the subversion of all metaphor.[1] Here and elsewhere Jesus attributes to the Father qualities we associate typically with a mother: reciprocal intimacy, compassion, gentleness, limitless willingness to forgive.

In highlighting what might be called God's softer side, Jesus is consistent with the Old Testament, where the Lord identifies to Moses "a God merciful and gracious, slow to anger, and abounding in steadfast love and faithfulness" (Exod 34:6). Where did the image of a stern, demanding God come from? Not from Scripture. As feminist theologian Elizabeth Johnson has reminded us: "Too often the predominant symbol has been interpreted in association with unlovely traits associated with ruling men in a male-oriented society: aggression, competitiveness, desire for absolute power and control, and demand for obedience. This is not the abba to whom Jesus prayed."[2]

Moreover, in the late twentieth century, the decline of the traditional family has burdened the Father metaphor with another "unlovely" association: *absence.* Among the outcomes of the campaign for inclusive language, in liturgical prayer and in theological discourse, perhaps the deepest and least conspicuous benefit has been the enriching nuance of God's image with which we enter prayer. Frequent repetition of John's Gospel as an entrée to contemplative prayer can foster a relationship with God that liberates us from all cultural stereotypes and dissolves false linguistic and theological dichotomies in that unity for which Jesus prayed. "As you, Father, are in me and I am in you, may they also be in us" (John 17:21).

Jesus' second metaphor follows from the first: he invokes God as generator of "eternal life" and then defines it: "And this is eternal life, that they may know you, the only true God, and Jesus Christ whom you have sent" (John 17:3). Using the verb "know" metaphorically in the biblical sense of the intimacy of sexual union, Jesus specifies a knowledge beyond intellectual information or analysis. Eternal life means knowing God as lovers know each other, in the reciprocal revelation of our innermost selves, and in the generation of a unique new "us" that is something more than our separate egos. In the final verse of the prayer, Jesus returns to this theme and further clarifies the kind of knowledge that is his gift to us: "Righteous Father, the world does not know you, but I know you; and these know that you have sent me. I made your name known to them, and I will make it known, so that the love with which you have loved me may be in them, and I in them" (John 17:25-26).

Having laid the foundation for prayer in this contemplative relationship, Jesus instructs us in the kind of intercessory prayer that flows from it. According to Jesus' example, intercession is not an inferior form of prayer, to be discarded when we reach a state of habitual union with God. Intercession is an outcome of that union which puts us in touch with the needs of others in the form of God's desires for them. Praying for others, in turn, puts us in touch with our own spiritual poverty. More importantly, intercessory prayer culminates in the challenge, "What can I do for the person, situation, world for which I pray?"

"You have a thousand prayers, but God has one,"[3] and it is usually through human agency that God's one prayer is answered. Just as Jesus seemed to move from prayer to public ministry and back again, so our own prayer functions in both "forward" and "reverse" modes.[4] Typically, we enter prayer in a state where "the world is too much with us"; then, as we "unwind" we deliberately let go of all external concerns and focus on the presence of God within us. Finally, refreshed after simply resting in God, we move out again through intercession and liturgical prayer to unite with the mission of the Church and the world it serves. Later, when an exaggerated sense of our own importance in mission begins to burden us with egotistical baggage, we revert to the inward spiral, but now we carry back with us to a loving God all those for whom Jesus prayed: "that the love with which you have loved me may be in them, and I in them" (John 17:26).

The intimate knowledge of and unity with the Father that Jesus calls "eternal life" encompasses all of *what* we pray for. This loving knowledge is the "truth" that "sanctifies us" and the hope subsuming all other intercessions. But the evangelist does not stop there. He has Jesus ask repeatedly for protection from "the world" in an insistence that might raise questions for some modern readers.[5] However, "the world" can be interpreted with contemporary relevance without indulging in erudite tangents attacking Hellenistic dualism. Regardless of the term's polyvalent associations, and maintaining fervently our reverence for "the world" as God's creation, we can pray for protection from "the world" if we translate the term as shorthand for *conformity* to the seductive fiction our materialist culture calls happiness. In this context it is legitimate to pray to Jesus, whose "kingdom" represents countercultural values, for the strength to resist pressure to conform to expectations for what is considered worldly success, expectations that threaten to separate us from spiritual fulfillment. And the world for which Jesus died will benefit from our resistance to its delusions.

The power to serve the world by transforming all our relationships in the love of God is the best legacy Jesus can leave us, and the best we can bequeath to those whom God has given us.[6] To his mother, his closest friends, and to those who would dedicate their lives to his mission Jesus left absolutely nothing of monetary value, not even a manuscript with his exact words.[7] But in the words with which John re-imagines Jesus' last testament, we find three gifts in particular that he bequeaths to his spiritual heirs: holiness rooted in truth, independence from "the world," and the radiant joy of those who love and know they are loved.[8]

Financial legacies enable us to continue doing good in this world after we have left it. But leaving loved ones our money does not automatically assure that they will inherit or remember our values. Only spiritual legacies perpetuate irreplaceable family assets, and often at times and in ways that we could never have anticipated. In addition to all that Jesus says with this Gospel, he also asks something: "Have *you* given any thought to your spiritual legacy?" Odds are strong that your children will take less time to dispose of your fortune than you took to amass it. But if your "effects" include a letter, a prayer, a journal of your own spiritual journey, then for generations after you have departed, you will continue to be more present in this world than any real estate, heirloom, or blue-chip portfolio. Having executed several modest estates that have included all the above, I can testify that your words will be your heirs' most treasured possessions.

The Poets Respond:

Charles Péguy (1873–1914) lacked only one of poetry's distinctive virtues: compression. His most famous work, "Mysteries," is literally voluminous: a single poem comprising three volumes. In these verses Péguy assumes the voice of God and endows the First Person of the Trinity with the personality, insight, and vocabulary of a French peasant. Although Péguy's American publisher broke the monologue down into shorter poems, their original form is, in fact, Péguy's attempt to articulate the Deity's uninterrupted, unpunctuated, unmediated relationship with humanity.

A Vision of Prayer

God Speaks: I am their father, says God. *Our Father who art in Heaven.*
   My son told them often enough that I was their father.
I am their judge. My son told them so. I am also their father.
I am especially their father.

. . . He who is a father is above all a father. . . .

Our Father who art in heaven, my son knew very well what he
   was doing that day, my son who loved them so.
Who lived among them, who was like one of them.
Who went as they did, who spoke as they did, who lived as they did.

Who suffered.
Who suffered as they did, who died as they did.
And who loved them so, having known them.
Who brought back to heaven a certain taste for man, a certain taste for the
     earth. . . .

He knew very well what he was doing that day, my son who loved them so
When he put that barrier between them and me, *Our Father* . . .
That barrier which my anger and perhaps my justice will never pass.
Blessed is the man who goes to sleep under the protection of
     that outpost, the outpost of those three or four words.
Those words that move ahead of every prayer like the hands
     of the suppliant in front of his face.
Like the two joined hands of the suppliant advancing before
     his face and the tears of his face.
Those three or four words that conquer me, the unconquerable.
And which they cause to go before their distress like two
     Joined and invincible hands.
Those three or four words which move forward like a beautiful
     cutwater fronting a lowly ship.
Cutting the flood of my anger.

And when the cutwater has passed, the ship passes, and back
     Of them the whole fleet.
That, actually, is the way I see them, says God. . . .

Because of that invention of my Son's, thus must I eternally see them.
(And judge them. How do you expect me to judge them now, after that.)
Our Father, who art in heaven, my son knew exactly what to do
In order to tie the arms of my justice and untie the arms of my mercy.
(I do not mention my anger, which has never been anything but my justice.
And sometimes my charity.) . . .
We know well enough how the father judged the son who had
     gone away and come back.
The father wept even more than the son.
That is the story my son has been telling them. My son gave them
The secret of judgment itself.
And now this is how they seem to me; this is how I see them
Just as the wake of a beautiful ship grows wider and wider
     Until it disappears and loses itself,
But begins with a point, which is the point of the ship itself, . . .
And the ship is my own son, laden with all the sins of the world.

And the point of the ship is the two joined hands of my son.
And before the look of my anger and the look of my justice
They have all hidden behind him
And all that huge cortege of prayers, all that huge wake
  Rows wider and wider until it disappears and loses itself.
But it begins with a point and it is that point that advances towards me.
. . . *Our Father* . . .[9]

—*Charles Péguy*

In cynical parody of the Lord's Prayer, the contemporary Puerto Rican poet and film critic Hjalmar Flax attacks "the world" by adopting the persona of a materialistic child addressing an absent father.

Our Father

Our Father who art in the office,
hallowed be thy name.
Thy will be done at home
as at thy desk.
Favor us in thy will.
Give us this day our steak, our French fries,
and chocolate ice cream.
Force not upon us the Brussels sprouts
and we shall forgive the cook
if our steak is too well done
and our fries uncrisp.
Endow us with sports cars;
keep away the police.
Exempt us from serving in the army.
For thine is the country,
the power and the dollars,
for ever and ever,
amen.[10]

—*Hjalmar Flax*

Since her death in 1997, Denise Levertov has become my companion not only in poetry but also in prayer.

On Reading Levertov's Last Poems

After a certain age, everyone living
Reminds us of someone who's dead
And every new day brings tokens
Of places to which we can never return.

But here in these verses
The last you have written
Everything aging reminds you of childhood.
And all your last rites become first communions.

I sit in the silence
Your words have created
And re-enter the womb of my own "great unknowing" [11]
Back to the *You* before other pronouns
Waiting as *then* dissolves into *now*
Listening to hear one original name.

—*Elizabeth Michael Boyle, O.P.*

NOTES

Resurrection

[1] Luke Timothy Johnson, *The Real Jesus* (San Francisco: Harper Collins, 1996) 134.

[2] Mary Oliver, "When Death Comes," in *New and Selected Poems* (Boston: Beacon Press, 1992).

The Easter Sunday Gospels

[1] The term "Easter Sunday Gospels" designates those that record scenes on the first Easter Sunday. In the Lectionary these events are distributed over several Sundays. Matthew 28:1-10 is used for both the Vigil Mass and sometimes Easter Day; Luke 24:13-35 and John 20:1-9 come on Easter Day in years A and B; John 20:19-31 and Luke 24:13-35 are read on the Second and Third Sundays of Easter, respectively.

² And fortunately, we do not have to, for "the New Testament never presents the resurrection of Jesus as resuscitation, i.e., a return to his former mode of terrestrial existence (like that, say, of Lazarus)." Joseph Fitzmyer, S.J., "How Do Contemporary New Testament Interpreters Deal with the Resurrection of Jesus?" in *A Christological Catechism: New Testament Answers* (Ramsey, N.J.: Paulist Press, 1982) 79.

³ T. S. Eliot, "Little Gidding," in *The Complete Poems and Plays* (New York: Harcourt, Brace and Company, 1952) 138. Some commentators, for example Pheme Perkins, interpret the whole scene with the angel as Matthew's rendering of a mystical experience in which the significance of the empty tomb was communicated to the women.

⁴ This structural analysis combines insights on the Fourth Gospel in G. R. Osborne, "Resurrection," in *Dictionary of Jesus and the Gospels,* ed. Joel B. Green (Leicester, Eng.: InterVarsity Press, 1992) 684, and Sandra Schneiders, *Written That You May Believe: Encountering Jesus in the Fourth Gospel* (New York: Crossroad, 1999) 192ff. The extrapolation of this structure to apply to Matthew and Luke and the hermeneutical application of the analysis are my own.

⁵ Karl Rahner, "Dogmatic Questions on Easter," in *Theological Investigations* (Baltimore: Helicon, 1966) 4:125.

⁶ John 20:14; 21:4, 7, 12; Luke 24:16, 31, 37; Acts 2:22-24; 10:40-42; 1 Peter 1:3-5, and elsewhere.

⁷ Schneiders, *Written That You May Believe,* 192. Pheme Perkins also suggests that Jesus no longer needs a body; it is now simply a way of communicating with his disciples. "Since the pre-existent One is not the less a person for lacking flesh and blood, the post-existent Christ does not require them either." *Resurrection: New Testament Witness and Contemporary Reflection* (Garden City, N.Y.: Doubleday, 1984) 394.

⁸ Karl Rahner, "The Life of the Dead," in *Theological Investigations* (Baltimore: Helicon, 1966) 4:353.

⁹ John W. Lynch, *A Woman Wrapped in Silence* (New York: MacMillan, 1945) 266.

¹⁰ Gerard Manley Hopkins, *Poems and Prose of Gerard Manley Hopkins* (Baltimore: Penguin Books, 1953).

¹¹ Lynch, *A Woman Wrapped in Silence,* 267–271.

¹² Rainer Maria Rilke, "Mary at Peace with the Risen Lord," in *Selected Works: Poetry,* trans. J. B. Leishman (New York: New Directions, 1967).

¹³ Rahner, "Life of the Dead," 353.

Second Sunday of Easter

¹ Denise Levertov, "Some Notes on Organic Form," in *New and Selected Essays* (New York: New Directions, 1992) 73.

² Catherine Sasanova, "Raise the Dead Inside My Given Name," *Image: A Journal of the Arts and Religion* (Spring 2001).

³ Czeslaw Milosz, "Six Lectures in Verse," in *The Collected Poems 1931–1987* (New York: Ecco Press, 1988).

[4] Denise Levertov, "Saint Thomas Didymus," in *The Stream and the Sapphire* (New York: New Directions, 1997).

[5] Paul Mariani, "Quid pro Quo," in *The Great Wheel* (New York: W. W. Norton, 1996).

Third Sunday of Easter

[1] Francis Thompson, "To Stars," in *Poems of Francis Thompson,* ed. Terence Connolly, S.J. (New York: D. Appleton-Century, 1941).

[2] In his essay "The Word and the Eucharist," Karl Rahner regrets the tendency of theologians to limit the meaning of "revelation" to doctrinal statements. Rahner prefers that the term embrace "revelatory actions and events in which God acts creatively to bestow grace . . . uttering his word in it" (the action). Karl Rahner, *Theological Investigations,* trans. Kevin Smyth (Baltimore: Helicon, 1966) 4:255.

[3] "But their eyes *were kept* from recognizing him" (Luke 24:16). This wording is an example of "the divine passive," that is, the grammatical construction for an act for which God is the unnamed agent. Luke uses the construction again in the final line of the story: ". . . he *had been made known* to them in the breaking of the bread" (Luke 24:35).

[4] Gabriela Mistral, "The House," in *Selected Poems of Gabriela Mistral,* trans. Doris Dana (Baltimore: Johns Hopkins University Press, 1971). Mistral notes taht, in her culture, bread is called "the face of God."

Fourth Sunday of Easter

[1] Leland Ryken, *Dictionary of Biblical Imagery* (Downers Grove, Ill.: Inter-Varsity Press, 1998) 784.

[2] See also Luke 10:3; John 10:1-6; Acts 20:28-29; 1 Peter 5:2.

[3] Biblical scholars analyze this chapter of John as the fusion of two parables. The first, vv. 1-10, focuses on access to the sheepfold and emphasizes the illegitimacy of other spiritual leaders. In vv. 11ff., the second parable emphasizes the relationship between the shepherd and his sheep. The first can easily be misunderstood as exclusionary, but "it would be a great mistake to allegorize . . . taking the fold as the Church and the sheep as the true believers." Barnabas Lindars, S.S.F., *The Gospel of John* (London: Oliphants, 1972) 356. See also Rudolf Schackenburg, *The Gospel According to John,* trans. Cecily Hastings and others (New York: The Seabury Press, 1980) 2:275–300.

[4] "I am the bread of life" (John 6:35, 41, 48, 51).
"I am the light of the world" (John 8:12; 9:5).
"I am the resurrection and the life" (John 11:25).
"I am the way, the truth, and the life" (John 14:6).
"I am the true vine" (John 15:1, 5).

[5] Lindars, *The Gospel of John,* 358, notes that Bultmann prefers "door."

[6] The Gospels for the Fifth, Sixth, and Seventh Sundays of Easter are all taken from Jesus' farewell discourse, which assures his disciples that he will continue to

enlighten and empower them through the Holy Spirit (John 14:15-25; 17:18-23), and on the Feast of the Ascension the Gospel is the "commissioning narrative," in which Peter and the apostles are commanded to preach and baptize (Matt 28:16-30).

[7] Karl Rahner, "Dogmatic Questions on Easter," in *Theological Investigations,* trans. Kevin Smyth (Baltimore: Helicon, 1966) 4:127.

[8] Gerard Manley Hopkins, "As Kingfishers Catch Fire," "Pied Beauty," in *Poems and Prose of Gerard Manley Hopkins* (Baltimore: Penguin Books, 1953).

Fifth Sunday of Easter

[1] Barnabas Lindars, "The Fourth Gospel: An Act of Contemplation," in *Studies in the Fourth Gospel,* ed. F. L. Cross (London: Mowbray, 1957) 23–35.

[2] See note 4, Fourth Sunday.

[3] Denise Levertov, "Some Notes on Organic Form," in *New and Selected Essays* (New York: New Directions, 1992) 70.

[4] Vassar Miller, "Accepting," in *If I Had Wheels or Love* (Dallas: Southern Methodist University Press, 1991).

Sixth Sunday of Easter

[1] As a classical literary genre, a farewell discourse includes a narrative setting, a summary of the master's teachings, and an exhortation to apply them in the future community.

[2] Karl Rahner, "Poetry and the Christian," in *Theological Investigations,* trans. Kevin Smyth (Baltimore: Helicon, 1966) 4:358.

[3] Denise Levertov, "Some Notes on Organic Form," in *New and Selected Essays* (New York: New Directions, 1992) 69–73.

[4] Dylan Thomas, "There Was a Saviour," in *The Poems of Dylan Thomas* (New York: New Directions, 1943).

[5] Ibid.

[6] Anna Akhmatova, "Knock with Your Little Fists," in *The Complete Poems of Anna Akhmatova,* vol. 2, trans. Judith Hemschemeyer (Somerville, Mass.: Zephyr Press, 1990).

[7] Robert Waldron, *Poetry as Prayer: The Hound of Heaven* (Boston: Pauline Books and Media, 1999) 70.

[8] Francis Thompson, "The Hound of Heaven," in *Poems of Francis Thompson,* ed. Terence Connolly, S.J. (New York: D. Appleton-Century, 1941).

Seventh Sunday of Easter

[1] Jung calls metaphor "the vernacular of the soul" and all statements of religious faith embedded in narrative "worthy of study for what they contain of truths anchored deep in the psyche." Carl Jung, "Answer to Job," in *Complete Works* 11, trans. F. C. Hull (Princeton: Princeton University Press, 1953–1978) 467.

Every Gospel passage in which Jesus uses the title "Father" provides an opportunity for preachers to point out (if necessary) that Jesus is not assigning a sex to the First Person of the Blessed Trinity. He is using the "soul's vernacular" to relate to a non-physical reality (Matt 5:48; 6:3, 9-13; Mark 14:36; Luke 10:21; 23:34, 46; John 11:41-54; 12:27-28; 17:1, 11, 24, 25). The only time Jesus does not pray to God as Father is when, feeling abandoned, he quotes Psalm 22:1: "My God, my God, why have you forsaken me." J. D. Dunn, "Prayer," in *Dictionary of Jesus in the Gospels* (Leicester, Eng.: InterVarsity Press, 1992) 619.

[2] Elizabeth A. Johnson, C.S.J., *She Who Is: The Mystery of God in Feminist Theological Discourse* (New York: Crossroad, 1997) 47–48.

[3] Anne Sexton, "Not So. Not So," in *The Awful Rowing Toward God* (Boston: Houghton Mifflin, 1975).

[4] By necessity, we express in linear, sequential terms relationships and events that in Jesus are, in fact, simultaneous. What is said here of prayer refers to the act of prayer, not the state of prayer.

[5] See John 17:11-12, 15. Evangelists, like everyone else, have Jungian profiles. Matthew and Luke exhibit extrovert characteristics, while John is obviously an intuitive introvert with a temperamental impulse to withdraw from the world. Wayne G. Rollins, *Jung and the Bible* (Atlanta: John Knox Press, 1983) 55.

[6] Jesus repeatedly refers to "those whom you gave me" (John 17:6, 9, 11, 24). Apparently John wants us to know that the Father did not deny his Son the gift of friends as well as colleagues.

[7] "The fact that the prayer cannot be proven to be the exact words of Jesus himself in no way detracts from its value. . . . John has a vivid sense of the union with Christ which his words describe." Barnabas Lindars, S.S.F., *The Gospel of John* (London: Oliphants, 1972) 317.

[8] "Sanctify them in the truth" (John 17:17); "They do not belong to the world, just as I do not belong to the world" (John 17:16); ". . . that they may have my joy made complete in themselves" (John 17:13).

[9] Charles Péguy, "Vision of Prayer," *God Speaks,* trans. Julian Green (New York: Pantheon, 1945).

[10] Hjalmar Flax, "Our Father," in *Anthology of Contemporary Latin American Literature: 1960–84,* ed. Barry J. Luby (Cranbury, N.J.: Associated University Presses, 1986).

[11] Denise Levertov, *This Great Unknowing: Last Poems* (New York: New Directions, 1999).

Chapter 4

TRANSFORMATION
Ascension Through the
Holy Body and Blood of Christ

ASCENSION

Acts 1:1-11   Matthew 28:16-20   Luke 24:44-53

The Gospel Speaks:

Today's first reading from Acts might make us feel like victims of a hoax. Luke invites us to a mountaintop for a spectacular vision. Then he reprimands us for accepting the invitation. "Why do you stand looking up toward heaven?" (Acts 1:11) The question almost provokes us to dismiss the rest of the story. If we did not come here to witness Jesus' final triumph, what exactly is the "point" of Ascension? Like most New Testament themes, the point is embedded in a paradox balancing both facets of an apparent contradiction. The Ascension *is* Jesus' definitive "leave-taking" from his bodily home on earth.[1] Yet, in the same act Jesus is fulfilling his promise never to leave us (Matt 28:20). Luke's compelling "lift-off" image signals not Jesus' separation from the earth, but a greater reality: the reconciliation of heaven and earth in a "redemption" that includes all creation.[2]

Obviously, when the New Testament pictures Jesus ascending into the sky (Acts 1:9; Luke 24:51), the author cannot be visually endorsing the myth that heaven is a *place* "up there." That would be to deliberately undermine Jesus' own campaign against localizing "the kingdom" (Luke 21:17). Such a literal interpretation also contradicts Jesus' repeated instructions to his friends about where to find him now, "down here," within and among us. Christian kerygma emphatically rejects Browning's oft-quoted bromide: "God's in his heaven / All's right with the world."[3] That line so provoked me as a teenager that I wrote an angry poem protesting God's exile from visible creation. Although my adolescent pantheism, rhyme scheme, and sexist language embarrass me a little now, my sense of God's earthly presence seems confirmed by contemporary "eco-theological" spirituality.

> God is *not* in his heaven!
> Thank heaven, he's right in his world.
> Through the lungs of all life God is breathing,
> With each child in the womb he lies curled.
>
> He has wedded his strength to our weakness
> And his love never rots in remorse.
> Though we to the marriage prove faithless
> Christ will not sue for divorce.

Well, then, what *does* the Ascension story mean, or more importantly, what does this story *do*? First, it signifies the climax of Jesus' resurrection in his "return to the Father." And because the Father has no mailing address, Luke employs the spatial metaphors embedded in the limits of language. Secondly, the ascending body of the Risen Jesus embodies and points toward our own ultimate goal: *perfect freedom.* The Ascension symbolizes freedom from the limits of time and space, of human intelligence and imagination, and from the contingencies and atrocities of the human will. Our goal, achieved in Jesus, is liberation from all that inhibits and distorts the image of God's freedom in us. Karl Rahner puts it beautifully: "All that's left after the 'angel of death' has gutted our spirit of all the useless rubbish we call our history" is "the essential core of freedom attained."[4]

Now let us consider the "earthly" side of the Ascension paradox. Precisely because the Father to whom the Risen Jesus has returned is *omnipresent,* he can remain with us. Once we really apprehend that complex reality, we are liberated from literalism[5] and can reconsider this whole narrative as a dramatic literary device to prepare us for something greater than we had imagined. No longer compelled to defend a concept with which adults have always been uneasy, we tear our eyes from the last glimpse of Jesus' toes disappearing into the clouds and focus instead on theological truths with solidity and staying power.

Luke, the only evangelist to write of the Ascension, has given us two different narratives—one that takes place on Easter Sunday evening and the other weeks later (Luke 24:51-52; Acts 1:1-9, 11).⁶ From a literary perspective, the different dates suggest a creative possibility. Perhaps Luke represents the *fullness of the Easter event* by historicising its theological complexity in narratives that render *separately* several things that happened *simultaneously*. According to this interpretation, Luke is saying that, in the same instant, Jesus rose bodily and spiritually, came to a "full concrete grasp of everything about himself," and returned to the glory of the Father.⁷

Before his physical departure, Jesus acted out *all the modes of his continued presence*. When he tells Thomas to touch his wounds and know that he is risen (John 20:27), he also tells us to touch the wounds of humanity and find him there. On the road to Emmaus, he shows us new depths of scriptural and eucharistic intimacy (Luke 24:32, 44-45). Above all, he promises, he will abide with and in us through the action of the Spirit (John 20:21-23; 21:15-17). This is the ultimate "pay-off" of the Ascension liturgy: it prepares us for the gift of the Holy Spirit, through whom the people of God continue Jesus' work on earth. Following a genre established in the Old Testament, the evangelists fashion three post-Resurrection appearances into "commissioning narratives." Typically, such a narrative contains a statement of authority, a commission, and a promise of continued support. When Jesus commissions the disciples to spread the kingdom, he also promises to empower them to fulfill that responsibility.

Christian evangelism traditionally focuses on the words "Go therefore and make disciples of all nations, baptizing them in the name of the Father and of the Son and of the Holy Spirit" (Matt 28:19). The text has inspired thousands of saintly zealots to invest their lives in the project of baptizing people in jungles, deserts, and ghettos all over the globe. Perhaps after centuries of significant success in energetically executing the command to baptize, it is time for Christians to underscore the full commission: "teaching them to obey *everything* that I have commanded you" (Matt 28:19). "Everything" Jesus commanded can be summarized in a single imperative: "This is my commandment, that you love one another as I have loved you" (John 15:12).

To love one another as Jesus loves, respecting individual cultures and consciences—that is a program our world, bleeding from excessive and distorted religious fervor, badly needs. To love that way, some would protest is not "natural." But the power of the Holy Spirit makes that kind of love both possible and urgent. Don't stand looking up to heaven. Look to the brothers and sisters of Jesus here on earth. Living in your own neighborhoods, yet calling to you in strange languages, living on far continents, yet present in your home via satellite—they need you to obey the commandment of love right now.

The Poets Respond:

Like many modern exegetes, Virginia Hamilton Adair envisions Ascension as the immediate consummation of Resurrection. Moving from the literal to the symbolic, her description "unwinds" the meaning beneath imaginative detail. The first trope, comparing the Resurrection moment to prayer, is reversible: in prayer we too can "slip through the narrow aperture" between death and life, time and eternity. Reading and rereading the poem, we realize that its whole movement embodies the "ascent" of prayer.

Beyond

In the stillness of the cave he stood
unwinding the cloth from his torn body.

Earlier the hired guards had moved the stone a little
to peer in, assure themselves of his death.

He slipped through the narrow aperture
as if in a dream or a prayer.

The opening in his side had closed;
holes in hands and feet were sealed in blood.

He looked back at the men
sleeping beside their empty wineskin.

He was somewhere else now, as if without walking.

The night wind seemed to lift him;
or was it only his hair stirring back from his forehead?

The sea breathed its freshness into his parched lips and lungs.
. . .
He began to climb the steps of the sea.

He walked for a while on the surface of the water
among angels of mist.

He rose through a cloud cover into the blue midnight.

This was the blue of a dress his mother used to wear;
her arms seemed to reach out to him as in his childhood.

Now he was walking on a highway of stars.

When he came to a dark portal
would there not be light beyond?

He stood at the doorway crying out,
"Father, I have come home."[8]

—*Virginia Hamilton Adair*

Denise Levertov, as is her custom, expresses paradox in "organic" imagery that simultaneously fuses and sunders heaven and earth, suggesting that Jesus' mixed emotions as he leaves the earth are replicated in "the torture and bliss" in each soul's struggle for wholeness.

Ascension

Stretching himself as if again,
through downpress of dust
upward, soil giving way
to thread of white, that reaches
for daylight, to open as green
leaf that it is . . .

Can the Ascension
　　not have been
　　　　arduous, almost,
as the return
　　from Sheol, and
　　　　back through the tomb
into breath?
　　Matter reanimate
　　　　now must relinquish
itself, its
　　human cells,
　　　　molecules, five
senses, linear
　　vision endured
　　　　as Man—
the sole
　　all encompassing gaze
　　　　resumed now,
Eye of Eternity.
　　Relinquished, earth's
　　　　broken Eden.
Expulsion,
　　liberation,
　　　　last
Self-enjoined task
　　of Incarnation.
　　　　He again
Fathering Himself.
　　Seed case
　　　　splitting.
He again
　　Mothering His birth:
　　　　torture and bliss.[9]

　　　　　　　—Denise Levertov

PENTECOST SUNDAY

Acts 2:1-11   1 Corinthians 12:3-7   John 20:19-20

The Gospel Speaks:

For high drama and "special effects," the Christian Pentecost story rivals most film scripts. But for shock value, Pentecost 2002 exceeded all previous scenarios. Once again, it seemed that Church leaders had locked the doors in fear (John 20:19). But this time information technology rendered all walls permeable. Fortunately, Jesus too penetrated walls of anxiety, anger, and betrayal to announce: "Peace be with you—even now." However, for his bishops, the Risen Jesus reserved a harsher language: he showed them his wounds (John 20:20). Then the opening verses of Acts provided an ironic commentary on the cataclysm that swept startled prelates onto the front pages of the secular press: "And suddenly from heaven there came a sound like the rush of a violent wind, and it filled the entire house where they were sitting" (Acts 2:2).

Indeed, Pentecost 2002 occurred in the midst of the most violent windstorm in memory. Yet, as spring advanced, little crocuses of hope began to sprout, and many began to herald the windstorm as a true coming of the Holy Spirit. Although the rain of fiery tongues pelting the hierarchy appeared at first to threaten schism, no event in Church history has so united the faithful with equal parts of wrath and loyalty. Throughout this "Second Coming," it was the "best" who exhibited both "conviction" and "passionate intensity"[1] as they proclaimed with one voice: "We are the Church."

Every Pentecost reminds us to claim that identity anew. As the rhythm of Jesus' life is repeated in his Mystical Body, the liturgical year releases the special grace of each mystery into the Christian community, into the existential situation that cries out for that grace again. Throughout history we discern an inexorable pattern in which crucifixion acts as a catalyst for grace. One of John's first references to the Holy Spirit establishes that the Spirit cannot come until Jesus has been "glorified" (John 7:39). And Jesus himself identifies the cross as his doorway to glory (Luke 24:26). The ferocity of media crucifixion eventually abated. But, fortunately, the people of God, shocked to attention by Pentecost 2002, now seem determined not to abandon a historic opportunity to "borrow . . . what rocks / faith founders on to build our house."[2]

The "rock" on which Jesus built his Church was neither virtue nor infallibility; that rock was *faith*, as Matthew's "proclamation narrative" at Philippi clearly demonstrates (Matt 16:13-19). Here Peter's declaration "You are the Messiah, the Son of the living God" elicits from Jesus the response, "Blessed are you, Simon, son of Jonah! For flesh and blood has not revealed this to you, but my Father in heaven. . . . You are Peter, and on this rock I will build my church, and the gates of Hades will not prevail against it" (Matt 16:16-18).[3] Founded on Jesus, the rock rejected by the builders who became the cornerstone, our faith can withstand even the historic erosion of clerical credibility (Acts 4:11; Ps 118).

To us, "the faithful," Jesus repeats his empowering words "As the Father has sent me, so I send you. . . . Receive the Holy Spirit" (John 20:22, 21). And to whom does Jesus send us this Pentecost? First of all, he sends us to our leaders. Relentless public exposure of the tragic consequences of secrecy and protectionism has finally commanded their attention. We must not miss the "teachable moment" to communicate truth to leadership, each in our own language. Once we are committed to do this, God will surprise us with opportunities. "To each is given the manifestation of the Spirit for the common good" (1 Cor 12:7). Those with access can "speak truth to power" respectfully, and above all patiently. Others may enlighten and encourage the media to press issues publicly, but also to demonstrate their own integrity by publicizing with equal ardor the nobler and less newsworthy efforts of the bishops in areas like economic justice and human rights.

Secondly, we are sent to each other. Paul reminds us that there are "varieties of gifts . . . services . . . activities, but the same God who activates all of them in everyone" (1 Cor 12:4-6). He goes on to enumerate faith, wisdom, discernment of spirits, healing, and miracles (1 Cor 12:7). We will need every one of these divine gifts. Some of us will serve best by calmly listening to victims and baffled laity. Others must seize the opportunity to promote communal study so that dialogue does not degenerate into a contest of entrenched opinions. If it is true that "John's gospel is a pristine theological creation flowing from a genius theologian who required no sources beyond the broad oral traditions of the community in which he lived,"[4] then cannot the community of believers continue to be a source of revelation? Clearly, God is trying to speak to our times through the reciprocal education of flock and shepherd, both of whom acknowledge that neither has the whole truth. While some are better suited temperamentally to support than to protest, all of us can intensify listening skills, prayer, and fasting.

"God is the fire my feet are held to," admits one poet.[5] Liability insurers put it more bluntly when they name every natural disaster "an act of God." If we use this historic moment "to give full scope / To what it means to live—not just cope,"[6] history will record the devastating windstorm of 2002 as "an act of God" that propelled our Church into a process of revolutionary reform that toppled an elitist power structure and unleashed the strength of the Spirit in the people of God.

The Poets Respond:

At the opening of the third millennium, both Scripture and ancient poetry seemed to comment on current events. Such is the case with this excerpt from Seamus Heaney's contemporary translation of an ancient Greek drama, obviously intended as a comment on the conflict in Northern Ireland. In the spring of 2002, a campus publication used it to comment on the tragedy of 9/11/01. Ironically, the publication delivered Heaney's message of hope just as the ecclesiastical tragedy referred to above began to supplant 9/11 in media attention.

From *The Cure at Troy: A Version of Sophocles' Philoctetes*

> History says, *Don't hope*
> *On this side of the grave.*
> But then, once in a lifetime
> The longed for tidal wave
> Of justice can rise up,
> And hope and history rhyme

So hope for a great sea-change
On the far side of revenge.
Believe that a farther shore
Is reachable from here.
Believe in miracles
And cures and healing wells.

Call miracle-self-healing
The utter self-revealing
Double take of feeling.
If there's fire on the mountain
Of lightning and storm
And a god speaks from the sky

That means someone is hearing
The outcry and the birth-cry
Of new life at its term.[7]

—*Seamus Heaney*

Even more appropriate to the emotions of Roman Catholics during the crisis are poems written specifically in praise of the Church, like those by the German convert Gertrud von Le Fort. Her poetry has long been out of print, but now her words seem painfully prophetic.

From *Hymns to the Church*

You have torn away my shores, you have done violence to
    The earth under my feet.
My ships are drifting out to sea, you have cut all their
    Moorings.
The chains of my thoughts are broken, they hang wild over
    the deep.
I flutter like a bird about my father's house, to find a crack
    That will let your strange light through.
But there is none on earth save the wound in my spirit—
I have fallen on the Law of your Faith as on a naked sword.
. . .

And behold the voice of your commandments speaks to me:

What I break is not broken and what I bend down to the
      dust that I raise up.
I have been without grace to you because of grace, and out of
      compassion I have been pitiless,
I have overshadowed you that you may no longer find your
      defenses,
As an island is swallowed by the sea so have I engulfed you
      that I might float you into eternity.
I have become a mock to your understanding and a violence
      to your nature,
That I might bolt and bar you like a prison and drag you
      before the gates of your spirit.
For where your inmost thirst would take you, the fountains
      of earth have ceased to flow.
Where your lost nostalgia fades blue, all the clocks of time
      are stopped.
See, I carry on my wings the white shadows of otherness,
And my forehead feels the breath of another shore.
It is for this that I must be a wilderness to your reason, and
      a nothingness on your lips,
But to your soul I am the start and the way home. . . .
      Where my feet refuse to take me, there will I kneel down.
And where my hands fail me, there will I fold them.
I will become a breath in the autumn of pride, and snow
      In the winter of doubt.
  . . . I have fallen on the Law of your Faith as on a naked sword.[8]

Traditional Christian art, limited by male imagination, often pictures Mary as the lone woman in the Upper Room with the apostles when the Spirit descended. Ruthann Williams, however, envisions a scene dominated by symbolic feminine imagery.

The spirit comes

    wings beating fire
    he plunges
    hard and deep
    a comet
    flashing
    intent on rendezvous

he sees them
in uncertain prayer
wanting
and wanting in the gift
he bears

tremulous disciples
weaving a chaos
of almost belief
of nearly doubt
but holding
to the mother's hope
laid like a bared breast
for them to suckle

the room quakes
at his approach
fills with sound
a wind
a gale
a flame

the fire
the light
the furious courage

stampeding the darkness
of fear
collected in the corner
of their hearts

spreads
blurs edges
into a single flaming moment
the rhythm of the spirit
burning out a hollow
to fill with life

male and female
he enters them
inflating souls
like pregnant bellies

bright veined against the tautness
eager
straining for the birthing
in this spirit

it comes

and men and women
newly valiant
spill out into the street
proclaiming the messiah
in tongues set free
unwinding grace
as dangerous as love

sons and daughters prophesy
some see visions
some dream dreams

believers come repentant
and are saved

while pharisees
locked in laughless law
tighten their phylactery bands
around their understanding
and walk away
to ponder punishment

in the power of the spirit
the day is terrible and proud

—*ruthann williams, o.p.*

FEAST OF THE BLESSED TRINITY

John 3:6-18   Matthew 28:16-20   John 16:12-15

The Gospel Speaks:

Anyone who attempts to "explain" the Blessed Trinity takes on a challenge even Jesus avoided. As poet Scott Cairns, warns,

> when addressing Second Person Quite
> Singular—if Triply so—the less one says the better.[1]

Throughout the Gospels we hear Jesus address the Father in prayer, promise to abide with us through the Spirit, and conclude Easter Sunday by commanding the apostles to baptize "in the name of the Father and of the Son, and of the Holy Spirit" (Matt 28:19). In the entire New Testament, however, a definition of the concept of one God in three divine Persons is "conspicuous for its absence." Instead, the Jesus of the Gospels, like a good poet, gestures toward revelation through imagery. These images invite us to *experience* the Trinity throughout our lifetime in a continual act of relationship. In Matthew, the allusion to the three divine Persons enticed Jesus' followers to ponder a concept, new to first-century Jews, which we have not yet fully apprehended: there is no God without *otherness* and no otherness without mutuality.

As Elizabeth Johnson points out, "Before Jesus could be professed as God by Christian believers, our very idea of God had to undergo transformation into Trinitarian form."[2] And since we are created "in the image of God," this Trinitarian theology carries implications for Christian anthropology as well: "created in the image of God" implies that "human beings are created to be persons in communion."[3] We can presume that Jesus did not expect to transform our idea of God overnight or perhaps even over centuries; in fact, his words and actions indicate that he anticipated the need for a continual revision of our idea of God, for each new age seems to recreate God in its own image.

In this reflection I shall interpret the Nicodemus text (John 3:6-18) as Jesus' timeless, elemental imagery for the Trinity.

First, the author of the Fourth Gospel provides a symbolic setting: Nicodemus comes to Jesus at night, as all who believe in the Trinity approach in the darkness of faith. In conversation with Nicodemus, Jesus points directly to a method for explicating his symbolic language. Just as we know the invisible wind by what it does, Jesus tells Nicodemus, so we know the invisible God by manifest divine activities (John 3:7). As the Gospel unfolds, the evangelist offers three concrete symbols that we shall use to represent the activity of the Trinity: womb, water, wind (John 3:4-8). We readily recognize these elements as metaphors, yet, indeed, so too are the titles Father, Son, and Spirit—all metaphors with which we attempt to name our invisible, unnameable God.[4] These three symbols have some things in common, yet each makes a distinctive contribution to human existence. Womb, water, and wind (on a smaller scale, breath and air) are all essential to natural life. Each image in its own way is also associated with pain and struggle or, like floods, hurricanes, and tornadoes, with natural disaster. In brief, our culture dubs such violent tragedies "acts of God."

At the outset Jesus identifies the First Person with the act of generating, nourishing, and renewing life, activities we ascribe to the Creator (John 3:3). We thank the First Person every time we greet our world born anew each morning, each spring, each time a child is born, whenever we discover new forms of creativity within us and in our culture. The evangelist's use of the feminine birthing metaphor subtly subverts our inclination to literalize the male metaphor with which Jesus consistently refers to the First Person. The birthing metaphor also segues gracefully into the second metaphor, water.

We associate water not only with the initiation and survival of life but also with cleansing, healing, refreshment. All these associations make water the ideal sacramental sign in the rite of baptism. As symbol of the cleansing, healing, life-sustaining action of the Son of God, water is transparently appropriate. Above all, it is as the vehicle for continual transformation that water expresses the activity we ascribe to the Second Person of the Trinity. At the molecular level, each individual drop of rain, snow, dew, or mist is a world in itself, yet all these worlds unite in a whole much bigger than their parts and participate in a multiform refreshment of our global ecosystem. In Christ Jesus the individual self becomes one with God, with herself, and with all humanity in a process that both achieves and transcends self-fulfillment. Carl Jung calls this the process of "integration" and identifies the Christ-life within each soul as the archetype of wholeness.[5] So when we baptize all nations in the name of the Son, we immerse humanity with all its glorious diversity and individuality in the teeming wholeness and interdependence of life-giving water.

Of all the biblical symbols for the Spirit, wind and / or breath is, perhaps, the most appropriate, for wind is totally invisible, known exclusively by its effects. And those effects are both benign and terrifying. Is there any rhythm that inspires more reverence than the inhalation and exhalation of an infant; any exhilaration cleaner than giving yourself to the wind-whipped sails that carry you across new horizons; any touch more relentless than the assault of a tropical storm; any shadow more menacing than the advance of a tornado? Feminist theologians like to point out that despite her notorious mood changes, or perhaps because of them, the wind of the spirit is always female, always a force for unifying mutuality, in both biblical and non-biblical ancient mythologies.[6]

The active presence of the Third Person is never more pervasive than in the life of Jesus: "The life of Christ is told as a 'biography of the Spirit' from first to last: Christ is born of the Spirit, driven into the desert by the Spirit, baptized in the Spirit; he preaches in the Spirit; in the end he submits his Spirit to the Father, and extends the promise of the Spirit to his followers."[7]

When Jesus fulfills that promise, "the rush of a violent wind" announces the arrival of the Spirit (Acts 2:2). With this symbol Jesus warns us that the Third Person comes to stir things up: to propel, topple, uproot, alter landscapes, renew the face of the earth. Some of these verbs make us uneasy, but all are signs of life. Pentecost celebrates the day the Holy Spirit came to the first Christians; Trinity Sunday celebrates the fact that the Spirit came to stay.

Even more awesome than what the Holy Trinity does is *where* the Trinity chooses to do it—within creation, in the Church, in historic events, and in unspectacular individual lives. From the moment the waters of baptism flow in the name of the Father, the Son, and Holy Spirit, the living water begins to flow *within you*. It is there that the Trinity dwells as your most intimate friend. In prayer the Trinity both speaks and listens to the individual and to the Church. Scott Cairns points out that the more we listen, the more we may observe

The Other also listening
Whose attention (we) would do well
not to interrupt.[8]

When we pray, the Blessed Trinity listens not merely to who we are as needy human beings judging ourselves by what we are not, but to the deeper reality of who we are in union with the triune God. And it is not fantasy when those who know how to listen in prayer hear God speak. In the Gospels Jesus assured us that he would not stop speaking when his body left this earth. In fact, he promised that through the indwelling Spirit he would tell us things that his disciples were not ready to hear. "I still have many things to say to you, but you cannot bear them now" (John 16:12). Today's feast celebrates the mystery of revelation continually evolving through the indwelling of the Trinity.

Baptism is not a static event. By making our souls the home of the three divine Persons, baptism empowers us to make our most pedestrian occupations a participation in the re-creation of our world in the image of Trinitarian love. Hence, when Jesus commissioned his apostles to baptize all nations in the name of the Trinity, he was not launching an advertising campaign, instructing his sales reps to conquer new territory or subordinate souls to a "corporate identity." He was commissioning them to unite all peoples in the name (that is, in the power) of the Father, the Son, and the Holy Spirit.

We make the sign of the cross so often that we need to do something to remind ourselves of its wondrous meaning. Years ago I tried to dramatize that meaning for my first class of second graders. Every morning I greeted them by bowing profoundly and praying aloud: "Glory be to the Father and to the Son and to the Holy Spirit within you, boys and girls." And they would joyfully chorus back: "Glory be to the Father and to the Son and to the Holy Spirit in you, Sister." Those second graders are grandparents now. I cannot remember another thing I taught them, and I pray that they don't either.

The Poets (Do Not) Respond:

Of all the poets cited in this book, only one attempted a few feeble verses about the Trinity. Poets, more than any of us, recognize the limits of poetry.

FEAST OF THE
BODY AND BLOOD OF CHRIST

John 6:51-58   Mark 14:12-16, 22-26   Luke 9:11-17

The Gospel Speaks:

When I was a child on my first visit to church, my mother pointed to the tabernacle and whispered, "See that little gold house? God lives in there." Like all children, being both logical and literal, I concluded that God was even smaller than I, since I could not imagine myself fitting into that miniature space. And young as I was, I resented that the space reserved for God was so tiny.

Today, as we celebrate the Feast of the Body and Blood of Christ, I trust that no adult still speaks of the tabernacle as the home of "the Real Presence." That kind of language locks God up in a very small space, in our lives, in the life of the Church, and in the life of the world. It also thwarts the purpose for which Jesus gave us the sacrament of his flesh and blood: to dramatize a truth we find hard to believe, namely, that our bodies and our world are tabernacles of the living God. Perhaps that is one of the reasons why in the mid-twentieth century, the Church mandated that tabernacles be removed from main altars and relocated in a subordinate space. Now, during the Liturgy of the Eucharist we focus on the consecrated bread and wine, and during the Liturgy of the Word we focus our attention on all the other forms of the "real presence" of God: in the continuing creation of all life; in individual souls by the gift of grace; in the sacramental love of husband and wife; as the Word, living and active in liturgical and private prayer; as creator and destroyer in the movements of history; wherever two or three are gathered to forgive and to decide in Jesus' name. In these and many other ways, we encounter and embody the Real Presence.

Why, then, did Jesus give us the sacrament of his Body and Blood? Is there a way in which Jesus' presence in the sacrament of the altar differs from other forms of God's presence in a sacramental universe? Yes, I can think of at least three ways in which Jesus is uniquely present in the sacrament: present in the human flesh he received from a woman;

present as food; and present as the continually renewed promise of eternal life. In the familiar prayer that Thomas Aquinas wrote for the first Feast of Corpus Christi, he defines the sacrament as "a sacred banquet in which Christ is received, the memory of his passion is renewed, the soul is filled with grace, and the pledge of future glory is given us." The Gospels chosen for today point the way to a comprehensive understanding of these mysteries of the Real Presence.

First of all, as a sign of his continuing intimate union with our humanity, Jesus chose to leave with us the flesh and blood he received from his human mother. The sacramental flesh and blood of the Word Incarnate signifies Jesus' special union with, and need for, women. Jesus could just as easily have remained with us in a way that demonstrated his divine independence from, or dominion over, everything earthly. By contrast, Mark's Gospel shows us a humanly dependent Jesus who needs to ask for help in the preparations for the meal at which he instituted this sacrament (Mark 14:12-16). We can infer that Jesus wants to make his presence felt in this world through our cooperation. He chose to communicate his presence in a ritual dependent on human agency, a ritual that symbolically destroys his body as a memorial of his greatest act of love on the cross. In the circumstances surrounding the first eucharistic supper, Jesus left us a reminder of human limitations; he gave us his humanity at the moment it was most vulnerable—and most generous: "This is my blood . . . poured out for many" (Mark 14:24). Jesus' timing underscores the fact that it is not in moments of personal triumph and fulfillment that we make Jesus real to others, but in those circumstances where we are most vulnerable, when we too suffer helplessness, abandonment, or betrayal by loved ones. Further, when we keep on loving the unlovable, we become the instruments for pouring out the blood of God's mercy. It is then that the eucharistic union, begun at the altar, fulfills its purpose in our lives and in our world.

Secondly, Jesus is present in the Eucharist as food. Food does not nourish us by remaining in our stomachs. Where is the food you ate yesterday? By now it has entered your bloodstream and has traveled to all parts of your body. Yesterday's food gave you energy to get up this morning and powered your rush to get to Mass on time. The food you ate yesterday is nourishing your brain cells and keeping you awake during this reflection. More importantly, where are the bread and wine that were transubstantiated into the Body and Blood of Christ last Sunday? You received the sacrament as food into your body, where it became your flesh and blood, bone and muscle and brain tissue. In the strongest possible metaphor, your participation in the eucharistic meal embodies Jesus startling promise: "Just as . . . I live because of the Father, so whoever eats me will live because of me" (John 6:57).

This brings us to the third gift of the sacred banquet: the pledge of eternal life. Through this sacramental food, Jesus fulfills and renews his pledge to live in us a life that defeats death. "Those who eat my flesh and drink my blood *abide in me, and I in them*" (John 6:56); "I am the living bread. . . . *Whoever eats this bread will live forever*" (John 6:51).

Hence our participation in the sacrament of Christ's Body must not conclude with the reception of Holy Communion. That would be locking God up in the cramped tabernacle of our own souls. Luke's Gospel makes it clear that the Eucharist empowers us to go out of ourselves to share the essence of life. Using the same language with which he describes the Last Supper, Luke narrates the story of the multiplication of the loaves and fishes (Luke 9:16; 22:17-20). Clearly, the writer is using a linguistic gesture to link the two scenes inseparably in our minds. Nourished by the love of Jesus, we too can feed thousands, for the very act of sharing multiplies our gift and magnifies it with a spiritual dimension. The author-aviator Antoine de Saint-Exupéry experienced a genuinely eucharistic meal when, downed in the desert, he prepared to consume his last supper—a piece of fruit. He tells us that slowly, and reverently, he savored his orange in the spiritual presence of all those with whom he had ever shared a meal and also with those who were hungry.[1]

We learn a lot about eucharistic sharing from those who are economically poor. Many months after the American disaster of 9/11/01, the people of a little Kenyan village heard about it. (No one in the village was rich enough to own a television.) To show their solidarity with the bereft Americans, they took up a collection for the children of the victims. Their relief fund consisted of fourteen cows.[2] The cow, the backbone of the village economy, is also the center of its liturgical life. Uneducated though they were, these Kenyan tribespeople knew enough to provide nourishment for both body and soul.

Jesus gave us the sacrament of his living body precisely because he resists being "reserved" in a chapel. He wants to go where we go, love those we love, weep, work, and wrestle with decisions everywhere we share life. Through us, Jesus yearns to be "bread for the world," and he will not feed the multitude without us.

The Poets Respond:

Vassar Miller's thanksgiving after Communion combines the language of traditional faith with the insights of contemporary psychology. Certain phrases trace adult "shadows" to the "tender and terrible" child cradled in the bone. Though the prayer begins with keen awareness of the need for mercy, the wisdom in the bone triumphs in a final dance of joy.

My Bones Being Wiser
A EUCHARISTIC MEDITATION

At Thy Word
my mind may wander
but my bones worship
beneath the dark waters of my blood
whose scavenger fish
have picked them clean.

Upon them
Thy laws are written,
the days are notched,
and against the soreness of my flesh
they cry out the Creed
crossing themselves

against the cold,
huddled together,
rubbing themselves,
taking the posture of penitence,
warmed with the breath
of Thy absolution.

My eyes weep,
my heart refuses
to lift its head.
Still at Thy Comfortable Words
my bones, thrice deniers, stretch high, singing
a triple holy.

They would keep if not their joy
at least their sorrow
secret, but lie on Thy altar,
a bundle of faggots
ready for burning.

My flesh is the shadow of pride
cast by my bones
at whose core lies cradled a child tender
and terrible, like the Lamb he prays
to have mercy
lest the hands held up
fall empty, lest
the light-as-air Host be only air.

Yet the Child within
my bones knows better.
though the dews of thanksgiving never
revive my mind, my heart, or my flesh—my blest bones dance
out the door with glory.
worn inside out.[3]

—*Vassar Miller*

NOTES

Ascension

[1] "Once we have realized that Jesus' resurrection has not been presented in the New Testament as a resuscitation or a return to terrestrial life or existence, but as a bodily resurrection to the glorious presence of the Father and that his appearances to the disciples were made from that glory, then his 'ascension' is readily understood as his final appearance, as his visible leave-taking from his assembled followers. . . . Henceforth, his presence among them would be through the Spirit . . . and in the breaking of the Bread." Joseph Fitzmyer, S.J., *A Christological Catechism: New Testament Answers* (Ramsey, N.J.: Paulist Press, 1982) 81.

[2] See Carol J. Dempsey, "Hope Amidst Crisis," in *All Creation is Groaning* (Collegeville, Minn.: The Liturgical Press, 1999) 269–284.

[3] Robert Browning, *Pippa Passes and Shorter Poems,* ed. Joseph E. Baker (New York: The Odyssey Press, 1947).

[4] Karl Rahner, *On Prayer* (Collegeville, Minn.: The Liturgical Press, 1993) 131–132.

[5] Karl Barth, among others, warns against visualizing the Ascension "as a literal event, like going up in a balloon." Rather we should understand the Ascension as "an entrance into a dimension of the created world provisionally inaccessible." Karl Barth, *Church Dogmatics: A Selection,* trans. G. W. Bromiley (New York: Harper, 1962) 153–154.

[6] Although Jesus' words are almost identical in both versions, Luke adds details that replicate features of the Transfiguration scene: mountain, cloud, and two white-robed men, who deliver heaven's final admonition. Luke's linking of these two episodes can be interpreted as two versions of his post-resurrection understanding of Jesus' divinity. William Kurz detects significance also in Luke's allusion to an Old Testament text to underscore the link between witnessing the Ascension and receiving the Holy Spirit. Kurz reads Acts 1 as an allusion to 2 Kings 2:4-15, where Elijah makes Elisha's empowerment by the Spirit *contingent on his witnessing* Elijah's ascent to heaven in the flaming chariot. William Kurz, S.J., "The Acts of the Apostles," in *The Collegeville Bible Commentary,* ed. Diane Bergant, C.S.A. (Collegeville, Minn.: The Liturgical Press, 1989) 1038.

[7] Fitzmyer, *Catechism,* 82. Elizabeth Johnson, *Consider Jesus: Waves of Renewal in Christology* (New York: Crossroad, 1991) 45. Jerome Kodell interprets Ascension as the physical signs of "exaltation," the completion of the Resurrection event, and points to Luke's first use of "they worshipped him" as an indication that this scene represents their first "recognition" of Jesus' divinity. Jerome Kodell, "Luke," in *The Collegeville Bible Commentary,* ed. Diane Bergant, C.S.A. (Collegeville, Minn.: The Liturgical Press, 1989) 936ff.

[8] Virginia Hamilton Adair, "Beyond," in *Beliefs and Blasphemies: A Collection of Poems* (New York: Random House, 1998).

[9] Denise Levertov, "Ascension," in *The Stream and the Sapphire* (New York: New Directions, 1997).

Pentecost Sunday

[1] "The ceremony of innocence is drowned / The best lack all conviction, while the worst / are full of passionate intensity." William Butler Yeats, "The Second Coming," in *The Collected Poems* (New York: MacMillan, 1956).

[2] Bryan D. Dietrich, "The Magician," *The Paris Review: Poetry Edition* (Spring 2000).

[3] The interpretation is valid even if we accept that Matthew retrojects Peter's post-Resurrection faith into a symbolic narrative.

[4] Peter F. Ellis, *The Genius of John: A Composition-Critical Commentary on the Fourth Gospel* (Collegeville, Minn.: The Liturgical Press, 1984) 4.

[5] Charles Wright, "Ars Poetica," in *Appalachia* (New York: Farrar Straus Giroux, 1998).

[6] Christopher Fitzgerald, "Sonnet 36," in *Sonnets to the Unseen* (Lansing, Iowa: Opus Bonum, 2001).

[7] Seamus Heaney, *The Cure at Troy: A Version of Sophocles' Philoctetes* (New York: Noonday Press, 1991).

[8] Gertrud von Le Fort, *Hymns to the Church* (New York: Sheed and Ward, 1938).

Feast of the Blessed Trinity

[1] Scott Cairns, "Public Prayer," in *Philokalia: New and Selected Poems* (Lincoln, Neb.: Zoo Press, 2002).

[2] Elizabeth Johnson, *She Who Is: The Mystery of God in Feminist Theological Discourse* (New York: Crossroad, 1997) 193.

[3] Mary Catherine Hilkert, O.P., *Imago Dei: Does the Symbol Have a Future?* Santa Clara Lecture, vol. 8, no. 3 (Santa Clara University, April 14, 2002) 7.

[4] ". . . even 'fatherhood' in God is completely divine and free of 'masculine' bodily characteristics proper to human fatherhood." John Paul II, *Mulieris Dignitatem,* Apostolic Letter "On the Dignity and Vocation of Women," *Origins,* vol. 18, no. 17 (October 6, 1988) no. 8, p. 267.

[5] Carl Jung, "Christ, a Symbol of the Self," in *Complete Works* 9, trans. F. C. Hull (Princeton: Princeton University Press, 1953–1978) 2.

[6] Elizabeth A. Johnson, *Women, Earth, and Creator Spirit* (Mahwah, N.J.: Paulist Press, 1993) 45–47. Johnson cites no less than twenty-three examples of the feminine characterization of the wind as Creator Spirit in a variety of mythological settings.

[7] Wayne G. Rollins, *Jung and the Bible* (Atlanta: John Knox Press, 1983) 88.

[8] Cairns, "Public Prayer."

Feast of the Body and Blood of Christ

[1] Antoine de Saint Exupéry, *Wind, Sand and Stars,* trans. Lewis Gallantière (New York: Harcourt Brace Jovanovich, 1967) 103–104.

[2] *The New York Times* (June 3, 2002) A1.

[3] Vassar Miller, "My Bones Being Water," in *If I Had Wheels or Love* (Dallas: Southern Methodist University Press, 1991).

Chapter 5

RECLAIMING THE POETRY OF ORDINARY TIME

"God employs several translators; some pieces are translated by age, some by sickness, some by war, some by justice; but God's hand is in every translation, and his hand shall bind up all our scattered leaves again for that library where every book shall lie open to one another."[1]

—John Donne

"Something almost unspeakably holy—I don't know how else to say this—underlies our discovery and confirmation of the actual details that made our world and also, in realms of contingency, assured the minutiae of its construction in the manner we know, and not in one of a trillion other ways, nearly all of which would not have included the evolution of a scribe to record the beauty, the cruelty, the fascination, and the mystery."[2]

—Stephen Jay Gould

Almost four centuries separate these two statements, the first by an Anglican priest-poet and the other by a secular science professor, but both speakers express the theme and spirit of this final chapter: scientists and theologians, confirming the intuitions of poets from the ancient psalmists to the neo-romantics of the third millennium, are asking us to listen to a gospel preached by the earth herself. That preaching embodies Raymond Brown's guideline cited earlier: "The basic hermeneutical principle is human need."[3] As those who have enjoyed the cross-pollination of poetry with Scripture in this volume prepare to reflect independently on the Gospels throughout the rest of the year, I trust that they will hear the voice of Jesus speaking with fresh urgency as he instructs us to listen to the lilies of the field, the birds of the air, the seeds in the soil.

In the opening pages I called creation "God's first language" and pointed to poets as the premier translators of that language. Many contemporary biblical scholars concur that creation is a primary source of revelation and that, therefore, the study of the natural sciences is the study of God. Commenting on the Fourth Gospel's lament that "the world did not know him," Bruce Vawter wrote: "These words are not to be restricted to the rejection of Christ by his own people. We may think, first of all, of the failure of the world to acknowledge the truth that God . . . had made known in creation."[4] For years now, voices from many secular disciplines have united to warn that dire consequences will befall a planet whose inhabitants ignore or defy the truths proclaimed by creation. Among these voices, three "translators," in particular, seem to have been rendering creation's wisdom in an increasingly poetic idiom: science, feminism, and biblical theology. All three seem to validate a vision of the natural world that the "hard sciences" once dismissed as pantheistic poetry.

Most of us are born pantheists. We worship naturally in wild, roofless cathedrals, where we feel at one with a Presence closer to us than we feel to ourselves. Traditional religious education instructed some of us in the distinction between pantheism (God in everything) and panentheism (everything in God.)[5] Today, however, respectable theologians are mining a rich lode of proof texts for creation theology: the poetic Wisdom literature of the Old Testament. Revisioning Christian theology in the light of contemporary cosmology, today's biblical scholars confidently make assertions that even fifty years ago would have been dismissed as careless thinking or "mere" mystical poetry. Jürgen Moltmann, for example, proposes that the experience of the Holy Spirit in the community of the Church "leads of itself beyond the limits of the church to the rediscovery of the same Spirit in nature, in plants, and in the ecosystems of the earth."[6] And Elizabeth Johnson does not hesitate to declare, "The whole world is the cosmic body of Christ."[7] Although Johnson does not cite Gerard Manley Hopkins, he would probably smile to hear her legitimize the kind of language that made his Jesuit colleagues nervous a hundred years ago:

> For Christ plays in ten thousand places
> Lovely in limbs, and lovely in eyes not his
> To the Father through the features of men's faces.[8]

Today theologians and scientists are talking like poets—and are being taken seriously. And the anguished poetry of a planet in pain is compelling scientists and preachers, conventional adversaries, to form a new partnership. In "Preserving and Cherishing the Earth," ecologists appealed to religious leaders to help prevent "crimes against creation," and without subscribing to any specific creed or cult, asserted that "efforts to safeguard and cherish the environment need to be infused with a vision of the sacred."[9]

During the same time period, a natural partnership between environmental activism and the feminist movement developed into eco-feminism. The rediscovery of mystical poets like Hildegard of Bingen strengthened eco-feminism's position and deepened respect for poetry's intuitive grasp of what has become the vision of modern science. Together, eco-theology, science, and eco-feminism have replaced the older interpretation of Genesis that focused on human "domination" with a more eco-sensitive version of the relationship between humanity and the other inhabitants of God's universe. Contemporary biblical scholars are reinterpreting the Genesis creation account through an ecological lens that highlights interdependence and mutuality. "Kinship" with creation, the traditional stance of poets, Franciscans, and natural mystics, has emerged as a pragmatic moral imperative for survival.

Long before molecular biologists and astrophysicists acquired the technology to demonstrate that not a single microscopic germ or extra-terrestrial fire dies without cosmic consequences, poets expressed the concept, sometimes soberly, sometimes playfully. Even Edith Sitwell, elegant tongue planted firmly in aristocratic cheek, heard the democratic gospel of creation aright:

> The dust is everything
> The heart to love
> And the voice to sing
> Indianapolis
> And the Acropolis . . .

And the Tyrant's ghost and the Low-Man Flea
Are emperor brothers (As are we)
And Attila's voice or the hum of a gnat
Can usher in eternity.[10]

Contemporary poetry both anticipates and reflects the latest stage in the continuing evolution of theology and Christology. Peggy Rosenthal concludes her study of the changing image of Jesus in two thousand years of poetry by observing that in the poetry of our age, the Jesus of the Gospels has been replaced almost completely by a sense of "an incarnational presence in our midst,"[11] and our best-known Christian poets proclaim the "sacramentality of the ordinary."[12]

I would like to conclude with a selection of less-familiar poets who find intimations of the sacred in the increasingly astonishing revelations of science. Just as ancient poets drew their metaphors for mysteries, human and divine, from visible creation, so these poets probe the mysteries of faith through metaphors drawn from the worlds-within-worlds now newly visible in contemporary laboratories and planetariums. These poets rarely respond to specific New Testament texts or episodes, yet I have found their words and images echoing in my mind as I read the Gospels.

The Annunciation

These beads we finger like distant stars—
why are they still called mysteries?
Is her story any harder to grasp
than fractals, fields of consciousness,
or intelligent energy?
Who among us has not known chaos—
neutrinos, undetected, blowing through us
like wings flapping;
like rearrangement of protons
and electrons;
Or the ecstatic surrender
to anyone's mercy?

This is not a parlor game—nature
acting out a charade. The clues are
assembled in equations
that add up to intuition.
Do the deaf not hear
a deeper voice? And what is faith
but the science
of infinite possibility—
new birth
and the atomic force
of redemption?

—*Rea Nolan Martin*

Whiplash

I would be lying if I said
I don't remember.
I do.
How could anyone forget
The sound of existence itself
splitting
with the force of conception.
And all at once

I

separated
even from myself,
traveling
through the prism
of the human idea,
racing
headlong
down
the flume
of archangelic radiance
through a contrivance
of space
into the invention
of time,

refashioned
into an appalling
density
of bones and flesh,
pressed further
into an emergency
of uncertain purpose
and handicapped
with an illusion
so real,
I could nurse at its breast?

By the time I recover, it will be time to leave.

—Rea Nolan Martin

Unified Theory

Funny Energy Einstein called it
Until he dismissed as impossible
That force he could only intuit,
Sassing gravity, spinning everything
Away from everything else
But here it comes again
Embarrassingly unthreading graceful theories,
Upending expectations, forcing us to face
The fact that the delicate balance is an illusion.
There is no heart of the matter,
Only ineluctable parting.
How odd our perpetual unraveling.
Is the fifth dimension loss?

What's really funny is we didn't get it,
Our own bodies spiraling slowly
The past fragmenting, flying away.
We are mirrors of the emptying cosmos,
Hope precarious on the back of heart break.

—Keven Bellows

Entanglement

"Where particles remain entangled light years apart"

I am searching
for an image
that will form itself
the way molten glass
responds to the glassblowers' breath
and becomes
the crystal container for claret

My amorphous thought
is wobbling in dark matter
an alternate universe
curled in ten dimensions
where no-thing is every-thing
blocked by light's limitation
where it doesn't matter
that there is no matter
and particles can not be detected
only known
in the wake of their effect

like God

bumping into this three dimensional universe
of spinning neutrinos
and warped time.
What magnificent symphony
of chemistry
plays itself out in the moment of belief
as if in the wild fields of chaos
a butterfly flaps its wings in Tokyo
and rain cascades from New York skies

possibility is infinite

they say
every action has a reaction
I think of J
her sudden death, cremation, gravesite service
finis

the one Mass card
making its way through the mail
how the family came
that cold January morning
and the stranger priest on the altar
reconstructed from the blueprint of faces
in the wooden pews
the architecture of her life
and gave her back to them
like light escaping from the black hole
of a collapsed star.

                    —*Marion I. Goldstein*

Redemption

Three thousand Beluga whales
are entombed
under a ceiling of ice
in the tundras of freezing fields.

In the luminosity of living
it is hard to heed a warning

blasting from the horn
of the Russian trawler.
The captain's order
bellowed from the bridge
is lost in thin air
but ah, a sailor with a phonograph
is climbing into the bridge

and from the throat of the ship's speaker
Beethoven's Ninth Symphony is floating
like grace
over the growing grave
notes lassoed by the wind
harness the herd
following the great hulk of metal
like the Good Shepherd
leading them home.

                    —*Marion I. Goldstein*

I offer my own final poem as a tribute to poets like those above who listen attentively to the gospel of the created universe.

Sunt Lacrymae Rerum

In the forest where
no ear listens
the tree falls
without a sound.
So say the monolingual philosophers.

But the tree knows better.
In each shriveled leaf
uptorn root
and still-born blossom
the tree, like other poets,
hears distinctly
the music of the "tears in things."

In one forest
no tree falls
without an echo
in song.

—*Elizabeth Michael Boyle, O.P.*

NOTES

Reclaiming the Poetry of Ordinary Time

[1] John Donne, "Meditation 17," cited by Jonathan Rosen in *The Talmud and the Internet* (New York: Farrar Straus, and Giroux, 2000) 5.

[2] Stephen Jay Gould, *The Structure of Evolutionary Theory* (Cambridge: The Belknap Press of Harvard University Press, 2002) 1342.

[3] Raymond E. Brown, S.S., "Hermeneutics," in *The Jerome Biblical Commentary* (Englewood Cliffs, N.J.: Prentice Hall, 1968) 71:54.

[4] Bruce Vawter, "The Gospel of John," in *The Jerome Biblical Commentary*, ed. Raymond Brown, S.S. (Englewood Cliffs, N.J.: Prentice Hall, 1968) 63:44.

[5] Thomas Aquinas, "God must be in all things in the most intimate way"; "God cannot be contained . . . pure being contains in itself all being." *Questiones Disputatae de Potentia Dei* 1, 2. "Things are in God more than God is in things," Summa I, q. 8.3. Collected in Joseph Pieper, *The Human Wisdom of St. Thomas: A Breviary of Philosophy from the Works of St. Thomas Aquinas,* trans. Drostan MacLaren, O.P. (New York: Sheed and Ward, 1948).

[6] Jürgen Moltmann, *The Spirit of Life: A Universal Affirmation* (Minneapolis: Fortress Press, 1992) 10.

[7] Elizabeth Johnson, *Women, Earth, and Creator Spirit* (New York: Paulist Press, 1993) 9.

[8] Gerard Manley Hopkins, "As Kingfishers Catch Fire," in *Poems and Prose of Gerard Manley Hopkins* (Baltimore: Penguin Books, 1953).

[9] "Preserving and Cherishing the Earth: An Appeal for Joint Commitment in Science and Religion," in *Billions and Billions,* ed. Carl Sagan (New York: Random House, 1997) 143–145. Cited in Mary Catherine Hilkert, O.P., *Imago Dei: Does the Symbol Have a Future?* Santa Clara Lecture, vol. 8, no. 3 (Santa Clara University, April 14, 2002) 8.

[10] Edith Sitwell, "Said King Pompey," in *The Collected Poems of Edith Sitwell* (New York: Vanguard Press, 1955).

[11] Peggy Rosenthal, *The Poet's Jesus: Representations at the end of a Millennium* (New York: Oxford University Press, 2000) 151.

[12] Ibid., 151–170.

EPILOGUE

Although I have enjoyed a lifetime relationship with literature, I have always kept it at a distance from my meditation on the New Testament. In the act of writing this book, the two passions of my life fused at a level I had not anticipated. I trust that I have led some readers into the same happy surprise, for every teacher's ultimate goal is to become unnecessary. If you have persevered through these pages from Advent to Trinity Sunday, you have by now developed habits of perception and habits of language that should empower you to interpret the Sundays of Ordinary Time on your own. I have discovered that weaving together lines of Scripture with lines of poetry—and sometimes with headlines from the media—we can participate over time in a midrashic process that Jonathan Rosen describes as "a sort of drift net for catching God, stretching out through time and space in ever widening spools."[1] As threads for that net, I offer ten brief epigrams and some additional sources that will assist you in your efforts to "catch God," however fleetingly, in language.[2]

❖ Reading poetry, we experience language as *cadenced expression;* thinking poetically, we experience Scripture, prayer, and living relationships as *cadenced perception.*

❖ Poetry, like architecture, generates sacred space by capturing "presence" in the form of changing light.

❖ A symbolic reading of a text is more revelatory than a literal reading.

❖ History itself is best understood as symbolic narrative.

❖ The Living Word rarely speaks in the passive voice.

❖ Preaching, like prayer, involves listening.

❖ A well-planned homily provides for silences.

❖ In the silences, imagery speaks to the unconscious in its native language.

❖ Authentic preaching, poetry, prophecy—all seek earthly justice and justice for the earth.

❖ Jesus used poetry to lead us to prayer, where neither words nor images matter. "I have said these things to you in figures of speech. The hour is coming when I will no longer speak to you in figures. . . ." (John 16:25).

NOTES

Epilogue

[1] Jonathan Rosen, *The Talmud and the Internet* (New York: Farrar, Straus and Giroux, 2000) 54–55.

[2] In addition to the anthologies listed in Works Cited, I would like to recommend several treasuries of poetry which, while not directly related to Scripture, radiate with spiritual inspiration for both preaching and prayer.

Hirsch, Edward. *Earthly Measures.* New York: Knopf, 1994.

Milosz, Czeslaw, ed. *A Book of Luminous Things: An International Anthology of Poetry.* New York: Harcourt Brace, 1996.

Paine, Jeffrey, ed. *The Poetry of Our World: An International Anthology of Contemporary Poetry.* New York: Harper Collins, 2000.

Rosenberg, Liz, ed. *Light Gathering Poems.* New York: Henry Holt, 2000.

Rothenberg, Jerome, ed. *Technicians of the Sacred: A Range of Poetries from Africa, America, Oceania.* Garden City, N.Y.: Doubleday, 1968.

_____. *Poems for the Millennium.* 2 vols. Berkeley: University of California Press, 1996–1998.

WORKS CITED

Adair, Virginia Hamilton. *Beliefs and Blasphemies: A Collection of Poems.* New York: Random House, 1998.

Akhmatova, Anna. *The Complete Poems of Anna Akhmatova.* Vol. 2. Trans. Judith Hemschemeyer. Somerville, Mass.: Zephyr Press, 1990.

Albright, W. F., and C. S. Mann. *Matthew: A New Translation with an Introduction and Notes.* The Anchor Bible 26. Garden City, N.Y.: Doubleday, 1971.

Atwan, Robert, ed. *Divine Inspiration: The Life of Jesus in World Poetry.* New York: Oxford University Press, 1998.

Auden, W. H. *The Collected Poems.* New York: Random House, 1972.

Barth, Karl. *Church Dogmatics: A Selection.* Trans. G. W. Bromiley. New York: Harper, 1962.

Barton, John, ed. *Oxford Bible Commentary.* Oxford: Oxford University Press, 2001.

Bergant, Diane, C.S.A., ed. *The Collegeville Bible Commentary.* Collegeville, Minn.: The Liturgical Press, 1989.

Berrigan, Daniel. *Selected and New Poems.* New York: Doubleday, 1973.

Berryman, John. *Love and Fame.* New York: Farrar Straus, and Giroux, 1970.

Bodo, Murray, O.F.M. *Poetry as Prayer: Denise Levertov.* Boston: Pauline Books and Media, 2001.

Brown, Raymond E., S.S. *The Birth of the Messiah: A Commentary on the Infancy Narratives in Matthew and Luke.* Garden City, N.Y.: Doubleday, 1977.

————. *The Gospel According to John.* The Anchor Bible 29, 29A. Garden City, N.Y.: Doubleday, 1966, 1970.

————, ed. *The Jerome Biblical Commentary.* Englewood Cliffs, N.J.: Prentice Hall, 1968.

————, ed. *The New Jerome Biblical Commentary.* Englewood Cliffs, N.J.: Prentice Hall, 1990.

————. *A Retreat with John the Evangelist: That You May Have Life.* Cincinnati: St. Anthony Messenger Press, 1998.

Butkus, Russell, "Sustainability: An Eco-Theological Crisis." In *All Creation Is Groaning: An Interdisciplinary Vision for Life in a Sacred Universe.* Ed. Carol J. Dempsey. Collegeville, Minn.: The Liturgical Press, 1999.

Cairns, Scott. *Philokalia.* Lincoln, Neb.: Zoo Press, 2002.

Chardin, Pierre Teilhard de. *The Phenomenon of Man.* New York: Harper Torchbooks, 1959.

Chesterton, G. K. *The Collected Poems.* New York: Doubleday, 1932.

Collins, Billy. *Sailing Alone Around the Room.* New York: Random House, 2001.

————. Personal Interview with Sister Elizabeth Michael Boyle. Caldwell College, April 2, 2001.

"Constitution on the Sacred Liturgy." In *Vatican II: The Conciliar and Post Conciliar Documents.* New rev. ed. Ed. Austin Flannery, O.P. Northport, N.Y.: Costello, 1998.

Craig, David, and Janet McCann, eds. *Place of Passage: Contemporary Catholic Poetry.* Ashland, Or.: Story Line Press, 2000.

Curzon, David, ed. *The Gospels in Our Image: An Anthology of Twentieth Century Poetry Based on Biblical Texts.* New York: Harcourt Brace, 1995.

Dempsey, Carol J., O.P., "Hope Amidst Crisis." In *All Creation Is Groaning.* Collegeville, Minn.: The Liturgical Press, 1999.

Diamond, Irene, ed. *Reweaving the World: The Emergence of Ecofeminism.* San Francisco: Sierra Club Books, 1990.

Doty, Mark. "Messiah: Christmas Portions." In *Sweet Machine.* New York: Harper Perennial, 1999.

Dunn, J.D.G. "Prayer." In *Dictionary of Jesus and the Gospels.* Leicester, Eng.: InterVarsity Press, 1992.

Edwards, Denis. "For Your Immortal Spirit Is in All Things." In *Earth Revealing—Earth Healing: Ecology and Christian Theology.* Collegeville, Minn.: The Liturgical Press, 2001.

Eliot, T. S. *The Complete Poems and Plays.* New York: Harcourt, Brace and Company, 1952.

_____. *On Poetry and Poets.* New York: Farrar, Straus, and Cudahy, 1957.

Ellis, Peter F. *The Genius of John: A Composition-Critical Commentary on the Fourth Gospel.* Collegeville, Minn.: The Liturgical Press, 1984.

Ferlinghetti, Lawrence. *A Coney Island of the Mind.* New York: New Directions, 1958.

Fitzgerald, Christopher. *Sonnets to the Unseen.* Schiller Park, Ill.: World Library Publications, 2001.

Fitzmyer, Joseph A., S.J., ed. *The Gospel According to Luke.* The Anchor Bible 28, 28A. New York: Doubleday, 1981.

_____. *A Christological Catechism: New Testament Answers.* Ramsey, N.J.: Paulist Press, 1982.

Flannery, Austin, O.P., ed. *Vatican II: The Conciliar and Post Conciliar Documents.* New rev. ed. Northport, N.Y.: Costello Publishing Co., 1998.

Flax Hjalmar. "Our Father." In *Anthology of Contemporary Latin American Poetry: 1960–1984.* Ed. Barry J. Luby. Cranbury, N.J.: Associated University Presses.

Freedman, David Noel, ed. *The Anchor Bible Dictionary.* New York: Doubleday, 1992.

_____. *Eerdmans Dictionary of the Bible.* Grand Rapids: Eerdmans, 2000.

Gasztold, Carmen de Bernos. *Prayers from the Ark and The Creatures Choir: The Voices of Animals Raised to God in Song.* Trans. Rumer Godden. New York: Penguin Books, 1976.

Goergen, Donald, O.P. "Preaching as Searching for God." *Dominican Ashram* (March 2000) 17.

Green, Joel B., ed. *Dictionary of Jesus and the Gospels.* Leicester, Eng.: Inter-Varsity Press, 1992.

Gulley, Norman. "Ascension." In *The Anchor Bible Dictionary.* New York: Doubleday, 1992.

Heaney, Seamus. *The Cure at Troy: A Version of Sophocles' Philoctetes.* New York: Farrar, Straus, Giroux, 1990.

Heidegger, Martin. "Language." In *Poetry, Language, Thought.* New York: Harper & Row, 1971.

Hilkert, Mary Catherine, O.P., *Imago Dei: Does the Symbol Have a Future?* Santa Clara Lecture. Vol. 8, no. 3. Santa Clara University, April 14, 2002.

Hill, Donald. *Richard Wilbur.* New York: Twayne, 1967.

Hill, Geoffrey. *New and Collected Poems.* New York: Houghton Mifflin, 1994.

Hirsch, Edward. "Poet's Choice." *The Washington Post Book World.*

Hong, Sara. "Hide and Seek." *Image: A Journal of the Arts and Religion.* Fall, 2000.

Hopes, David Brendan. *The Glaciers' Daughters.* Amherst: University of Massachusetts Press, 1981.

Hopkins, Gerard Manley. *Poems and Prose of Gerard Manley Hopkins.* Baltimore: Penguin Books, 1953.

Impastato, David. *Upholding Mystery: An Anthology of Contemporary Christian Poetry.* New York: Oxford University Press, 1997.

John Paul II. "The Ecological Crisis: A Common Responsibility." World Peace Day, January 1, 1990.

_____. "Mulieris Dignitatem." Apostolic Letter on the Dignity and Vocation of Women. *Origins.* Vol. 18, no. 17. October 6, 1988.

Johnson, Elizabeth A., C.S.J. *Consider Jesus: Waves of Renewal in Christology.* New York: Crossroad, 1991.

_____. *She Who Is: The Mystery of God in Feminist Theological Discourse.* New York: Crossroad, 1997.

_____. *Women, Earth, and Creator Spirit.* New York: Paulist Press, 1993.

Johnson, Luke Timothy. *The Real Jesus.* San Francisco: Harper Collins, 1996.

Jung, Carl. "Answer to Job," "Christ, A Symbol of the Self," "On the Relation of Analytical Psychology to Poetry." In *Complete Works* 11, 9, 15. Trans. F. C. Hull. Princeton: Princeton University Press, 1953–1978.

_____. *Man and His Symbols.* New York: Doubleday, 1971.

Kodell, Jerome, O.S.B. "Luke." In *The Collegeville Bible Commentary.* Collegeville, Minn.: The Liturgical Press, 1989.

Ku, Sang. *Wasteland of Fire: Selected Poems of Ku Sang.* Trans. Anthony of Taizé. London: Forest Books, 1989.

Kurz, William S., S.J. "The Acts of the Apostles." In *The Collegeville Bible Commentary.* Collegeville, Minn.: The Liturgical Press, 1989.

Lectionary of the Canadian Conference of Catholic Bishops: New Revised Standard Version. Conacan, Inc., 1992.

Le Fort, Gertrud von. *Hymns to the Church.* New York: Sheed & Ward, 1938.

Levertov, Denise. *New and Selected Essays*. New York: New Directions, 1992.

_____. *The Stream and the Sapphire*. New York: New Directions, 1997.

_____. *This Great Unknowing*. New York: New Directions, 2001.

Lindars, Barnabas, S.S.F. *The Gospel of John*. London: Oliphants, 1972.

Lynch, John W., S.J. *A Woman Wrapped in Silence*. New York: MacMillan, 1945.

Mann, C. S. *Mark: A New Translation with Introduction and Commentary*. The Anchor Bible 27. New York: Doubleday, 1986.

Marcello, Leo Luke. *Nothing Grows in One Place Forever*. St. Louis: Time Being Books, 1998.

Mariani, Paul. *The Great Wheel*. New York: W. W. Norton, 1996.

Merton, Thomas. *The Tears of the Blind Lions*. New York: New Directions, 1949.

_____. *Man in a Divided Sea*. New York: New Directions, 1946.

Miller, Vassar. *If I Had Wheels or Love*. Dallas: Southern Methodist University Press, 1991.

Milosz, Czeslaw. *The Collected Poems: 1931–1987*. Trans. Robert Haas. New York: Harper Collins Ecco Press, 1988.

Mistral, Gabriela. *Selected Poems of Gabriela Mistral*. Trans. Doris Dana. Baltimore: Johns Hopkins University Press, 1971.

Mitchell, Stephen. *Parables and Portraits*. New York: Harper Collins, 1990.

_____. Trans. and ed. *The Selected Poetry of Rainer Maria Rilke*. New York: Vintage Press, 1989.

Moltmann, Jürgen. *The Spirit of Life: A Universal Affirmation*. Minneapolis: Fortress Press, 1992.

Noyes, Alfred. *The Golden Book of Catholic Poetry*. New York: J. B. Lippincott, 1946.

Oliver, Mary. *New and Selected Poems*. Boston: Beacon Press, 1992.

Paz, Octavio. *The Other Voice: Essays on Modern Poetry*. New York: Harcourt Brace Jovanovich, 1991.

Péguy, Charles. *God Speaks*. Trans. Julian Green. New York: Pantheon, 1945.

Perkins, Pheme. *Resurrection: New Testament Witness and Contemporary Reflection*. Garden City, N.Y.: Doubleday, 1984.

Petrement, Simone. *Simone Weil: A Life.* Trans. Raymond Rosenthal. New York: Pantheon, 1976.

Pieper, Joseph, arr. *The Human Wisdom of Saint Thomas: A Breviary of Philosophy from the Works of Saint Thomas Aquinas.* Trans. Drostan MacLaren. New York: Sheed & Ward, 1948.

Plante, Judith, ed. *Healing the Wounds: The Promise of Ecofeminism.* Philadelphia: Fortress Press, 1984.

Poelman, Roger. *Times of Grace: The Sign of Forty in the Bible.* Trans. D. P. Farina. New York: Herder & Herder, 1964.

Radcliffe, Timothy, O.P. "Letter to the Order." *International Dominican Information* 128. May 2000.

Rahner, Karl. "Dogmatic Questions on Easter," "The Life of the Dead," "Poetry and the Christian," "The Word and the Eucharist." In *Theological Investigations* 4. Trans. Kevin Smyth. Baltimore: Helicon, 1966.

————. "Easter: A Faith That Loves the Earth." In *The Great Church Year.* New York: Crossroad, 1993.

————. *On Prayer.* Collegeville, Minn.: The Liturgical Press, 1993.

————. "The Resurrection of the Body." In *Theological Investigations* 2. Trans. Karl H. Kruger. Baltimore: Helicon, 1963.

Rees, Richard. *Simone Weil: A Sketch for a Portrait.* Urbana, Ill.: Southern Illinois University Press.

Rilke, Rainer Maria. *Rilke's Book of Hours: Love Poems to God.* Trans. Anita Barrows and Joanna Macy. New York: Riverhead Books, 1997.

————. *Selected Works.* Vol. 2: *Poetry.* Trans. J. B. Leishman. New York: New Directions, 1967.

————. *Translations from the Poetry of Rainer Maria Rilke.* Trans. M. D. Herter. New York: W. W. Norton, 1962.

————. *The Selected Poetry of Rainer Maria Rilke.* Trans. Stephen Mitchell. New York: Vintage Press, 1989.

Rollins, Wayne G. *Jung and the Bible.* Atlanta: John Knox Press, 1983.

Rosen, Jonathan. *The Talmud and the Internet.* New York: Farrar Straus and Giroux, 2000.

Rosenthal, Peggy. *The Poets's Jesus.* New York: Oxford University Press, 2000.

————. *Praying the Gospels through Poetry: Lent to Easter.* Cincinnati: St. Anthony Messenger Press, 2001.

Rozewicz, Tadeuz. "Unknown Letter." In *Unease*. Minneapolis: New Rivers Press, 1981.

Ryken, Leland, ed. *Dictionary of Biblical Imagery*. Downers Grove, Ill.: Inter-Varsity Press, 1998.

Sagan, Carl, ed. "Preserving and Cherishing the Earth: An Appeal for Joint Commitment in Science and Religion." In *Billions and Billions*. New York: Random House, 1997.

Saint Exupéry, Antoine de. *Wind, Sand and Stars*. Trans. Lewis Gallantière. New York: Harcourt Brace Jovanovich, 1967.

Salzman, Mark. "The Transcendent in Contemporary Fiction." Auburn Theological School Lecture. New York, November 5, 2001.

———. *Lying Awake*. New York: Alfred A. Knopf, 2000.

———. Personal Interview with Sister Elizabeth Michael Boyle, November 6, 2001.

Sarton, May. "Lazarus." In *Collected Poems 1930–93*. New York: W. W. Norton, 1966.

Sasanov, Catherine. "Raise the Dead Inside My Given Name." *Image: A Journal of the Arts and Religion*. Spring 2001.

Schnackenburg, Rudolf. *The Gospel According to St. John*. Vol. 2. Trans. Cecily Hastings. New York: The Seabury Press, 1980.

Schneiders, Sandra M., I.H.M. *Written That You May Believe: Encountering Jesus in the Fourth Gospel*. New York: Crossroad, 1999.

Sexton, Anne. *The Awful Rowing Toward God*. Boston: Houghton Mifflin Company, 1975.

Shaw, Luci. *Writing the River*. Colorado Springs: Pinon Press, 1994.

Smith, Dinita. "The Eerily Intimate Power of Poetry to Console." *New York Times*, October 1, 2001. E1–4.

Smith, Sister Pamela, S.S.C.M. *Waymakers: Eyewitnesses to Christ*. Notre Dame, Ind.: Ave Maria Press, 1982.

Spong, John Shelby. *Liberating the Gospels: Reading the Bible With Jewish Eyes and Freeing Jesus from 2000 Years of Misunderstanding*. San Francisco: Harper Books, 1997.

Szymborska, Wislawa. *Sounds, Feelings, and Thoughts: Seventy Poems by Wislawa Szymborska*. Princeton: Princeton University Press, 1981.

Thomas, Dylan. *The Poems of Dylan Thomas*. New York: New Directions, 1943.

Thompson, Francis. *Poems of Francis Thompson.* Ed. Terence Connolly, S.J. New York: D. Appleton-Century, 1941.

Unamuno, Miguel de. "The Christ of Velasquez." In *The Last Poems of Miguel de Unamuno.* Madison: Fairleigh Dickinson University Press, 1974.

Waldron, Robert. *Poetry as Prayer: The Hound of Heaven.* Boston: Pauline Books and Media, 1999.

Weil, Simone. *Waiting for God.* Trans. Emma Crauford. New York: Harper Torchbooks, 1973.

Wilbur, Richard. *Advice to a Prophet and Other Poems.* New York: Harcourt Brace, 1988.

————. *Conversations with Richard Wilbur.* Ed. William Butts. Jackson, Miss.: University of Mississippi Press, 1990.

————. "Interview with Paul Mariani." *Image: A Journal of the Arts and Religion.* Issue 12. Winter 1995. http://www.imagejournal.org/wilburframe.html.

Wojtyla, Karol. *Collected Poems.* Trans. Jerzy Peterkiewicz. New York: Random House, 1979.

Yeats, William Butler. *The Collected Poems.* New York: MacMillan Company, 1956.

Works Recommended

Atwan, Robert, ed. *Chapters into Verse.* New York: Oxford University Press, 2000.

Countryman, L. William. *The Poetic Imagination.* Maryknoll: Orbis Press, 1999.

Lawrence, *Imaging the Word.* Kenneth T. Cleveland: United Church Press, 1994.

Morneau, Bishop Robert. *Ashes to Easter.* New York: Crossroad, 1997.

————. *Fathoming Bethlehem.* New York: Crossroad, 1997.

PERMISSIONS

Adair, Virginia Hamilton: "Communion," "Beyond," from *Beliefs and Blasphemies* by Virginia Hamilton Adair. Copyright © 1998 by Virginia Hamilton Adair. Used by permission of Random House, Inc.

Akhmatova, Anna: "Knock with Your Little Fist," from *The Complete Poems of Anna Akhmatova*, translated by Judith Hemschemeyer, edited and introduced by Roberta Reeder. Copyright © 1989, 1992 by Judith Hemschemeyer. Reprinted by permission of Zephyr Press.

Bellows, Keven: "In the Desert," "Unified Theory." Printed by permission of the author.

Berrigan, Daniel: "In Memoriam," from *Selected and New Poems* by Daniel Berrigan. Copyright © 1973 by Daniel Berrigan. Used by permission of Doubleday, a division of Random House, Inc.

Boyle, Elizabeth Michael, O.P.: "Skytides," "The Desert Speaks," "Ages of Faith," "What the Star Said," "Moscow's Secret," "The Climb," "The Price," "Question," "Easter to Pentecost," "On Reading Levertov's Last Poems," "Sunt Lacrymae Rerum." Printed by permission of the author.

Duguid, Sandra: "The Road to Emmaus." Originally published in *America*, April 27, 2003. Reprinted with the permission of America Press, Inc. americamagazine.org.

Doty, Mark: "Messiah: Christmas Portions," from *Sweet Machine*. Copyright © 1998 by Mark Doty. Reprinted by permission of HarperCollins Publishers, Inc.

Ferlinghetti, Lawrence: "Christ Climbed Down," *A Coney Island of the Mind*. Copyright © 1958 by Lawrence Ferlinghetti. Reprinted by permission of New Directions Publishing Corp.

Fitzgerald, Christopher: Sonnets 31, 41, 54, 66, from *Sonnets to the Unseen*. Copyright © 2001 by World Library Publications, 3825 N. Willow Drive, Shiller Park, IL 60176. All rights reserved. Used by permission of World Library Publications.

Goldstein, Marion I.: "Design," "In the Absence," "Uncertainty Principle," "Entanglement," "Redemption," from *Psalms for the Cosmos*. Johnstown: Pudding House Publications, 2003. Reprinted by permission of the author.

INDEX OF POETS AND POEMS

GOSPEL INDEX